The Life and Times of King Cotton

Le Bureau de Coton a La Nouvelle Orleans, de Degas

DAVID L. COHN

The Life and Times of King Cotton

GREENWOOD PRESS, PUBLISHERS
WESTPORT, CONNECTICUT

Library of Congress Cataloging in Publication Data

Cohn, David Lewis, 1896-1960.
    The life and times of King Cotton.

        Reprint of the ed. published by Oxford University
    Press, New York.
        1. Cotton growing--United States. 2. Cotton manu-
    facture--United States. 3. Cotton trade--United
    States. I. Title.
    HD9076.C56 1973   338.1'7'3510973   73-11996
    ISBN 0-8371-7115-6

Originally published in 1956 by Oxford University Press, New York

Reprinted with the permission of Oxford University Press

Reprinted in 1973 by Greenwood Press,
a division of Williamhouse-Regency Inc.

Library of Congress Catalogue Card Number 73-11996

ISBN 0-8371-7115-6

Printed in the United States of America

for L.M.C.

Foreword

I HAVE SOUGHT TO DISCUSS HERE a few of the many aspects of American cotton culture over a period almost contemporaneous with the life of the republic. So far as possible, I have dealt with men rather than with statistics; the millions of men, women, and children, white and Negro, slave and free, whose lives gave fecundity to the nation's cotton crop or were nurtured by it.

Cotton alone, of all the products of our soil or industry, stirs the emotions of whoever contemplates it. Furs, cattle, oil, gold, wheat, corn, railroads — the tale of all these on this continent excites the imagination as one perceives with what courage and adventurousness men have bent the resources of nature to their use. But it is the melancholy distinction of cotton to be the very stuff of high drama and tragedy, of bloody civil war and the unutterable woe of human slavery.

So, too, cotton alone, of all the products of our soil or industry, fashioned the thinking and way of life of a whole great region and, despite marked diversities existing among its various parts, made it one. Twenty-five years ago, Anne O'Hare McCormick, writing in *The New York Times Magazine*, said: 'For cotton is something more than a crop or an industry; it is a dynastic system, with a set of laws and standards always under assault and peculiarly resistant to change. It is map-maker, trouble-maker, history-maker . . . It was cotton that made the South into a sec-

tion . . . On cotton . . . the South built up a social and political economy essentially different from that prevailing in the rest
of the country.'

Ninety years after the event, the imagination of the country
continues to be stimulated and beguiled by the Civil War as by
nothing else in the history of the nation. Men are still bemused
by their visions of the vanished life of a vanished age in the Old
South: its white-columned mansions, the proud men and women
who occupied them, the scores of slaves, the candelabra of mag-
nolia trees burning waxen-white in the passionate nights, the duels
and the balls and the palatial steamboats on the Mississippi
bound downriver to glittering New Orleans — French-speaking,
music-loving, pleasure-loving, Roman Catholic — a Latin-Roman-
Mediterranean island in a Protestant, Anglo-Saxon, 'American' Sea.

And if this be but fanciful? Does it really matter? Are not fic-
tions and illusions the bread and wine of the spirit?

Never was there a swifter flowering and a swifter dying, for the
Old South was dominant for only about twenty years before '61.
But it had pride and cruelty and dignity. It had style and beauty
and romance and melodrama and a touchy sense of personal honor
and was no stranger to ritual; all this endured in an excessive
landscape of the mind starred by tiger-bright jungle. Yet these
are things that strangely stir men, the heart turning in upon itself, and so it is that the Old South of the cotton plantations still
beguiles them.

As fibers of various lengths may appear in a bale of cotton, so
the fabric of cotton culture is highly complex. It contains
elaborately intermingled elements of politics, finance, business organization, social organization, soil and insect chemistry, race relations, and the politico-economic policies of the nation in its
international relations with other peoples.

A complete study of cotton culture in the United States would
properly involve a detailed study of all these factors. It would
require not one volume, but many volumes. Such an inquiry is beyond the aim of this book. Here I have attempted merely to tell
something of an agriculture that fashioned the life of a great region
and profoundly affected the destiny of the whole American people.

D. L. C.

New York, 29 June 1956

Contents

The Life and Times of King Cotton

I

A Young Man Goes Tutoring and Shakes the World

On an October morning in 1792, a young man named Eli Whitney — aged 28 and just graduated from Yale — took ship at New York bound for Savannah, Georgia. No one could then have guessed that a machine of his invention was to set in motion world-shaking forces. Whitney had no technical training nor had he ever seen cotton fields. But he soon invented the cotton gin and a contemporary notable among inventors — Robert Fulton — said that Whitney was one of three who had accomplished more for mankind than any other men of their age.

The gin's direct and indirect effects at home and abroad were prodigious. Here it stopped the slow dying of Negro slavery and stimulated it anew on a huge scale, started a westward cotton movement that is still in progress, founded a cotton plantation system that profoundly affected the culture and politics of a great region, fostered the controversy that ended in civil war, and fastened on the United States a massive race problem. It made possible great cotton exports from the United States to Europe and enormously advanced the industrialization first of England, and later of continental European states, as cotton became the basis of vigorous industries. At the same time, cotton became a principal element in American economic relations with Europe, the

3

most important item in the American trade balance, and it also affected European interests in the United States by becoming a factor in international politics and economics.

Beneficial effects of the gin might have been foreseen but its malefic effects could scarcely have been anticipated. No machine is born into Original Sin. But in this case it was as though some wicked spirit had brooded over the young Connecticut Yankee's device and ordained: 'Evil, be thou my good.'

Eli Whitney was born on a New England's winter day — 8 December 1765. (A century later, in April 1865 when spring came flooding up the Shenandoah Valley, Lee surrendered the Army of Northern Virginia at Appomattox.) His was a farm family living at Westborough, Worcester County, Massachusetts, and it soon became evident that he was born to make things with his hands. A mere boy during the Revolutionary War, with his father's consent he set up a forge and made nails for which there was an insistent demand. After the war he manufactured more profitable hairpins. The skill he acquired in drawing out steel for the pins was useful when he came to fashion the wire teeth of his cotton gin.

Mechanically precocious, Whitney was at the relatively ripe age of 19 when he began to seek a liberal education. (In eighteenth-century America a boy of 19 was much 'older' than a boy of the same age is today.) It took him nearly ten years to get it and at 28 he was graduated from Yale. There he had spoken of preparing himself to become a lawyer, but it was with little enthusiasm or sense of conviction.

Whitney's father, who like most New England farmers of his day saw little cash, helped him through college. Eager to conform to the details of dress and deportment that marked more affluent students, he found that conformity was expensive. Today's student may slop around the campus in levis and nondescript sweater and shoes, but the eighteenth-century Yale student was expected to dress well. His wardrobe, for example, had to include at the minimum a pair of pantaloons of mixed cotton and wool, a pair of fine shoes, and cambric handkerchiefs — items costing in the aggregate almost $15. Laundry came to $3 a quarter, board $1.60 a week. Every ten weeks the student had to pay $5 for a room in Connecticut Hall, $3 for sweeping, making the bed, and general damages, plus $5 for bed and bedding. He also had to have pocket money and fees for membership in such societies as the Rinonian of which Whitney was 'scribe.' At least $1,000 was needed to go through Yale, and although Whitney earned some money by tutoring more prosperous students, his financial troubles constantly appear in letters to his father: 'I am, Sir, in the most straitened circumstances . . .' But before commencement his father had paid his last bills.

Commencement, in the rural New England of that day, took second place to agriculture, coming only when some crops had been gathered and others had been laid by. For Eli Whitney it was the second Wednesday in September 1792. He was immediately engaged as tutor to the children of a Major Dupont of South Carolina and in the next month sailed for Savannah. Aboard the same schooner was the wealthy widow of the Revolutionary War general, Nathanael Greene, who was returning with her family to Mulberry Grove plantation after a summer spent in the North. As the schooner sailed southward, a pleasant friendship began between the young Yale graduate and the wealthy matron, and she invited him to visit at her plantation before going to South Carolina.

Mulberry Grove was a great plantation near Savannah. It had been 'liberated' from its former British owners during the Revolution and afterward given General Greene for his services by the state of Georgia. Maintained lavishly, with a retinue of 50 Negro servants, the plantation with its broad fields of rice and corn and patches of watermelons and pumpkins stretched along the river. At night, in the slave quarters, Negroes often sat in a circle lit by a flaming torch and drowsily picked seeds from 'vegetable wool.'

Eli Whitney, a young man whose poetic disposition had revealed itself at college, found himself the guest of hospitable Southerners, living in an exotic environment of great beauty that must have stirred his imagination. But the friendly people who dropped in at Mulberry Grove often discussed a practical problem that faced them. So urgently did they talk that, as Whitney later recorded, he fell involuntarily to thinking of solutions to the problem even as he listened to their conversation.

What was then the plight of Southern agriculture, the place of cotton in it, the condition of slavery? It is one of the unhappy paradoxes of man's economic estate that while war often brings 'prosperity,' equally often peace brings depression. So it was that the decade following the peace of 1783 brought depression to the plantations. Tobacco, upon which half the South's population depended in large or small degree, dropped to ruinously low prices. These low prices continued for many years and exports remained nearly stationary. Indigo production, once stimulated by a subsidy no longer effective, fell into eclipse. Rice culture was painfully affected by the slow transition to the new tide-flow system.

Wool? George Washington had encouraged wool growing and kept a sheep flock of six to seven hundred head. But large-scale production of sheep for wool alone, without a good market for mutton, did not pay; since sheep were constantly attacked by wolves and dogs they had to be watched by day and penned up by night. Flax? The manipulation of it into yarn required more cheap labor than was available. Yet linen was widely used and some of it was indispensable for making the linsey-woolsey clothing worn by most people.

Planters had even tried sericulture. Using Virginia mulberry trees and silkworms imported from France, Italy, and Spain, they had produced some silk. Georgia, in the year after Eli Whitney's birth, had shipped 1,084 pounds of silk to England, but thereafter the industry waned. Sericulture demanded an abundance of cheap, skilled labor that was not at hand, and the market for silk was limited because its high price made it available only to the rich.

Southern agriculture was weak in all its branches. It was logical that the price of slaves — a prime capital investment — fell sharply. At the end of 1794 George Washington advised a friend to shift from slaves to some other form of property, and concluded by stating his own position: 'Were it not that I am principled against selling negroes, as you would cattle in a market, I would not in twelve months hence be possessed of a single one as a slave. I shall be happily mistaken if they are not found to be a very troublesome species of property ere many years have passed over our heads.'

In these circumstances, the prosperity of Southern agriculture, and the salvaging of investments in slaves, depended upon the coming of a new, important cash crop. It could be cotton if . . .

Nearly all of the cotton used in colonial America was West Indian. In 1640 the General Court of Connecticut declared: 'It is thought necessary for the comfortable support of these plantations, that a trade in cotton wooll be sett uppon . . .' and it recommended building ships for importing cotton. During the Revolutionary War, however, every effort was made to grow and manufacture at home, with some success. In 1786, Jefferson wrote: 'The four southernmost States make a great deal of cotton. The poor are almost entirely clothed in it winter and summer . . . The dress of women is almost entirely of cotton . . .'

Long before this time, Alexander Hamilton, born in the cotton-growing West Indies, had said that 'several of the Southern colonies' might some day 'clothe the whole continent.' But this day seemed remote at the time Eli Whitney was visiting Mulberry Grove.

Southern planters had experimented unsuccessfully with several varieties of cotton until they imported seed from the Bahamas that produced a fine fiber and brought a high price. It grew well and enriched some South Carolina planters when its price in Liverpool rose to five shillings a pound toward the end of the eighteenth century, and it sold for 50 to 75 cents a pound at home. One planter — William Brisbane — earned so much in two years that he retired and spent several years traveling. Then he sold his plantation to William Seabrook. Neighbors thought that Seabrook would soon go broke because of the high price he had paid for the plantation, but the proceeds of two crops made him free of debt.

Here, then, was a potential source of farm gold. The long silky fibers of sea-island cotton brought far higher prices than upland cotton. And — greatest advantage of all perhaps — its seeds could be easily removed by squeezing the cotton between simple rollers.

But, alas, black-seed, or sea-island cotton, flourished only on islands off the coasts of Georgia and South Carolina and on certain lowlands adjacent to the coasts.

Green-seed, or upland, cotton, the short-staple variety, offered a more exhilarating prospect. It could be grown on millions of untilled acres, and though it brought less than sea-island cotton, the yield per acre was far greater. It had long been cultivated in the colonies for domestic use but on a scale so tiny that American home-spinners — among them George Washington — sometimes imported raw cotton from England. Green-seed cotton was occasionally grown as a garden plant, but more often by farmers who made a coarse cloth from it after they had laboriously removed its tenaciously clinging seeds from the fiber. Seed-picking was usually an after-supper job carried on beside the fireplace that shed heat and light. Toiling late after a day in the fields, heads often nodded, and prodding was sometimes needed to complete the task. Farmers often relieved the monotony and tedium of the work by organizing cotton-pickings. Young people met at one house or another to pick seeds at night. Logs were stacked high in the fireplace until there was a roaring blaze and the cotton was spread out to dry so that its seeds could be more readily separated from the fiber. It was divided into parts and there was eager competition among pickers to be the first to finish the allotted task. The winner was hailed champion. And — a more practical reward — he might kiss any girl he chose.

Rebecca Latimer Felton, in her *Country Life in Georgia in the Days of My Youth,* describes the fibers and clothing available on early antebellum plantations: (Born while Jackson was still in the White House, she lived to become, in 1922, the first woman senator of the United States:) 'When my grandmother, Lucy Swift, began housekeeping, wool and flax were the dependence of housekeepers for clothing their families. Silk culture was exploited in General Oglethorpe's time, but the use of cotton was handicapped. Before there were any cotton gins the cotton lint was picked from the seed by human fingers. The lint was then carded by hand, spun on homemade wheels, then reeled into . . . "hanks" . . . then the warp was prepared for the homemade loom by a variety of processes, all tedious and slow, and all the work done by the house-mother and her helpers. In this way all the wearing apparel of the masses was constructed. Well-to-do men generally contrived to get a broadcloth coat, maybe once in a lifetime. Silk dresses were scarce . . . and they were worn only occasionally, at weddings or brilliant occasions . . .'

How tantalizing was the planter's prospect as the eighteenth century moved to its close. Cotton is the whitest and most versatile of fibers. Strong, durable, washable, cleanable, easy to dye, spin, weave, adaptable to clothing and industrial uses, the world awaited the coming of cotton cloth in huge volume at modest prices. The soil and climate of the South made cotton cultivation simple on millions of unused acres. In England men named Crompton, Hargreaves, Arkwright, and Cartwright had recently revolutionized textile manufacture. Machinery operated by steam or waterpower engines had inaugurated the factory system that made possible the production of cotton cloth for the world market, a market that was rapidly growing to meet the needs of an increasing population. So avid was the demand for cotton cloth that Britain's cotton manufactures were beginning to rival her famous woolen production. Statistics are eloquent: in the period 1783–90, Britain's cotton imports jumped more than threefold, from 9 million pounds in 1783 to 28 million pounds in 1790. But — to the intense regret of Southern planters — little or none of the cotton came from the American South.

This must have been maddeningly frustrating. They could grow cotton. An apparently insatiable market wanted it. The factory system assured an ever-widening demand for it. And they urgently needed an important cash crop. But before they could enter the agricultural heaven that they glimpsed, they had to solve the problem of green-seed cotton. Its price would remain prohibitively expensive as long as it took a man a whole day to produce one pound of fiber free of seeds. Now if someone should invent a machine that could quickly, economically remove the seeds from cotton . . .

These considerations filled the tabletalk at Mulberry Grove. Among those who came to the plantation during Whitney's visit were former officers who had served with General Greene and who now lived in the 'up country': Majors Pendleton, Forsythe, and Bremen. They pictured the great Southern prosperity that would come if a way could be found to separate the seeds from green-seed cotton as roller gins, evolved from the Hindu 'churka,' separated the seeds from sea-island cotton. At one point, tradition says, Mrs. Greene called young Whitney from his room, presented him to the gentlemen, and told them that he could 'make anything!' By way of proof she showed them an embroidery frame that he had made for her and toys he had made for the children. (Later she gave him a room where he could work.) Eli Whitney wrote to his father of the disappointment he had suffered with respect to his tutoring job and his interest in the planters' problem.

'There were a number of very respectable gentlemen at Mrs. Greene's who all agreed that if a machine could be invented which would clean cotton with expedition, it would be a great thing both to the inventor and to the country. I involuntarily happened to be thinking on the subject and struck out a plan of a machine in my mind.'

The would-be inventor communicated his plan to Mr. Miller, 'who is agent to the executors of General Greene and resides in the family, a man of respectability and property.' Miller urged Whitney to experiment at his expense and they agreed that any profits from the enterprise should be shared equally. Whitney was spurred on not only for this reason but also because, as he told his father, 'Previous to this I found I was like to be disappointed in my school; that is, instead of a hundred, I found I could get only fifty guineas a year. I, however, held the refusal of the school until I made some little experiments.' He went to work and, he writes, 'In about ten days I made a little model for which I was offered . . . a hundred guineas. I concluded to relinquish my school and turn my attention to perfecting the machine. I made one . . . which required the labor of one man to turn it and with which one man will clean ten times as much cotton as he can in any other way before known . . . This machine may be turned by water or with a horse . . . It makes the labor fifty times less, without throwing any class of People out of business.'

When he had completed drawings for the gin, and a working model, Whitney went to the nation's capital — Philadelphia —

to apply for a patent. On 20 June 1793, he wrote a letter of application and enclosed a fee of $30, addressing himself to the Honorable Thomas Jefferson, Secretary of State, whose office was charged with the duty of issuing patents.

'. . . Mr. Jefferson,' Whitney wrote his father, 'agreed to send the patent as soon as it could be made out.' Then he speculated on the profits his invention might bring: 'It is generally said . . . that I shall make a fortune by it . . . I am now so sure of success that ten thousand dollars would not tempt me to give up my right and relinquish the object. I wish you, sir, not to show my letter nor communicate anything of its contents to anybody except my brother and sister, enjoining it on them to keep the whole a *profound secret.*'

Whitney did not stay in Philadelphia to finish his business because of the prevalence of yellow fever. He went to New Haven, where he took the precaution to appear before Elizur Goodrich, alderman and notary public, who certified: 'He does verily believe that he, the said Whitney, is the true inventor and discoverer of the machine for ginning cotton.'

Jefferson took a personal interest in the gin, an interest expressed when he wrote Whitney reminding him that, to comply with the law, he must offer a model of his machine: 'As the State of Virginia, of which I am, carries on household manufacture of cotton . . . as I do myself . . . permit me to ask information from you on these points: Has the machine been thoroughly tried in the ginning of cotton? What quantity of cotton has it cleaned on an average of several days? What will be the cost of one of them to be worked by hand? Favorable answers to these questions would induce me to engage one of them to be forwarded to Richmond to me.'

Rarely does a great invention proceed almost directly from conception to execution. Whitney went through no long, tortuous process of trial and error to invent the gin. He finished a model of it within ten days after going to work, and a year later it was being manufactured. The machine consisted of a cylinder with wire teeth which drew seed cotton through a wire screen that separated seed from lint, and was fitted with a revolving brush to remove lint from the teeth of the cylinder. This design is still the basis of today's gins.

Phineas Miller married his wealthy employer, Mrs. Greene, and Whitney, supplied with money, established a gin factory in New Haven. Miller toured the up-country looking for suitable gin sites, and wrote Whitney urging haste in producing gins: 'The people of the country are running mad for them . . . When the present crop has been harvested there will be a real property of at least fifty thousand dollars lying useless unless we can enable the holders to bring it to market.' The coming of the gin had sharply stimulated cotton growing, and it is believed that in 1793 two or three million pounds of upland cotton were gathered in the Piedmont.

The firm of Whitney-Miller, operating under its patent, both manufactured and monopolized the gin. Instead of selling it outright, they ran their business on the principle of the grist-mill operator who takes compensation in grain. For example the Georgia *Gazette* of 6 March 1794 carried the following advertisement:

COTTON GINNING

The subscriber will engage to gin in a manner equal to picking by hand, any quantity of the green seed cotton, on the following terms, viz. for every five pounds delivered to him in the seed he will return one pound of clean cotton fitted for market.

For the encouragement of planters he will also mention that ginning machines to clean green seed cotton on the above terms will actually be erected in different parts of the country before the harvesting of the ensuing crop.

PHINEAS MILLER
Mulberry Grove, Near Savannah

By 1797 Miller had 30 gins operating in Georgia, but a rebellion against the monopoly had started even before this date. The situation was explosive. Men believed that fortunes awaited them in the cotton fields, and they did not propose to be hampered by a monopoly whose charges they regarded as exorbitant. Our patent laws were then weak, communications were poor, and the frontier was not concerned with niceties of law enforcement. Men ignored the Whitney patent, rival machines appeared everywhere, and the patentees found themselves involved in endless lawsuits. They did, however, receive a grant of $50,000 from South Carolina in exchange for their patent rights in that state, and smaller grants from North Carolina and Tennessee. But most of these monies went to pay for legal entanglements and other costs.

Lawsuits were vexatious for Whitney because he had to leave Connecticut to appear at the trials. William Scarborough has left us an eyewitness account of Whitney when he appeared in the Federal Circuit Court sitting at Louisville, Georgia: 'Mr. Whitney entered the Court with a small package, enveloped in a silk handkerchief . . . this he carefully deposited under the court table.'

After the defendant presented testimony that appeared conclusive, Whitney got up to make some explanations: 'He took his package from under the table, and opening the handkerchief, presented to view an exquisitely beautiful model of his gin . . . with several handfuls of seed cotton. He handed up both to the judge, and spreading out the silk handkerchief to prevent the escape of the ginned cotton, desired the judge to turn the crank, which he seemed to do with great delight, and in a very few seconds the cotton was separated from the seed . . .

'Mr. Whitney then inquired of the judge and jury if it was not in that state the cotton that was exported for the purpose of manufacture in . . . England . . . Which being assented to, he handed the ginned cotton to the judge, requesting him to strive and force the cotton again between the slats, which it was found impossible to do without breaking the model all to pieces. Thus by the most conclusive ocular demonstration, he proved . . . that the machine used in Europe could have no sort of affinity, let alone identity, with his invention.'

But men found it easy to reproduce the Whitney gin because of its simple principle and construction, and soon there were in operation ten times more bootleg than patented gins. Bootleggers competed not only with Whitney but with one another, and sharply drove down ginning prices. Yet they did not stop there. They spread the rumor — at home and in cotton-importing Britain — that the Whitney gin ruined cotton fiber.

Gins — bootleg, Whitney-made, homemade — spread over the South. A letter written by a traveler in 1797 mentions a gin in the Alabama Territory and gives us a glimpse of early cotton culture in the Lower South: 'I took a view of Mr. Grierson's farm . . . He had a treadle gin sent him from Providence . . . He finds no difficulty in hiring the Indian women to pick out the cotton . . . He gave half a pint of salt, or three strans [sic] of mock wampum beads a basket . . . When the cotton was fully open, they could pick two to three baskets a day.'

Gin-makers too sprang up all over the South. Thus in 1830, William Martin advertised in the Huntsville (Alabama) *Democrat*: 'The subscriber avails himself of this opportunity of saying to the public that he has established himself as a GIN MAKER, on Nubben Ridge . . . Gins of every description that may be required can be had on terms to suit purchasers.'

Long before this time Eli Whitney, bedeviled by lawsuits, had expressed his vexation at the South in a letter written in 1803 to Judge Josiah Stebbins: 'I have a set of the most Depraved villains to combat and I might almost as well go to *Hell* in search of *Happiness* as to apply to a Georgia Court of Justice.'

On another occasion the disappointed inventor discussed his troubles in a letter to another disappointed inventor, Robert Fulton: 'The difficulties with which I have had to contend have originated principally in the want of a disposition in Mankind to do justice . . . My invention was new and distinct . . . I have always maintained that I should have had no difficulty in causing my rights to be respected if it had been less valuable and used only by a small portion of the community.'

No one knows precisely what sums were earned by the inventor-banker firm of Whitney-Miller, but it seems likely that the invention and initial manufacture of one of the world's great machines brought inventor and financial backer little more than several years of toil, worry, and disillusion. Their error lay perhaps in seeking to bring about a monopoly of an invaluable machine; an error the greater because they attempted to apply it to free-swinging frontiersmen decades before their tamed descendants would come to accept trusts and monopolies as matters of course.

Whitney, unable to make a living from the gin, at last turned to new fields and in 1798 received a government contract to manufacture and deliver within two years 10,000 muskets. The musket is a relatively complicated instrument, and the federal armory at Springfield, Massachusetts, was turning out only about 250 a year.

At this rate it would take Whitney years to fulfill his contract. But he introduced a method of manufacture that tremendously affected the United States and the world — the principle of interchangeable parts. As the first step in this process he invented the milling machine. The kingpin of machine tools, it enabled workmen to cut metal according to pattern. This was the foundation stone of his system of interchangeable parts. Now he could make the same parts of different guns as identical as 'the successive impressions of copper-plate engraving.' Thus he introduced the system of interchangeable parts into American industry, substituted the uniformity of the machine for the skill of the craftsman, and greatly decreased the cost and selling price of manufactured goods.

Through this principle forces were set in motion that gave the United States its industrial dynamism, made it the world's mightiest workshop, enormously improved its standard of living, and permitted it twice within a generation to turn the tide in two world wars as it came tardily to the battlefields riding the invincible horses of Pittsburgh and Detroit.

In the moment at Mulberry Grove when the young Yankee schoolmaster put a few cotton bolls into his machine and turned the crank, there was proclaimed on this soil an era of incalculable economic, social, and historical change. On the day before, so to speak, as the French traveler Chastellux wrote, 'They [slaveowners] are constantly talking of abolishing slavery, and of contriving some other means of cultivating their estates.' But by the end of the first quarter of the nineteenth century, the cotton kingdom was coming into being, thousands of slaves were cultivating cotton on hundreds of thousands of Southern acres, and 450,000 workers in English cotton mills were spinning and weaving the produce of this labor.

Midway in the nineteenth century, Daniel Webster sought the origins of the major political issue of the day. What had created proslavery attitudes in the South? What had caused Negro slavery to become a cherished institution — 'no evil, no scourge, but a great religious, social and moral blessing?' Mr. Webster's answer was in terms of Southern prosperity: 'I suppose this is owing to the rapid growth and sudden extension of the cotton plantations of the South. It was the cotton interest that gave a new desire to promote slavery, to spread it, and to use its labor.'

And it was, of course, the gin that gave life to the 'cotton interest' which in turn 'gave a new desire to promote slavery.' Ten years later, Senator Hammond of South Carolina warned the North and the world: 'Cotton is king! You dare not make war upon it.'

The creator of the cotton gin was dead at 60, after a short career of only 30 years. But Macaulay would say of him: 'What Peter the Great did to make Russia dominant, Eli Whitney's cotton gin has more than equaled in its relation to the power and progress of the United States.'

II

England Weaves for the World

THE INVENTION OF THE GIN was explosive, coinciding as it did with the English industrial revolution. The gin stimulated large-scale cotton culture in the South. 'The whole interior of the United States,' said Mr. Justice Johnson of the Supreme Court, 'was languishing, and its people were emigrating for want of some object to engage their attention and employ their industry when the invention of this machine [the cotton gin] set the whole country in motion . . . Individuals who were depressed with poverty and sunk in idleness have suddenly risen to wealth and respectability. Our debts have been paid, our capitals increased, and our land trebled in value.'

On one side of the ocean was a huge area unsurpassed for cotton growing; on the other side was the British factory system. Because it could inexpensively manufacture cotton cloth for a cloth-hungry world, cotton growers were now sure of a constant, ever-widening market. The interplay of these factors produced astounding results.

Short-staple (upland) cotton soon became the South's most valuable crop and the basis of its economy. During each decade production approximately doubled, from 100,000 bales in 1801 to 4.5 million bales in 1859. By that date United States cotton pro-

duction was two-thirds of the world total, and raw cotton had
become the nation's leading export commodity. Eventually the
growing, selling, and manufacturing of cotton and cottonseed
products employed 8 per cent of the country's population in a
$15 billion cotton industry. Because this expansion of American
cotton culture from the time of Eli Whitney to the Civil War
was so dependent upon its relationship to British cotton-textile
production, let us turn to some of the circumstances of English
industrial growth.

From the thirteenth century to the sixteenth century, wool
dominated British textiles. The British grew it and wore it. Exports of raw wool and woolen cloth to the Continent were of
the greatest importance to British economy, and a Venetian, writing home from England in 1500, spoke of the wealth that the
British derive 'from their extraordinary abundance of wool, which
bears such a high price and reputation throughout Europe.'

Wool's dominance had not been threatened, nor was there
any intimation of change, when in 1599 a charter was granted
to the East India Company and a few tiny ships sailed on a six
months' voyage to the East. Although the Dutch and Portuguese
had preceded the British, soon thereafter Indian-made cotton
fabrics appeared in the markets of that strangely gifted people
of the small islands set in northern seas who managed to be not
only superb playwrights, poets, colonizers, soldiers, and lawgivers
but also astute shopkeepers.

Cotton had been immemorially grown in India, as on the
other side of the world it had been grown in Peru. It was used
in the Indus Valley as early as 3,000 B.C. While night still lay
upon a primitive Europe, Hindus had invented the churka, or
roller gin, to separate seed from cotton, and a foot-propelled
loom. They wove cotton lint into yarn, and yarn into cloth —
often of surpassing beauty. Some cloths were so gossamer that
they were called 'webs of the woven wind.' Garments made of
them could be drawn through a moderate-sized finger ring. A
seventeenth-century English traveler describes 'calicuts,' 'so fine
you can hardly feel them in your hand.' Another tells of a muslin
of such delicate texture that 'when a man puts it on, his skin shall

appear as plainly through it, as if he were quite naked; but the merchants are not permitted to transport it, for the governor is obliged to send it all to the Great Mogul's seraglio.'

If wars often degrade warriors, they sometimes exert a civilizing influence upon them and cause unexpected economic change. Thus, the then for the most part rude English had first encountered the silks, steels, and damascened wares of Arab culture when they went to Palestine during the Crusades. They had brought home specimens of these things — marvels beyond the telling. Later, in India, they sent home Indian cottons for sale whose price was within reach of the ordinary man's purse. The delicate textures, exotic designs, and bright colorings brought something of tropical warmth and Eastern wonder to a people living among northern fogs and darkness. There was an instant demand for Indian cottons, a demand that rose annually along with the howls of English wool men. At their pressure Parliament passed an act that matches even some of our tariff regulations in absurdity, such as when Congress, in 1929, levied tribute on Chinese preserved duck eggs presumably to protect our duck-egg foundries. In 1666 Parliament decreed that the dead should be buried only in woolen shrouds. (Perhaps, however, no proper Englishman would have wanted to appear in heaven wearing 'foreign' cloth.)

Yet though wool men thundered and those given to deploring deplored, cotton's vogue increased. Then Parliament, as our Congress has so often done under tariff pressures, sank to the occasion. In 1720 it 'outlawed' calico, forbade its use, and enlisted armies of snoopers. The snooper who informed upon his calico-using neighbor was awarded five pounds sterling at the law-breaker's expense. Thus was patriotism made profitable.

If this was foolish legislation in its own time, coming events made it appear even more foolish. The revolution that transformed rural, agricultural England into urban, industrial England began in little more than a generation. Britain became the world's workshop, moved far ahead of continental Europe in industrial power, and grew wealthy as the world's foremost producer of cotton textiles.

Men are sometimes brutal in search of profits. They are also sometimes ridiculous. When it was once proposed to abolish the English duty on the importation of raw cotton, flax-spinners protested. Anxious for the virginity of English maidens and the chastity of English wives, they said that the wearing of cotton gave rise to erotic sensations!

Nothing, however, could stop the triumphant march of English cotton textiles. Soon they flooded the markets of the earth, including those of India. For nearly 3,000 years India had made cottons for home and export markets, but now she lost most of her trade to English machine-made cottons. By 1860 Britain was exporting to India nearly 242 million pounds of yarn and cotton goods, the manufacturing costs only one-fourth of the Indian. British cotton textiles, usually made from American cotton, were to bring great riches to a few English textile lords, incalculable misery to thousands of textile workers, and to change the face of English districts as the 'dark satanic mills' rose in the once green valleys. And about a century after the beginning of the industrial revolution, Britain's huge demand for American cotton became the subject of a tragic miscalculation by Southern secessionists. But in 1720 these events were obscured by the impenetrable curtains of the future.

The industrial revolution ended an age based upon England's centuries-old monopoly: the almost universal use of her woolen cloths and the skills of her woolen workers. Woolen cloth had been a treasure constantly replenished — as marketable and current as gold all over the world. It had been an invaluable part of Britain's world trade which, ever since the seventeenth century, had been making England greater than the French or Spanish empires, and richer than the carrying trade of the Netherlands. England's empire was raised on the foundations of village industry, and to the end of the eighteenth century, woolen cloth made up one-third of both her exports and her total output. But cotton, the new staple of industry, was gaining fast and was to overtake wool at the turn of the century.

Woolen cloth-making was a handicraft culture that employed simple tools and was conducted as a cottage industry. Cloth was made by men whose capital was a loom and perhaps a week's supply of wool, whose labor was their own plus their families'. When pieces of goods had been made they were collected by hamlets; larger collections went to the towns where they were dispatched in rude vehicles over bad roads to seaports. If weavers prospered, they might buy an extra loom or two, and hire hands to work them, but they remained well-to-do master workmen and rarely became clothiers. These men evoked the praise and admiration of Daniel Defoe. A fine reporter, in addition to his other great gifts, he held up the weavers of the West Riding wool country as models of industry and the pride of society, at the same time giving us a glimpse of how they lived and worked: 'The land was divided into small enclosures from Two Acres to six or seven each . . . Every three or four Pieces of Land had a house belonging to them — hardly an House standing at Speaking-distance from another . . . Every one generally keeps a Cow . . . for his Family . . . The Houses are full of lusty Fellows, some at the Dye-vats, some at the looms, others dressing the Cloths; the women and children carding or spinning; being all employed, from the youngest to the oldest.'

All this was to be ended by the invention of the cotton gin and the successive, close-knit British cotton-machine inventions that were achieved in little more than 20 years. Kay's flying shuttle more than doubled the weaver's capacity, while the Hargreaves spinning jenny increased productive power eightfold. Arkwright's spinning frame and inventions for carding and spinning made large-scale production possible in factories operated by massed, disciplined labor. The machines were driven by Watt's steam engine which burned British coal. Britain's moist climate was excellent for textile-making, and soon a cloth-hungry world clamored for the output of her cotton mills.

In 1781, Watt's partner, Boulton, wrote him: 'The people in London, Manchester and Birmingham are *steam mill mad* . . .' The application of steam to machinery destroyed the village-cottage industry and led to the establishment of the factory town. As horsepower came to be exalted and an almost bucolic age was passing to the hissing of steam and the clanking of machines, William Blake wrote:

The Villages lament: they faint, outstretch'd upon the plain.
Wailing runs round the Valleys from the Mill & from the Barn.
The Horse is of more value than the Man.

Cotton began to displace wool as Britain's principal textile manufacture, and manufacturers became fearful that their raw-cotton demands, almost exclusively supplied by the Levant and the West Indies, would outrun the supply. Between 1780 and 1800 they had increased their cotton imports tenfold. Textile men urged the East India Company to expand Indian cotton cultivation. But before such a project could be got under way, rescue came from an unexpected quarter: from His Majesty's former North American Colonies now called the United States of America. As she grew to be the world's greatest producer of raw cotton, her exports in large measure displaced other cottons in the British market, and she became an unfailing source of supply to British manufacturers, however large their demands.

In 1763 Britain's prestige was high everywhere. But 20 years later when, after an unsuccessful war with her North American colonies, she signed away an empire her prestige sank. Even such powerful, intelligent rulers as Josef of Austria, Catherine of Russia, and Frederick of Prussia believed that her sun had set. Men talked of George III, Chatham, North, Edmund Burke, and Charles Fox. But few mentioned the obscure inventors who were then toiling in Britain and the United States. Yet as Britain was losing an empire, these men were initiating changes that were to raise her to world industrial and banking supremacy, give her the power to stand the long strain of the Napoleonic wars, and, leader of a grand coalition, enable her to destroy the would-be world conqueror.

Under the impetus of the industrial revolution, based principally upon iron and cotton, Britain's population nearly doubled within a generation. The population of such manufacturing centers as Liverpool, Manchester, and Glasgow grew even more rapidly. Writing of the Lancashire of this period in *The Cotton Famine*, R. A. Arnold said: 'For years and years she has wanted "hands" . . . and her demand was not made in vain. Nowhere else upon an equal space of God's earth has population obeyed the summons of capital to an equal extent . . . From north, east, and south, numbers have flocked to share the profits of the cotton trade; and from the west . . . crowds of Irish — fleeing from a poverty at home which would seem starvation to an Englishman, — have swollen the army of cotton-workers.'

In 1828 James Dobbs' comic song on the growth of Birmingham — 'I Can't Find Brummagem' — was a great hit:

> *Full twenty years, and more, are past,*
> *Since I left Brummagem;*
> *But I set out for home at last,*
> *To good old Brummagem.*
> *But every place is altered so,*
> *There's hardly a single place I know;*
> *And it fills my heart with grief and woe,*
> *For I can't find Brummagem.*
>
> *I remember one John Growse,*
> *A buckle-maker in Brummagem:*
> *He built himself a country house,*
> *To be out of the smoke of Brummagem:*
> *But though John's country house stands still,*
> *The town itself has walked up hill,*
> *Now he lives beside of a smoky mill,*
> *In the middle of the streets of Brummagem.*

We hear of population growth in the cotton districts from Sir Robert Peel, who had brought calico printing to a high state of efficiency. In 1806 he said: 'In the cotton trade, machinery has given birth to a new population; it has promoted the comforts of the population to such a degree that early marriages have been resorted to, and a great increase of numbers has been occasioned by it . . .'

Although industry did add to the comfort and wealth of the total population, the new class of urban workers led a life of almost unrelieved misery. Peel, a humane man, tried to mitigate the growing horrors of the smoky mill towns, but his contemporaries in the first generation of industrial chiefs were generally rough, callous men. Carlyle coined the term 'captains of industry' to describe them. Their notion of hell was simple. It was the condition, they said, of 'not making money.' They believed with Lord Brougham that 'Charity is an interference with a healing process of nature, which acts by increasing the rate of mortality, thereby raising wages.' The friend of labor, therefore, was the man who let workmen starve to death, for when many workers died, labor became scarce and wages rose.

Children were quite often employed in the textile mills, working until they died or reached an age when their labor became unprofitable. 'Strappers' flogged drowsy children of six and seven years who toiled sixteen hours a day, and 'groups of pallid mites could be seen supporting each other as they dragged their limbs up the dark lanes of Lancashire and Yorkshire valleys.'

At Dundee, spinning-mill girls, some of them barely eight-years old, worked from six in the morning until eight-thirty at night. During a six-week 'brisk-time' their hours were from three in the morning until ten at night. But when Lord Shaftesbury aired these horrors and said that steam should be prevented from escaping into rooms where women and children worked, employers ridiculed him and Lord Brougham remarked, 'Really, my Lords, I feel this is great nonsense.' Similarly, in the 1840s, as thousands starved in the midst of a great depression, the Duke of Norfolk outdid Marie Antoinette's prescription 'Let them eat cake.' He suggested that the poor might stay their hunger and warm their stomachs with an inexpensive soup composed of curry powder dissolved in hot water.

By 1860 the condition of child workers had been legally 'improved.' The Factory Laws then declared that from eight to thirteen years of age operatives were to be classified as 'children'; from thirteen to eighteen years of age as 'young persons,' a class that included women of all ages. 'The army of King Cotton,' wrote R. Arthur Arnold, a contemporary observer, 'is recruited without reference to stature, and as to age, eight years is sufficient. At thirteen the operative attains his majority and becomes a "full-timer."'

Since the ever-expanding cotton mills needed an ever-expanding labor supply at low wages, mill owners sought to breed the needed supply on the spot. 'For the last fifty years,' Arnold wrote in 1864, 'the cotton manufacturer has given such encouragement to matrimony as never existed elsewhere. And it must be admitted that . . . the operative class has fulfilled the Scriptural demand. They have been fruitful, they have multiplied . . . No one who has ever attended morning service at Manchester Cathedral will forget the ceremony of asking the banns of marriage . . . Boy-husband and girl-wife — themselves often not fully grown — become the parents of weakly children, specially requiring what they rarely get, a mother's care. The husband and wife . . . can rent a house which is wind and weather proof, though a filthy roadway may rise high above the door-sill — though the paved floor be perpetually damp, and through the back door, fever-seeds are wafted from the pestiferous "midden," which is "Lancashire" for that unwholesome combination of an open cesspool and an ashpit, usually to be found at the back of their houses.'

While Britain was moving from cottage to factory industry, the usual order of labor was reversed. The male breadwinner was left at home. His wife and children worked in the cotton mills. Obviously the woman who worked thirteen hours a day in a factory had no time to give to her children, and immediately after confinement some women were forced to return to work. Arthur Bryant in *Pageant of England 1840–1940* tells us how mill workers looked: 'Monotonous and unnatural working conditions resulted in permanent curvature of the limbs. Whole families went about with crooked legs or twisted shoulders. Every street had its company of cripples, of . . . youths bent double and limping, of haglike girls with deformed backs and hips . . . The factory population of Lancashire seemed more like some ill-fated race of pigmies than normal human beings . . .'

Few paid any attention to a grave, bearded man then taking notes on the working conditions of cotton-mill hands. The notes were preparation for a book. Written by Karl Marx, it was to be entitled *Das Kapital*.

The British cotton-textile trade grew constantly throughout the first half of the nineteenth century. In 1859–60, while the United

States consumed only 953,000 bales of its home-grown cotton, Britain took over two million bales. As our Civil War began, she accounted for more than half of the world's consumption of cotton.

A world market for cotton textiles, Britain also — at Liverpool — became a world market for raw cotton. She re-exported a considerable part of the staple she imported. Russia bought about three-fourths of her cotton supply in Liverpool; so did Belgium, the Prussian *Zollverein*, and countries of southern Europe. Here buyers had the advantage of a market that sensitively registered fluctuations in worldwide supply and demand. British fiber classification was believed to be more accurate than any other, and British merchants obligingly extended long credits to their customers. Hence Liverpool grew into the world's leading cotton market, a dominance which was shaken in the twentieth century only by governmental restrictions, at home and abroad, upon the free cotton market.

The industrial revolution and the factory system were established on the Continent, and while these countries continued to import much of their cotton through Britain, they sought at the same time to escape dependence upon her for textiles. Their efforts opened new markets to American cotton. Thus, for example, French imports of American cotton jumped from 27 million pounds in 1821 to 168 million pounds in 1855, and in 1856 we shipped relatively large amounts to Holland, Spain, Genoa, Naples, and other Italian States.

For a long time, American cotton growers had a flourishing market in Britain, and Britain had a flourishing textile trade based on American cotton. But 'resentments' developed and bit deep into cotton men on both sides of the ocean. Americans welcomed continental competition not only because it widened their markets but also because they did not like the so-called British monopoly. At the same time, however, British economic and political leaders were deeply concerned by America's constantly increasing predominance in the production of cotton. Their concern deepened at every crop shortage, and it became a matter of the gravest anxiety as the United States moved nearer and nearer to sectional conflict.

Britain's anxiety was well founded. She had a great textile empire that was a source of immense profit to her. But it was an empire largely at the mercy of American cotton growers who, as the Civil War approached, supplied it with three-fourths of the cotton it consumed. Britain therefore sought to develop new sources of supply elsewhere and as an agency to further this end in 1857 formed the Cotton Supply Association of Great Britain.

Four years later the United States plunged into the civil conflict that British textile men had so long feared. American cotton then became an objective for the highest British diplomacy as it had also been a prime consideration of Southern secessionist leaders. How the issue was decided might shape the future not only of the United States but of much of the world.

III

'My Head Is Bendin' Low'

THE RISE OF AMERICAN COTTON to international importance was based upon a number of factors: the cotton gin, the industrial revolution, Negro slavery, and the Southern environment — particularly soil and climate. Ullrich Phillips wrote: 'Let us begin by discussing the weather, for that has been the chief agency in making the South distinctive. It fostered the cultivation of the staple crops, which promoted the plantation system, which brought the importation of Negroes, which not only gave rise to chattel slavery but created a lasting race problem.'

If the South's long, hot growing season was favorable to cotton culture, it also affected men's lives. For, says Phillips, 'In the tedious heat, work is hard, indolence easy; speech is likely to be slow and somewhat slurred; manners are soft; and, except where tempers are hot, the trend is toward easygoing practices.' As the South's warm, enervating climate differed from the colder, more bracing climate of the North, so also its broad, fertile coastal plain, so different from the rocky New England soil and the rolling, upland territory of the Middle Atlantic states, naturally led to the establishment of large agricultural areas — the plantation system. Into this environment, favorable for cotton culture on a wide scale, came an adequate labor supply in the form of African slaves.

For nearly three centuries white Europe and America ravaged
black Africa for slaves. They were the great nations: proud,
enlightened, strong, and — Christian. Decade after decade stinking
slave ships of the English, the French, the Portuguese, the Dutch,
the Spanish, the Danes, the Americans stood off Africa's coasts.

Slave trading is an old, primitive form of commerce, and in
what might be called its modern period, the British were its pre-
eminent practitioners. One of its pioneers of the Elizabethan Age
was John (afterward Sir John) Hawkins. He turned from pillaging
Spanish galleons to slaving in his ship the *Jesus* (of Lübeck) lent
by Queen Elizabeth in exchange for shares in his expeditions.
Negroes whom the ship's men were trying to capture, said a
member of the expedition in his diary, used to flee at their
approach, 'leaping and turning their tailes, that it was most
strange to see and gave us great pleasure to behold them.' The
slaves were gathered by force, and Hawkins sometimes sold them
by force. When the Spanish citizens of Rio de la Hache, a West
Indies port, pretended that they could not pay cash for slaves,
Hawkins threatened them with a hot English 'breakfast of
javelins and arrows.' Whereupon the reluctant customers found
cash and bought slaves. Hawkins sailed away only to return, kill
the citizens, plunder the town, and go home to a knighthood.

Hawkins' sailing orders to the captains who accompanied him
were: 'Serve God daily — love one another — preserve your victuals
— beware of fire — and keepe good companie.' Once, when he was
becalmed with a cargo of Negroes, God, he felt, came to his
rescue: 'Almighty God, which never suffereth his elect to perish,
sent us the ordinary breeze.' And once after he had captured full
cargoes of slaves in Sierra Leone, sold them in the Spanish islands,
and reached home, the chronicler said: 'God be thanked! in
safety: with the loss of twenty persons in all the voyage; as with
great profit to the venturers in the said voyage, so also to the
whole realm, on bringing home both gold, silver, pearls, and
other jewels in great store. His name therefore be praised for
evermore! Amen.'

Black slaves, ungrateful that they were being taken into white
civilization, died on the voyage, maimed themselves, committed
suicide. Captain Thomas, who commanded the ship *Hannibal* of

London, in 1693, comments in his journal upon the ingratitude of his cargo: 'We spent in our passage from St. Thomas to Barbadoes two months eleven days, in which time there happened such mortality among my poor men and negroes, that of the first we buried 14, and of the last 320 . . . the Royal African Company losing ten pounds on every slave that died, and the owners of the ship ten pounds ten shillings, being the freight agreed upon to be paid . . . for every negro delivered alive . . . at Barbadoes . . .'

Captain Thomas is moved to self-pity: 'No gold-finders can endure so much noisome slavery as they who carry negroes; for these have some respite and satisfaction but we endure twice the misery; and yet by our mortality our voyages are ruined, and we pine and fret ourselves to death, to think that we should undergo so much misery and take so much pains to so little purpose.'

During the eighteenth century the slave trade loomed large in the world's economic life. Every Atlantic community, including the American, engaged in it and competed vigorously with one another for sources of supply and sale. As demand increased, prices rose. In the mid-eighteenth century a sturdy slave brought £10 on the Gold Coast and sold for £30. Twenty-five years later a slave of similar quality brought £27 and sold for £50.

As sharp demand reduced the supply of prime slaves, larger proportions of old and infirm Negroes were included in the cargoes. Slavers 'dressed up' Negroes to make them look younger and healthier than they were. Drugs were used to bloat them so that they looked fat. They were 'sweated with powder and lemon juice, and oiled to impart a gloss to the skin.' When slaves were offered for sale, the men and women stark naked, the ship's surgeon examined them for defects. Those who were rejected were killed by their owners or patched up to be offered for sale again.

Slaving ships could not make more than one or two trips a year, and efficiency dictated that they be packed tight with Negroes. The look and stench and horror of such a ship at sea is portrayed for us by an eyewitness — the Reverend R. Walsh. In 1807–08 Britain and the United States forbade their nationals to engage in slave trading, and the Reverend Mr. Walsh was aboard a naval patrol vessel when it captured a slaver bound for Brazil. It had left Africa with a cargo of 562 persons, and after being out for 17 days, had thrown overboard 55. 'The slaves,' our clergyman tells us, 'were all inclosed under grated hatchways between decks . . . They were stowed so close together there was no possibility of their lying down . . . or changing their position . . . As they were shipped on account of different individuals, they were all branded . . . with the owner's marks . . .'

The slaves, instinctively feeling that they had fallen among friends, 'immediately began to shout . . . They could not contain their delight; they endeavored to scramble upon their knees, stretching up to kiss our hands . . . Some, however, hung down their heads in apparently hopeless dejection . . . and some, particularly children, seemed dying.'

In the holds 'The heat . . . was so great and the odor so offensive that it was quite impossible to enter.' The slaves were brought on deck for fresh air and water although the slaver's mate feared that he and his fellows would be murdered. There were '517 fellow creatures of all ages and sexes . . . all in a state of total nudity, scrambling out together to taste the luxury of a little fresh air and water.' When water was brought, 'They all rushed like maniacs toward it. No entreaties or blows could restrain them . . . they fought with one another for a drop of this precious liquid.'

The slavers' risks were those of the perils of the sea, slave rebellion, and disease among his cargo. When rebellion flamed it sometimes became necessary to destroy many of the rebels and with them a large part of the profits of the voyage. Occasionally epidemics swept slave ranks. As the pink pimples that herald the coming of smallpox appeared on a slave's face, he was thrown overboard. Ophthalmia frequently afflicted slaves and whole cargoes became blind and were destroyed. Sometimes ship's crews caught the disease. Chronicles depict blind crew, blind Negroes, and blind ship drifting upon blind ocean. Occasionally a slaving vessel caught fire at sea. Then the crew took to the boats, while slaves died between crackling columns of fire and the illimitable expanse of the pitiless sea.

Yet this highly speculative traffic was immensely lucrative — the

profits of a single voyage often ran to 1,000 per cent — and gains
from the trade enhanced the commercial capitals of both England
and New England. Slaving profits were the underpinning of some
of the great English middle-class families of the eighteenth and
nineteenth centuries, and it has been estimated that in 1750,
English slave traders were deriving an annual return of £1.2 million
on £800,000 invested in the traffic.

As slaving became big business, it was no longer conducted by
such hotheaded feudal captains as John Hawkins, but by cool-
headed businessmen — especially Liverpool merchants. Thus, the
Royal African Company was well financed by English merchant
capitalists and invested with a monopoly charter. Through the
defeat of the Spanish in 1713, England obtained the right to
the exclusive transport of Negro slaves to the Spanish-American
possessions for 30 years. Capital became readily available for out-
fitting ships and stations were established on the West African
coast. A chain of middlemen was devised. Sound businessmen
ran the trade along sound economic lines. Under their guidance,
Liverpool, which in 1751 had 87 ships with a capacity of 25,000
slaves, in 11 years acquired 878 ships taking 303,737 slaves to
the Indies, a cargo valued at more than £15 million.

The slave trade was brutal, but success in it was not just a
matter of physical force. Liverpool men were especially successful
in the trade, and Miriam Beard in a *History of the Business Man*
accounts for it in these terms: 'In the region about Liverpool there
was much Puritanism, later merging into Methodism . . . Pos-
sibly the Puritan temperament triumphed here; it was because
these Liverpool men were so thrifty, figuring their expenses to
the last shilling, that they beat the more reckless Portuguese
and other Catholic competitors in the field . . .

'The slave trade called for the best qualities of the sea-pirate
as well as the Puritan-Bourgeois; only the English had this well-
balanced mixture of traits, enabling them to wrest the lion's
share of the trade away from Spanish, Dutch and French and
hold it until it was legally abolished, even continuing the smug-
gling until far into the nineteenth century.'

Americans, not to be left out of such a profitable enterprise,
entered the slave trade in 1683 when the ship *Desire*, built at

Marblehead, set sail. Yankee capacity for trading soon astonished
the world and made many New Englanders rich. Their ships came
swarming into the Gulf of Guinea, using markets frequented by
the English: Sierra Leone, the Grain Coast (Liberia), the Ivory,
Gold, and Slave Coasts, the Niger Delta, Cameroons, Gabon,
and Loango. Here slaves, gathered in the huge fan-shaped hinter-
land, were herded together.

Slave-trading was a three-way traffic with a potential three-way
profit. English slavers traded Manchester and Yorkshire goods for
Negroes in Africa. Then they exchanged the Negroes in the
West Indies for spices, rum, and other commodities which they
sold in England. Or they disposed of their slaves for cash and
bought West Indian goods for English sale. Americans purchased
West Indian molasses, distilled it into rum in New England,
traded the rum for slaves in Africa, and sold the slaves in the
West Indies or at home. In 1750 there were about 350,000 slaves
in His Majesty's North American Colonies; by the year of independence the number was about 500,000.

In a draft of the Declaration of Independence, Jefferson
indicted George III for waging 'cruel war against human nature
itself, violating its most sacred rights . . . in the persons of
distant people, who never offended him, captivating and carrying
them into slavery in another hemisphere, or to incur miserable
death in their transportation hither.' But this passage never became
part of the Declaration. It was deleted because the South had
not attempted to suppress slavery, and because men in the North
('our Northern brethren') were engaged in the trade.

There was a sentimental opposition to slavery among some
Southerners, especially those who derived their philosophy from
the idealistic Age of Enlightenment, and nourished the principles
that underlay the French and American revolutions. In his *Notes
on Virginia*, written in 1781, Jefferson denounced slaveholding
in terms that were afterward employed with great effect by
abolitionists: 'With what execration should the statesman be
loaded who, permitting one-half of the citizens thus to trample
on the rights of the other, transforms these into despots and
those into enemies . . . Can the liberties of a nation be thought
secure when we have removed their only firm basis, a conviction

in the minds of the people that these liberties are the gift of God? That they are not to be violated but with his wrath? Indeed I tremble for my country when I reflect that God is just; that his justice cannot sleep forever.'

Jefferson, Madison, George Mason, the Randolphs, Patrick Henry, and Richard Henry Lee all opposed slavery in principle and favored its early extinction. George Washington expressed his hope that 'slavery may be abolished by slow, sure and imperceptible degrees.' But antislavery feeling in Virginia and Maryland was animated by a purely practical reason. It was that the change from specialized farming to general farming left many planters with surplus labor, and their dilemma was expressed by Washington when he wrote: 'It is . . . clear, that on this Estate [Mount Vernon] I have more working negroes . . . than can be employed to any advantage in the farming system . . .'

Washington did not, however, want to sell or lease them except by families. Unfortunately the demand was only for individual laborers, and the worried master of Mount Vernon wrote: 'Something must be done or I shall be ruined; for all the money (in addition to what I raise by crops, and rents) that has been *received* for Lands, sold within the last years, to the amount of Fifty thousand dollars, has scarcely been able to keep me afloat.'

But Jefferson's Virginia, upon attaining independence, prohibited the importation of slaves within her borders. By 1807 all the states had legally abolished the foreign slave trade, although in South Carolina it had been revived when the opening of Louisiana in 1803 and other factors offered, as Du Bois put it, 'fortunes to planters and Charleston slave-merchants.' But Congress on 2 March 1807 prohibited the importation of slaves into the United States after 1 January 1808, and Britain passed a similar act at almost the same time — 25 March 1807.

Yet prohibitory legislation did not automatically put a stop to so profitable a business. Where there are great profits to be made, men will be found to take large risks. Hence the slave trade went on, and it was not completely halted even though in 1820 Congress placed the importation of slaves on the same basis as piracy and made it an offense punishable by death. United States naval vessels hunted down slavers, but when illicit cargoes were confiscated, the government was faced with an embarrassing problem. The captured slaves could not be returned to their homes and there was no other place to send them. Finally in 1822 the colony of Monrovia, a section of modern Liberia, was founded by a philanthropic group as a home for repatriated slaves.

More than a generation after Congress 'outlawed' the foreign slave trade, it was still being carried on by venturesome Americans — usually from New England — who would not give up a good thing despite the risks. In 1843 Horatio Bridge was an officer of an American naval vessel off the West African coast, and his *Journal of an American Cruiser* tells us: 'More vessels come to . . . Africa from Salem than from any other port in the United States; although New York, Boston and Providence, all have their regular traders . . . All the vessels bring New England rum, tobacco, powder, guns, large brass pans and cloth . . .

'The bills of Pedro Blanco, the notorious slave-trader at Gallinas . . . are taken as readily as cash. Some of the large English houses give orders to their captains not to traffic with men reputed to be slave-dealers; but if a purchaser comes with money in his hand, it requires a tenderer conscience and sterner integrity than are usually met with on the coast of Africa, to resist the temptation . . . It is quite an interesting moral question . . . how far either Old England or New England can be pronounced free from the guilt . . . of the slave trade, while, with so little indirectness, they both share in its profits and contribute aid to its prosecution.'

Americans continued to bring slaves here until the very eve of the Civil War. In 1860, a Congressional report said: 'Almost all the slave expeditions for some time past have been outfitted in the United States, chiefly in New York. Large sums were involved and foreign opinion of this country was scandalized by the illicit slave-trade.' The British were especially perturbed by this illegal participation in an activity that had long been abolished by the great trading nations. In 1860, Lord John Russell, Britain's foreign minister, told Washington that 'United States capital has been more and more employed in this [slave] traffic.' Vessels flying the American flag could not be halted by British cruisers and, said Russell, 'The master [of the slaver] often taunts the captain of a British cruiser with impunity [sic] from capture.'

The Quakers had announced their opposition to slavery toward the end of the seventeenth century, but this did not become a widely held opinion in New England and the Northern states until one all-important fact had been established. It was that slavery was *unprofitable* north of Maryland.

Yankee artisans, who had prospered during the Revolution, raised their voices, not against slavery, but against non-agricultural slavery. They hoped that manufacturing would increase and they did not want to compete with slave labor. Their demands combined with various other pressures caused many states to legislate against the slave trade, but the Lower South disapproved and in 1786 Jefferson wrote: 'The disposition to emancipate them [slaves] is strongest in Virginia . . . In Maryland and Georgia a very few are disposed to emancipate. In South Carolina and Georgia, not the smallest symptom of it.'

Ullrich B. Phillips comments sharply upon the motivations of North and South with respect to slavery: 'While the rising cotton industry was giving the blacks in the South new value as slaves, Northern spokesmen were frankly stating an antipathy of their people toward negroes in any capacity whatsoever . . .' Even if Negroes had not continued to be brought here illegally for 50 years after the foreign trade was abolished, there was an abundant seed-stock of about a million slaves in 1808. And, says Phillips, 'had no man invented a cotton gin their natural increase might well have glutted the market for plantation labor.' But the banning of slave imports increased the value of Negroes already here while slaveowners found themselves with large 'inventory profits' when the coming of the gin, coinciding with the industrial revolution in England, brought a huge demand for raw cotton and for slaves to grow it.

At first American slaveowners had taken slaves of any tribal origin as long as they looked healthy enough to stand hard work. But trial and error led them to specify the kind they wanted. Since slave raiding occurred over large African areas tribesmen of various states of culture were caught in the slavers' dragnet, but they were not all equally desirable to the slaveowner. Senegalese, for example, intelligent and often with a strong Arabic strain in their ancestry, were valued for domestic service and responsible positions. But Gold Coast Coromantees were little wanted because they were likely to become 'troublemakers.' Strong of mind and body, courageous, ferocious, and stubborn, they might stir up dreaded insurrections. Mandigoes, on the other hand, were gentle. Their flaw was that they were gifted thieves.

The most valuable of all were the hardworking, cheerful, docile, submissive Whydahs, Nagoes, and Pawpaws of the Slave Coast. Eboes were desirable too, except in one respect. In slavery they were markedly suicidal.

Before 1808, slavers usually sold their cargoes through merchants who charged a 10 per cent commission of the sale price for their services. The following advertisement published at Charleston in 1785 is typical of the trade: 'GOLD COAST NEGROES. On Thursday, the 17th of March instant, will be exposed to public sale near the Exchange . . . the remainder of the cargo of negroes imported in the ship *Success* . . . consisting chiefly of likely young boys and girls in good health, and having been here through the winter may be in some degree seasoned to this climate . . .'

'Seasoning' was important, a fact first discovered in the colonies when indentured servants newly arrived from England died during the summer 'like cats and dogs.' Sometimes slaves perished soon after their arrival of diseases they had brought from Africa, committed suicide, or, consumed by longing for their lost homes, could be put to doing only light work. It was often necessary to take great pains to keep up the spirits of newly arrived slaves, and the difficulty of the task is pointed out by an observer familiar with conditions in South Carolina and Georgia in 1740. He reported that the value of an unseasoned slave's life might be estimated at no more than seven years.

For more than a century — impelled by a luscious combination of 'religion' and dividends — the ships of New England slavers journeyed great distances carrying outward cargoes of rum and hardware and inward cargoes of Negro slaves.

Newport, Rhode Island, was a well-known slaving port during the eighteenth century. Her slave-ship owners seem to have worked primarily for God and only secondarily for profit, because when their ships arrived laden with slaves who had escaped the perils of the long voyage from Africa, they thanked God that another cargo of heathen had been brought to a Christian country where they might enjoy the sweet dispensations of organized religion.

The Negroes who were brought as slaves to the United States long, long ago, and those who brought them, are dust. Yet from remote vistas of time, down endless corridors of space, swell the overtones of melancholy that are heard today in so much of the singing of cotton-plantation Negroes. Alexander Falconbridge, who was a member of a slave-ship's company, wrote in 1788 that 'the poor wretches are frequently compelled to sing, but when they do so, their songs are generally lamentations of exile from their native country.'

IV

'Picture Tonight'

W<small>HENEVER</small> <small>PEOPLE</small> of the Old South gather for a party they are not unlikely — especially after they have been touched to mellow nostalgia by that noble beverage, bourbon whiskey — to sing softly:

> Picture tonight,
> A field of snowy white,
> Darkies are singin' soft an' low . . .

'Men,' says Santayana, 'create what they imagine and love what they create.' Here the singers lovingly recall the never-never land of the fabled Befo'-the-Wah plantations: the planter and his lady, their beautiful daughter and desperately handsome son; the stately mansion filled with family portraits, Chippendale, and old silver, its grounds sloping through bird-haunted formal gardens to the steamboat-burdened Mississippi; the courtly Negro butler (such as William Veal of Stark Young's *So Red the Rose*), slaves in the 'quarters,' and cotton fields blowing white to the farthest horizon.

Yankee troubadours of New York's Tin-Pan Alley, who have long made songs about fields o' cotton, git-tars on the levee, and the *Robert E. Lee*, together with the mockingbird school of Southern lady writers and overwrought homegrown romantics, have distorted the image of the antebellum cotton South. It was a land, according to them, wholly composed of great plantations whose hordes of happy slaves sang their heads off in an atmosphere half *Ivanhoe,* half honeysuckle.

At the cost of doing violence to an amiable legend, it must be said that the truth is less 'romantic.' Big planters were a tiny minority among cotton growers. Yet the South of their day was a 'fabric of cotton' upon which they wrought something of a miracle. For their influence upon the legislation, codes, and manners of the region was out of all proportion to their numbers. So it was that millions of non-slaveholders followed the leadership of a handful of slaveholding planters even into the fiery furnace of civil war.

We cannot here discuss the many ways in which slavery and the plantation system affected the lives of the Southern people before '61, and still affects them. But one of the most notable results was familism. In the isolation of plantation life, the home, the family, and the small domestic world of the 'big house,' became the center of everything. There developed what W. J. Cash calls 'an unusually intense affection and respect for the women of the family — for the wife and mother upon whose activities the comfort and well-being of everybody greatly depended.'

Writing of the effects of slavery in the United States and Brazil, the Brazilian scholar, Gilberto Freyre, says in *Foreign Affairs:* 'I suggested that the Roman Catholic devotion for the Virgin Mary glorified as Queen — Regina — seems not to have become as intense in any other Roman Catholic area of the world as in Brazil. This was a result . . . of that extreme idealization of aristocratic women (and even of Negro women in the shape of old mammies) as basic or vital sentimental parts of the plantation family complex developed in slavery days. In this particularly intense devotion to the Virgin Mary we detect a sublimation or idealization of the cult of women that has found other means of expression in the United States, including an identification of the cult of the purity of women with the cult of race purity . . .'

Technologically, the plantation system was in advance of its times. According to Gray, it was the nation's first large-scale organization of agriculture, in fact the first great experiment in this field since the Roman Empire. It attempted to manage scientifically a relatively large number of workers tilling large acreages under unified direction. It thus anticipated today's giant, 'rationalized' agriculture in the United States.

The plantation system was marked by the following characteristics:

Cotton was its basic cash crop.

It was a monoculture which could employ labor during the greater part of the year.

It employed a slave labor force that produced a surplus value over and above the cost of its keep.

It used extensive rather than intensive methods of cultivation because it had to extract a maximum current income from the capital invested in slaves.

It relied heavily upon outside credits to keep it going.

Gray points out the many weaknesses of this system in his great study of the plantations. Thus, for example, because it stressed maximum current money income, it was not favorable to the accumulation of wealth over a long period. This resulted in a failure to provide for soil conservation, and a disregard for the small economies that contribute toward an accumulation of wealth. This waste of the soil periodically necessitated heavy expenses for the purchase of new land, and the large profits of 'good' years stimulated personal extravagance among planters.

The South in general, and particularly the Lower South, was continuously in debt because it always needed new capital for expansion. But the relative poverty of the South, as compared with the North, was the result of this system of rural economy that was wasteful in both production and consumption, a system that concentrated a large proportion of the money income in the hands of a relatively small percentage of the population. One effect of this was to push a great number of the white inhabitants into isolated regions where they pursued an almost totally self-sufficing economy.

Yet, for all this, the mantle of 'romance' that has been thrown about the planter makes it difficult for us to see him realistically.

We do not, for example, associate him with anything as drab as capitalism. We reserve this identification for industrialists with their workers, factories, and shares sold on stock exchanges, and although we have had 'captains of industry,' we have never used the term 'captains of agriculture.' Yet some prewar planters merited it; among them, Francis Surgett of Natchez. At his death shortly before 1860, he owned, among other things, 75,000 acres of fertile lands in Louisiana, Arkansas, and Mississippi — his estate worth several million dollars. Other planters of the section were nearly as rich.

A man farming huge areas, using large numbers of workers, and employing extensive bank credits and capital is scarcely either the modest Jeffersonian farmer or the cavalier scornful of all worldly values. But hothouse romanticism and down-on-the-levee-hey-hey songwriters have kept capitalism away from the planter's door.

Yet the plantation system was capitalist agriculture giving unified direction to slave labor in the production of a commercial crop. On the plantation the functions of employer and laborer were sharply differentiated. Negroes tilled fields; white men directed them. But on the farm, the whole family worked alongside hired hands and, in the early days, their slaves. Among farmers who had only two or three slaves, slavery sometimes seemed to approach the Arab system that gives slaves a quasi-family relationship. Thus, Hundley, in his *Social Relations in Our Southern States*, says of early small slaveowning farmers: 'You will invariably see the negroes and their masters ploughing side by side in the fields; or bared to the waist, vieing with one another who can cut down the broadest swath of yellow wheat . . .'

The farmer farmed not so much for profit as to 'bread' himself. Whatever acreage remained was devoted to cash crops. But the plantation system was concerned solely with commercial agriculture. It produced a staple crop: one that was usually exported. Its producers sought, not a mere living, but a money profit, and a plantation's degree of self-subsistence varied according to its owner's wishes.

If men generally do not regard large-scale farming as 'capitalism,' neither did the planter. He usually thought of himself as a landed aristocrat remote from the (to him) vulgarities of the market place, and sometimes expressed, or affected, a scorn for its values. Yet he invariably measured his success as the businessman measures it: by the ratio of net money income to capital investment.

The experience of the cotton-producing South since 1865 has dispelled the notion that cotton culture was in any way, except by force of circumstances, dependent upon Negro labor, slave or free. The plantation system did not create slavery, nor did slavery create the plantation. But cotton culture did put slavery in the forefront of the great historical drama whose climax was the Civil War.

Slavery in America long antedated the cotton plantations. It had existed in the English North American colonies for 150 years before anyone dreamed that cotton cultivation was to become the principal occupation and preoccupation of the South. Slavery was planted on American soil by the British and the Dutch who planned to build agriculture colonies in the Western Hemisphere that could produce food and raw materials for the homelands and serve as markets for home manufactures. For these purposes cheap labor seemed necessary, and a double advantage might be gained because the transport of Negroes from Africa to America employed homeland shipping while it supplied colonists with labor.

Slavery was the product of a certain time and place. It had the general ethical sanction of its age and of preceding ages. The Constitution, when enacted, enfolded equally slave and free states. Ten Presidents were slaveholders: Washington, Jefferson, Monroe, Madison, Jackson, Tyler, Polk, Taylor, Johnson, and Grant. Both legally and ethically, slavery influenced many domestic commercial policies, and Europe invested heavily in the slave trade. Once introduced it became a *raison d'être* for the plantation system, a system brought to vigorous life, as we have seen, by the simultaneous coming of the cotton gin in America and the industrial revolution in England.

Foreign slave trading was marked by sharp competition. Although planters usually paid cash for slaves, the aggressive Royal African Company brought an innovation to the business by offering Negroes on the installment plan. Its advertisements translated into modern jargon might have read: 'High quality slaves direct from trapper to user. Save middleman's costs by dealing with us.

Under our easy-payment plan slaves earn money for you while you pay for them.'

Europeans also competed with one another as moneylenders to planters, a factor leading to rapid extension of the plantation system, and often to ruinous land practices and bankruptcy. But lenders made high profits and pursued prospective borrowers as doggedly as our more frantic bankers of the 1920s, who begged foreigners to take American money at 8 per cent interest or more.

Once there was an active demand for cotton, the planter preferred the slave to the indentured servant. Initially the slave was a little more expensive than the servant but — so the argument ran — his services were for life as opposed to the servant's four years. Slaves, moreover, multiplied. They had some value even at birth. It cost something to break in the 'brute' Negro to field work: that is, to acclimate him to an alien civilization. But he was soon as efficient as the servant and — an important matter — was more tractable. He also cost less to keep than the servant. De Bow estimated that $15 would cover the average slave's keep for a year.

The net profit made from a slave was the value of his produce less the cost of his keep, and this was an advantage to the planter of the slave over the indentured servant. The latter could enter into contractual relations with his master, and therefore was not able to be stripped of the entire surplus of his labor. Then there were the women. Slave women could be employed in the cotton fields, but servant women could be employed only in domestic labor.

There were certain conditions precedent to the profitable employment of slave labor, and cotton culture conformed notably to them. For instance, growing cotton was an extremely simple process since it employed few tools and no machines. Before 1860 planting was done mainly by hand, the hoe was used to 'chop cotton' and cultivate it, and harvesting was done by hand. Even the brute Negro could soon learn to 'make' cotton. But he could not, under slavery, quickly acquire the knowledge and techniques necessary for diversified farming. Hence slave labor could be employed most profitably only in the cultivation of one crop, or crops whose methods of culture were alike.

One-crop farming exhausts the soil so that in order to use slave labor efficiently, there had to be new, fertile lands to which men could turn as the old fields were exhausted. Cotton again seemed an ideal answer. Rice, sugar cane, and tobacco demanded soil and climatic conditions that prevented their extension over all the available territory, but cotton could be grown on most of the tillable lands of the South. Even when limited to the most fertile soils a huge expanse was open to it. Ultimately, however, the limitation of fertile lands led the cotton-growing South to demand extension of the national domain.

Profitable use of slave labor required a certain stable or predictable type of employment for the slave represented both capital and labor. The slaveowner, out of self-interest, had to sustain his slaves throughout the year and hence provide work for them that would permit him to use his property steadily. Cotton served him well because its culture lasts a large part of the year; when Negroes were not tilling the fields they were kept busy clearing lands for cotton. Of course the profitable use of slaves called for large-scale labor organization. The slave required constant supervision because his only impulse to work was fear of punishment. But a considerable slave force on a large plantation required little more superintendence than a lesser number on a smaller plantation.

Contemporary observers of the slave era and modern scholars generally agree that slavery in the South did not pay; that, among other things, slave laborers were only about two-thirds as efficient as free laborers. In 1826 Thomas Cooper said: 'It [slave labor] is all forced, and forced too from a class of human beings who have the least propensity to voluntary labor even when it is to benefit themselves alone.' So, too, study has confirmed Hammond's assertion: 'As a general rule . . . free labor is cheaper than slave labor.'

Many planters — those who had fertile lands in a good location, solid banking connections, and who knew how to manage their assets efficiently — remained solvent and made large profits from their operations. It seems that in every period of crisis some men have prospered when the majority of their fellows floundered. Yet, taken as a whole, the plantation cotton economy possessed no restorative powers within itself; too much of its capital was tied up in slaves. In the 1850s, when slave costs rose out of all proportion to prices received for cotton, the essential contradictions of the system became painfully clear. Gray points this out:

> One of the serious disadvantages of the slavery system was the slow accumulation of capital.
> Scarcity of capital retarded the adoption of labor-saving devices, and thereby intensified the scarcity of labor in the latter part of the period.
> The labor supply being scarce in proportion to the land supply, the land resources and human resources of the cotton South were inadequately used.

The slavery system capitalized a large part of the labor of the cotton country, profoundly disturbing its economic life. Free labor moved from one region or one industry to another as better opportunities for earning more money were offered, but slave labor was attended with no such mobility. The great capital values represented by the capitalization of the future value of the slaves had to be realized in any transfer of their labor. And — an important matter — public opinion opposed transferring slaves by sale. Thus the process of economic expansion was more disturbing to the South than to the North. For the process of expansion, rather than the institution of slavery, was mainly responsible for the industrial demoralization of the cotton South. Basically, however, slavery deprived the South of the immigration and industrial diversification which in the North alleviated the 'growing pains' of agricultural expansion. 'Hence,' concludes Gray, 'we have the near-paradox of an economic institution completely effective under certain conditions, but essentially regressive in its influence on the socioeconomic evolution of the section where it prevailed.'

Although the question of the profitability of cotton culture has not been exhaustively studied, the evidence suggests that even large-scale planters teetered constantly between solvency and insolvency, and this was even more true in the case of small planters whose costs were proportionately higher.

The prewar South was overwhelmingly rural. In 1860 it had only three cities of more than 100,000 inhabitants and 27 towns with a population above 4,000. Only 8 per cent of the South's population lived in towns and cities.

The plantation system had little use for an expanding population, and this had marked effects on the prewar and postwar South. Relatively few immigrants cared to chance a system that did not welcome them, and they were repelled by slavery and did not want to compete with slave labor. In 1850, there were about 378,000 foreign-born living in the slave states, while the non-slave states had nearly three times as many. They constituted about 4 per cent and 14 per cent, respectively, of the total population of each section. Thus cotton culture (and slavery) deprived the South of an admixture of foreign-born men and women whose gifts enriched the life of the North in every department of living from the artistic to the industrial. At the same time many young Southerners tended to migrate to other sections because there were few opportunities for them as a large free labor group.

Wherever the plantation system and slavery spread, there was a strong tendency for them to displace other forms of rural economy and labor. A contemporary described the process: 'As one man grows wealthy and thereby increases his stock of Negroes, he wants more land to employ them on; and being fully able, he bids a large price for his . . . neighbor's plantation, who by selling advantageously can raise enough money to go into the back country . . . and speculate or grow rich by industry as he pleases.'

In Mississippi, Joseph and Jefferson Davis 'assembled' an enormous plantation by buying the farms of men who sold either because of the encroachments of the plantation system or the pressure of hard times. C. C. Clay, Senator from Alabama, wrote of the relentless process of removals, sales, and exhaustion of lands before 1850 in the wake of the ever-moving plantation. Of his native county of Madison, he said: '. . . Our small planters, after taking the cream off their lands, are going farther west and south in search of other virgin lands which they . . . will despoil in like manner. Our wealthier planters . . . are buying out their poorer neighbors . . . The wealthy few, who are able to live on smaller profits and to give their blasted fields some rest are thus pushing the many who are merely independent.'

In Dantesque overtones, Senator Clay describes some of the

effects of this process: 'In traversing that county [Madison] one will discover numerous farm houses, once the abode of industrious and intelligent freemen, now occupied by slaves, or tenantless, deserted and dilapidated. He will observe fields, once fertile, now unfenced, abandoned, and covered with those evil harbingers, fox-tail and broom-sedge. He will see moss growing on the mouldering walls of once thrifty villages; and will find "one only master grasps the whole domain" that once furnished happy homes for a dozen white families . . . A country in its infancy . . . is already ex-hibiting the painful signs of senility and decay apparent in Virginia and the Carolinas. The freshness of its agricultural glory is gone, the vigor of its youth is extinct, and the spirit of desolation seems brooding over it.'

The removal of small farmers from commercial agricultural areas were also accelerated by a social factor. Once they had worked, as we have seen, in the fields with their slaves, but tabus of the evolving society dictated a division of labor into 'white men's jobs' and 'nigger jobs.' (Indeed Jefferson had said: 'No man will labor for himself who can make another labor for him . . . Of the proprietors of slaves, a very small proportion are ever seen to labor.') The former were, roughly, white-collar tasks; the latter were heavy labor and menial tasks. Now not even poor whites, whom the 'quality' disdained and who in turn disdained Negroes, would work alongside black men.

Man is more than an economic animal, and a powerful non-economic force contributed to the growth of the plantation system. In the antebellum South land ownership was the accepted criterion of social prestige, as it has generally been a condition precedent to 'aristocracy' in the Western world. For instance, as English industrialists rose to riches and often to the peerage, many of them nailed down an 'aristocracy' by buying large estates. It was natural, then, that men of English extraction looked back to the old country where the stellar aristocracy was rooted in land hold-ings and sought to emulate this by becoming landed proprietors. The impulse to do so was, of course, keenest in the great majority whose social status, or that of their families, in the old country had been something less than distinguished.

Another factor besides the drive for aristocratic status spurred the growth of the plantation system. Land abundance and the comparatively high price of labor led to extensive rather than intensive soil cultivation. The applied principle was stated in a letter from one planter, Thomas Jefferson, to another, George Washington. 'Where land is cheap and labor dear, the same labor spread in a slighter culture over 100 acres will produce more profit than if concentrated by the highest degree of culture on a small portion of the land.' So cheap was land that even Jefferson held that manuring was not necessary to good farming practice in Virginia, 'because we can buy an acre of new land cheaper than we can manure an old one.'

In 1860, C. W. Howard of Georgia, editor of an agricultural magazine, observed that although the one-crop system and extensive cultivation severely injured the land, planters were disinclined to change their methods. 'The system is such that the planter scarcely considers land as part of his permanent investment. It is rather a part of his current expenses . . . He buys land, he uses it until it is exhausted, and then sells it . . . for whatever it will bring . . . It is something to be worn out, not improved . . . The period of its endurance is . . . estimated in its original purchase, and the price is regulated accordingly.'

Yet the compelling fact is — however much we blame antebellum planters for wastefulness — that intensive land culture has never been resorted to by any people as long as the extensive system has proved to be more profitable. Labor and capital in a new country are too scarce to permit men to employ any system but the extensive and, if they are pioneers in an empty continent, they rapidly come to believe 'there's always more where that came from.'

Since land was cheap and labor dear, 'Planters,' says Gray, 'bought land as they might a wagon — with the expectation of wearing it out.' Some who expected to use land profitably for only 20 years depreciated it at the rate of 5 per cent a year. Such men often moved several times within a generation, and passed like devouring hosts from Virginia to Texas.

Under extensive cultivation, planters strove for maximum production per hand rather than per acre. The farmer, however, tried to make two ears of corn grow where only one had grown before. Hence planters were often contemptuous of 'book farming' for books emphasized the intensive methods of European agriculture.

The specialization of the plantation system early led it away from crop diversification, household manufactures, and even food production for home use. The process was hastened as manufactures became cheaper after 1815 and railroads were developed. Large areas of the two Carolinas and Georgia had been almost self-sufficing before cotton culture became their dominant occupation. This engaged their land so that they had to rely on the border and more remote parts of the South for great quantities of food and livestock.

South Carolina had become a large importer before 1850. Yeomen farmers of Kentucky and Tennessee sent to her plantations their flour, corn, oats, peas, hay, bacon, butter, cheese, and livestock. The coastal counties of North Carolina went farther afield. They imported Northern flour and New York pork, and horses, mules, hogs, and oxen were brought to the cotton areas in ever-increasing droves. The Lower South — composed of rich riparian lands that might have produced almost everything needed for plantation use — came to rely increasingly upon other regions for food. Its dependence was even more complete than that of the Upper South, because the land was extraordinarily suitable for cotton growing, and food could easily be brought by water from border states.

Many contemporaries thought that all this was economic insanity and they said so without, however, changing things in the slightest. Thus, in 1840, *The Carolina Planter* wrote: 'Most men . . . say nothing if the overseer gets in the quota of cotton. They sell their cotton and buy corn, and *sometimes* they buy pork or bacon. But on these plantations it is a rare thing for a regular allowance of meat to be given out . . . with most planters a large crop of cotton is aimed at, and habit and faith in advance of the market always make them look to cotton alone.'

Other factors stimulated a one-crop economy. Great Southern areas were more suited to cotton production than any other part of the world, and planters who scorned the injunction against putting all your eggs and so forth, often made large profits. Such men did not want to employ labor that could be producing cotton to grow food for other laborers and themselves. Then too cotton culture itself imposed a certain limitation upon crop diversification. Cotton requires a long growing season and much hand labor so that generally there was no labor surplus to care for other crops that might have come along at the same time.

Force of habit also contributed to maintaining the one-crop South. Everybody — overseers, labor, even work stock — was trained to grow cotton. Frequently other crops could not be marketed. There was no mechanism for the purpose and many districts lacked adequate water or rail transportation. When shortly before '61 west Tennessee planters grew a big wheat crop, they found it could not be shipped economically. Even though wheat flour was then bringing exorbitant prices in nearby Mississippi, they made little on their crop.

The planter also enjoyed other benefits from his one-crop monopoly. He could obtain credit, buy supplies in quantity at low prices, employ superior management. His capital, or credit, enabled him to acquire the best lands, tools, and overseers. He also had marketing advantages. Constantly in touch with commission merchants who knew the markets, he shipped his cotton at the most favorable times and, a large customer, he was favored by steamboat and railroad companies.

We owe much of our knowledge of the plantation system to Frederick Law Olmsted who traveled widely in the South and Southwest during the decade preceding the Civil War. In Texas he observed costs of cotton culture and notes that in fencing and tillage the planter's costs were lower than the farmer's. 'The planter,' he continues, 'has . . . a better knowledge of the most successful forms of cultivation . . . he has a gin and press of his own . . . to which he can carry his wool [cotton] at one transfer from the picking; by which he can put it in order for market expeditiously, and at an expense much below that falling on the farmer, who must first store his wool, then send it to the planter's gin . . . and have it prepared at the planter's convenience, paying, perhaps, exorbitantly therefor; and, finally, to the fact that the planter deals directly with the exporter.'

So it was that in the mid-1850s, when cotton sold at New Orleans for approximately 11 cents a pound, big plantations could grow it for 5 cents. The difference was enough to return a profit to the planter after paying all expenses. But at the same time, the cost of growing cotton on small farms — especially those located in the less favorable regions — was 8 cents a pound. Here the margin between profit and loss was uncomfortably thin, and the farmer was close to the brink of insolvency.

Olmsted saw that the plantation system was hastening a concentration of slave ownership, especially in the Lower South and Southwest. He describes the results of superior management on plantations along the Mississippi, Red, and Brazos rivers: 'The soil was a perfect garden mould, well drained and guarded by levees against the floods; it was admirably tilled; I have seen but few Northern farms so well tilled . . . They [the Negroes] had good tools; their rations . . . were brought to them in the field . . . They had the best sort of gins and presses, so situated that from them the cotton bales could be rolled in five minutes to steam-boats . . . They were superintended by skillful . . . overseers. These plantations were all large, so large as yet to contain much fresh land, ready to be worked as soon as the cultivated fields gave out in fertility.'

Little wonder that as the plantation system expanded a Scotsman, traveling in the South at the height of its flowering (1857) wrote home and said: 'Niggers and cotton — cotton and niggers; these are the law and the prophets to the men of the South.'

Nonetheless constant purchases of lands and slaves by planters, their cavalier disregard of self-sufficiency, and their personal extravagance kept much of the South — especially the Lower South — a debtor region. These aspects of the system were bemoaned by many critics, among them General George McDuffie of South Carolina. He pleaded for increased plantation self-sufficiency, argued that this did not prevent high cotton production, and denounced credit obtained at usurious interest rates. Turning to South Carolina planters, he said: 'We cannot compete with the planters of Alabama and Mississippi in a wild and destructive system, by which even they have sunk under embarrassment and ruin, with all their advantages of soil and climate . . . While they are exhausting their soil and preventing the natural increase of slaves by a reckless system of pushing and driving, let us improve the facility of the one, by resting and manuring it, and increase

the number of the other, by moderate working and by providing
everything necessary for their health and comfort.'

These words were written in 1840. Planters either decried them
or ignored them. The dull virtue of prudence had little appeal for
men who prided themselves on their cavalier dash, had an instinct
for command, and a high capacity for the excessive. They were
forced into temporary cautiousness only when hard times came,
when panics struck down the price of cotton, and banks failed.
But when good times returned, they resumed their old ways.

We get a glimpse of prewar plantations from the diaries of
planters and their families, and the journals of travelers. Observations of the latter vary widely. Olmsted, for example, found little
of the famed Southern hospitality. 'Only once or twice,' he says,
'in a journey of four thousand miles . . . did I receive a night's
lodging or a repast from a native Southerner, without having the
exact price in money which I was expected to pay for it stated to
me by those at whose hands I received it.'

He rarely saw or entered any of the legendary white-pillared
mansions. Of a long journey between the Mississippi River and the
upper James River, he writes: 'Nine times out of ten . . . I slept
in a room with others, in a bed which stank . . . I washed with
utensils common to the whole household; I found no garden, no
flowers, no fruit, no tea, no cream, no sugar, no bread (for corn
pone . . . is not bread); no curtains, no lifting windows . . . no
carpets or mats. For all that, the house swarmed with vermin.
There was no hay, no straw, no oats, no care, no honesty . . .'

It has been said of Olmsted that he neglected the more gracious
aspects of Southern civilization in his preoccupation with the common life of the South and therefore painted a picture almost un-
relievedly dark. Yet, whatever merit there may be in this charge,
there were few great planters living in great houses. The slaveowning aristocracy was distinguished by its scarcity.

Timothy Flint, who preceded Olmsted to Louisiana in the 1820s
visited planters and found among them a considerable opulence
and sophistication at a time when these qualities were generally
lacking in most of the nation. He also noted that Southern hospitality was no legend. 'The opulent planters are hospitable to an

eminent degree . . . It is taken for granted that the guest is a gentleman and that he will not make improper use of the great latitude that is allowed him. If he does not pass over the limits which just observance prescribes the more liberties he takes and the more ease he feels within these limits, the more satisfaction he will give to his host . . .'

We get a glimpse of the gaiety common to many Louisiana plantations in a diary entry dated 7 February 1842: '. . . Came on to my House for dinner. Sent and collected the neighbors. A. G. Barrow and family. Miss Swift. Flower and family. Miss Mary Barrow. Miss Sophia Johnson. Mrs. Collins. 12 or 13 gentlemen. Danced all night by the piano and violin.'

The party went on and on. The violinist broke down and was replaced by another. The following entry, made the next day, reads: 'Would not let any leave — got a violin player from town. "Norman." Let them rest and nap during the day . . . At dark began to dance. Anything but dance they wouldent [sic], retired at 2, nearly all broke down and so perfectly free, easy, and happy for two days and nights . . . Never enjoyed myself so much.'

The tropically exuberant moods of Louisiana planters — many of them of Latin blood — were probably more extravagant than those of their counterparts farther north, but Flint's commentaries have validity for the large group of Gulf state planters. Many of them shared with their slaves little sense of interest in the past or the future. Flint writes: 'The present is their day and "a short life and a merry one" their motto. Their feelings are easily exhausted. Tears flow. The excitement passes away and another train of sensation is started. In the pulpit they expect an ardor, an appeal to the feelings which a calmer and more reflecting man of the North would hardly tolerate.'

In this excessive atmosphere 'The men,' says Flint, 'are "sudden and quick to quarrel." The dirk or pistol is always at hand. Fatal duels frequently occur. They are . . . excessively addicted to gambling . . . A Louisianian will forego any pleasure to witness and bet at a horse race . . .'

Planters, of course, varied in class origins, education, temperament, intelligence, and character. They were *arrivistes* and aristocrats, plain men and pretentious, educated and nearly illiterate, and were marked by both inhumanity and *noblesse oblige*. They lived and endured against the extraordinary background of their environment.

The huge Southern hinterlands had slumbered from the founding of Jamestown in 1607 until the invention of the cotton gin nearly 200 years later. It was 1820 before the plantation system began sweeping across the Appalachians to the Gulf and westward to Texas. It encountered great difficulties, but none more potent than the diseases that lay in its path. One was malaria which, of all human diseases, has most evilly afflicted mankind throughout the ages. The other was yellow fever that ravaged great Southern regions decade after decade and was not to be conquered until the early twentieth century. In 1878 it struck hard in the classical plantation region of the Mississippi Delta.

When the stricken began to vomit black and cough up their life's blood in thick clots, and when their chests turned yellow and their enfeebled bodies were stormswept with dreadful retching, the living could do nothing for the dying except pray at their bedsides and await the coming of merciful death. Safety, they knew, lay in flight to the north. Many would not go, others could not go. Through the long, hot, melancholy summer of 1878 hundreds sickened and died of yellow fever while the rest, worn with pain and grief, nursed the sick and buried the dead. The hand of death was not stayed until, as the Greenville (Mississippi) *Times* reported in November of that year: 'A big white frost last Monday morning was a glorious sight for our people to see. To those within the infected districts it was a token of rescue and rest; to those who were shut off from their homes it was an assurance that their exile would soon be over . . . With what agony of heart the white robes of the blessed frost was watched and prayed for, none can know save those who passed the fearful hours within the death-haunted districts, and friends and relatives who watched and waited for the dark clouds to pass away.'

A hundred and fifty miles to the north of this area lay the important banking and cotton-market town of Memphis. When it was stricken by yellow fever in 1878, after having suffered severely from the disease in 1873, 25,000 of its inhabitants rushed madly from the city, and so great was the panic that in many cases fathers deserted wives and families. Many of the neighboring towns in self-defense kept the refugees from their doors with shotguns, refused to permit trains to stop and even compelled some of the refugees to camp in the forest without food or shelter. It is estimated that of the 20,000 people who remained in Memphis during the epidemic, 17,600 were stricken with yellow fever and 5,150 died.

Thousands of people who fled the city never returned. Memphis went bankrupt and in 1879 surrendered its charter and became a state tax district. Twelve years passed before it again became a chartered municipality.

Less dramatic, but less fatal, the far more pervasive and blighting plague of malaria spread over huge areas of the cotton country. In spring and summer, often until late fall, great numbers of men, women, and children, white and Negro, burned with the fever and froze with the chills of malaria. In the intervals between the attacks that came every third or fourth day the victims were listless, too dull to think, too weak to work. Travelers noted the debility of the people. Some ascribed it to unknown causes. Others said the people were just shiftless, and so contributed to the stereotype of the lazy, good-for-nothing Southerner. But malaria went its way decade after decade, taking an immeasurable toll in pain and death and retarding the development of the country.

There were vine-and-tree-entangled jungles to be cleared, huge forests to be felled, swamps to be drained, ditches to be dug. There were the unconquered and apparently unconquerable Mississippi, its tributaries, and dozens of lesser rivers that periodically flooded the country and swept away everything that men had built. But neither heat nor torrential rains nor disease nor floods stayed the men who wanted to grow cotton, and they conquered a hostile environment with headlong intrepidity and swiftness. As W. J. Cash put it in *The Mind of the South*: 'From 1820 to 1860 is but forty years — a little more than the span of a single generation. The whole period from the invention of the cotton gin to the outbreak of the Civil War is less than seventy years — the lifetime of a single man. Yet it was wholly within the longer of these periods, and mainly within the shorter, that the development and growth of the great South took place. Men who, as children, had heard the war-whoop of the Cherokee in the Carolina backwoods lived to hear the guns of Vicksburg. And thousands of other men who had looked upon Alabama when it was still a wilderness and upon Mississippi when it was still a stubborn jungle, lived to fight — and to fight well, too — in the ranks of the Confederate Armies.'

Forty years for the taming of an empire, or, if you like, 70 years, little more than a generation or two. It is not extraordinary, then, that this should have been a rough-edged country, marked with the turbulence, violence, and chicanery of the frontier. Flamboyant reports had gone forth of the marvelous fertility of the soil, and men came flocking from everywhere in the Union, especially from the older slaveholding regions. In this new country adventure and fortune were to be found and even if a man had little cash and nothing to recommend him, he could still get credit.

'Credit was the thing of course,' says Judge Baldwin of Alabama in *Flush Times in Alabama and Mississippi*. 'To refuse it . . . was an insult for which a bowie-knife was not too summary a means of redress. The state banks were issuing their bills by the sheet . . . and no other authentication was asked of the applicant for a loan than his great distress for money.'

Judge Baldwin tells us what happened: 'Prices rose like smoke . . . lands bought at the minimum cost of Government, were sold at thirty to forty dollars an acre . . . Money got without work . . . turned the heads of its possessors. The new era had set in . . . the era of credit without capital and enterprise without honesty . . . The condition of society may be imagined; vulgarity, ignorance, arrogant pretension, unmitigated rowdyism, bullying violence, if they did not rule the hour, seemed to wield unchecked domain.'

Among the planters there were Cotton Snobs, boors, and parvenus. Yet amid the violence of the frontier with its host of grabbers and adventurers, there were planters of solid worth: men who, out of all relation to their tiny number, deeply affected the life of the region. Often well-educated but rarely 'intellectual,' they

respected learning and the learned, and were much given to conversation, especially about farming and politics. They were elected
to local governing bodies, state legislatures, and Congress. Some of
them traveled in Europe, spent summers in Northern watering
places, or lavishly entertained their cosmopolitan friends and other
planters. Their houses were quietly elegant.

The manner of their living bred in them a capacity for command and self-reliance. But the servility of slaves and the obse-
quiousness of social inferiors affected some of them with a false
pride. Yet self-restraint and gentleness were held to be marks of
good breeding and pride was often tempered by religion.

One of the worst features of this society was absenteeism.
Some planters spent only a portion of their time on their lands
because of the prevalence, in summer, of malaria or yellow fever.
Others preferred to travel or reveled in the life of great cities such
as New Orleans. But absenteeism led almost inevitably to bad
farming practices and often to the maltreatment of slaves who
were left to the none-too-tender mercies of overseers.

A model prewar plantation was that of Thomas S. G. Dabney.
In 1835 Colonel Dabney, who had spent his early manhood on his
ancestral Virginia estate, emigrated to Mississippi. He was a member of a group perhaps unparalleled among pioneers. Here were
no lean men marching with rifle, ax, wagon, families, and small
possessions across the plains, no refugees from the Germany of '48,
no Irish of the potato-famine years, empty-handed and eagerly
looking for a new home in the New World. Dabney and his counterparts, educated and cultivated, pioneers with means, were prop-
ertied men moving with their families, slaves, and possessions like
princely patriarchs of the Orient.

Colonel Dabney owned a plantation of 4,000 acres in Hinds
County, Mississippi. A devoted Unionist, he nonetheless supported the Confederacy and was financially ruined by the War.
His daughter, Susan Dabney Smedes, in her *Memorials of a Southern Planter*, writes of him: 'Thomas was never an early riser. He
maintained that it did not matter so much when a man got up as
what he did after he was up . . . Everyone knew when he was

awake by the merry sounds proceeding from his chamber. He did
not go in to breakfast till he had danced the Fisher's Hornpipe for
the baby . . . All the nursery flocked about him at the signal, one
or two of the little tots joining in the capering . . .'

Men visited Dabney to study his methods. When asked how he
made his Negroes do good work 'His answer was that a laboring
man could do more and better work in 5½ days than in six. He
used to give half of Saturdays to his negroes . . . and distributed
prizes of money among the cotton pickers . . . A very tall and
lithe young woman . . . was the best cotton picker at Burleigh.
At Christmas Nellie's share of the prize money was over $17.00.
Her pride in going up to the master's desk to receive it, in the
presence of the assembled negroes . . . was a matter of as great
interest to the white family as to her own race.'

Planters have always tried to get their cotton picked quickly
before it is harmed by rainy weather. On Dabney's plantation 'The
negroes were helped in every way to gather the cotton . . . Some
. . . men were detailed to carry the great hampers to the wagons
that the pickers might lift no weights. Water carriers . . . went
up and down the rows handing water to the pickers. They would
get so . . . excited over the work that they had to be made to
leave the fields at night, some of the ambitious ones wishing to
sleep at the end of their rows, that they might be . . . at work
in the morning earlier than their rivals.'

Many plantations permitted slaves to grow or make things for
sale and keep the money. On the Dabney plantation 'The negroes
sold all the chickens they did not eat . . . thrifty negroes made
so much on their chickens, peanuts, popcorn, molasses cakes, baskets, mats, brooms, taking in sewing, that they were able to buy
luxuries. Some of the women bought silk dresses. They had the
clothes of the master and the mistress in addition and . . . as the
house grew full of young masters and mistresses they were added
to . . .'

On rainy days the general plantation custom was for Negro men
to work at indoor tasks while the women often came to the 'big
house' either to make clothes, if they were proficient, or to learn
how to sew if they were beginners. 'Then Mammy Maria,' says

Mrs. Smedes, 'who was . . . a field marshal on such occasions, gave out the work . . .'

Mammy Maria's kind is disappearing from the changing Southern plantation, but her counterpart is still to be found there: the firm, just woman of character. 'She was,' we learn, 'far more severe in her judgment of misdemeanors than the master or mistress. The place that she made for herself was one that would, in a character less strong or true, have brought on herself the hatred and distrust of her race. But they knew her to be just . . . and with so warm and compassionate a heart . . . that she grew into a kind of prime minister, and it was well known that if she espoused a cause and took it to the master it was sure to be attended to at once, and according to her advice.'

It was illegal to teach slaves to read but apparently few planters abided by the law. On the Dabney plantation slaves learned to read and taught others, 'among them a slave named Virginius who taught in the kitchen by the light of pine torches . . .

'Virginius did not spare the rod. His beatings were received with shouts of laughter . . . the scholars dodging to escape the young pedagogue's stick.' One graduate student wanting to read history, the teacher suggested *Robinson Crusoe* and lent his copy. But 'after reading 100 pages, Joe . . . said, "Did you say dat book was history?" The teacher explained as well as he could what fiction was, on which Joe said, "I bin mistrustin' all 'long some o' de things what Robinson Crusoe say wa'nt true." '

Slaves were property. Their value was based upon the value of the male prime field hand; that is, the male between the ages of 18 and 30. His price, in turn, was based upon the price of his hire. In general the average price of slaves was about 40 to 50 per cent of the value of prime field hands. Infants were sold by weight, sometimes bringing $7 to $10 a pound. Boys and girls were often valued by their height and weight. The price of the prime field hand was put at six to eight times his annual rate of hire.

The planter took an annual inventory of his slaves and in 1850, E. T. Capell, owner of Pleasant Hill Plantation in Mississippi, wrote out his inventory composed of the following men and boys:

NAME	AGE	VALUE AT COMMENCE-MENT OF THE YEAR	VALUE AT END OF THE YEAR
John	70	$50.00	$75.00
Tone*	49	1,000.00	1,200.00
Sandy	38	600.00	800.00
Edmund	45	1,000.00	1,300.00
Tiny	40	700.00	950.00
Solomon	38	700.00	950.00
Peter	(age not given)	700.00	950.00
Isaac	30	700.00	950.00
Anthony	25	800.00	950.00
Scott	25	800.00	950.00
George	20	750.00	1,000.00
Jim	27	800.00	950.00
Detson	20	700.00	900.00
Bill	18	700.00	900.00
William	24	1,000.00	1,100.00
Charles	10	500.00	650.00
Henry	9	375.00	400.00
Henderson	8	300.00	350.00
Johnson	6	250.00	275.00
Stephen	4	200.00	225.00
Tom	5	250.00	275.00
Monroe	4	200.00	225.00
Daniel	2	150.00	175.00
Sim	2	150.00	175.00
Aaron	3	175.00	200.00
Jerry	1	75.00	100.00
		$13,625.00	$16,975.00

The planter had an 'inventory profit' on his slaves of more than $3,000. All increased in value during the year from John at 70 to the infant Jerry. But the niceties of calculation that moved the planter to increase the value of George, aged 20, by $250, while increasing the value of Detson, age 20, by only $200 are not available to us.

The planter's female slave group was composed, with one exception, of young women and children. Whether this was because a high proportion of slave women died in childbirth — as did white women in that day when little was known about infection — is not recorded. This, however, is the list;

NAME	AGE	VALUE AT COMMENCE-MENT OF THE YEAR	VALUE AT END OF THE YEAR
Hannah	60	$100.00	$125.00
Mary	34	800.00	900.00
Fanny	23	800.00	900.00
Rachel (Senior)	32	675.00	750.00
Martha	27	675.00	750.00
Celia	25	675.00	750.00
Rachel (Junior)	24	675.00	750.00
Diana	31	600.00	700.00
Chaney	32	600.00	675.00
Lucy	28	600.00	750.00
Let	28	550.00	650.00
Azaline	13	600.00	700.00
Amanda	13	400.00	600.00
Sarah	9	350.00	450.00
Harriet	8	300.00	400.00
Bet	7	350.00	400.00
Hannah	7	350.00	450.00
Maryan	7	275.00	300.00
Ellen	6	200.00	250.00
Louisa	5	175.00	200.00
Susan	4	200.00	250.00
Melissa	3	100.00	125.00
Matilda	5	200.00	225.00
Jinny	3	150.00	150.00
Caroline	3	150.00	150.00
Frances	2	100.00	125.00
Laura	1	100.00	125.00
Amarintha	1	75.00	100.00
Saraan	6 mo.	75.00	100.00
Rose	6 mo.	75.00	100.00
Ann	(no age given)		100.00
Delia	" " "		100.00
		$10,975.00	$13,100.00

Here again the planter had a considerable inventory profit. A record of cotton picked during one week affords us some clue to valuations put upon individual slaves by the master. Azaline and Amanda were both 13 but Azaline's pickings exceeded those of Amanda so perhaps she was considered to be worth more. Even Sarah, aged 9, did some picking, as did Hannah, aged 60, although she was absent one day because of sickness.

The overseer was the villain of the plantation piece, and some of the blackest criticisms of slaveholding were inspired by his often brutal treatment of slaves. Deriving from English estate managers (bailiffs), he was indispensable to the absentee owner or the resident owner who owned several plantations but could not personally supervise them all. Yet most planters hired overseers in any event because they detested punishing slaves, driving them in the fields, or cluttering their own lives with management detail.

Since overseers as a class were held in contempt by planter and community, intelligent, educated men of character rarely worked as such. The task usually fell to illiterates from the ranks of poor whites who despised Negroes as planters despised overseers. Considering their origins and low place in society, it is not surprising that many overseers were dishonest, unreliable, cruel, petty tyrants who beat male slaves and forced their attentions upon female slaves. The contemporary press complained of the overseer system and individual overseers and George Washington's attitude is indicative of the general planter attitude toward them.

He wrote of the 'insufferable conduct of my Overseers,' and 'of the little dependence there is on such men when left to themselves.' They must be kept at a distance, 'for they will grow upon familiarity, in proportion as you sink in authority, if you do not.' *The Carolina Planter* reported: 'The planter looks down upon his overseer as one of an inferior and degraded caste.'

Overseers constituted a small agricultural class, numbering only about 19,000 in 1850, but their place in the plantation system gave them an importance disproportionate to their number. A consideration of them will illuminate some aspects of human relations on the plantation, and the manner in which planters tried to control overseers and insure good treatment of Negroes.

Overseers' salaries ranged from $200 a year to $2,000 for an exceptionally able man. The average salary was between $400 and $600. The real wage of the overseer, however, was higher. He got free shelter, food, and firewood for himself and his family, free fodder for his horse, and was often assigned slaves for his personal convenience.

Elisha Cain was overseer for Retreat Plantation, in Georgia, in the 1830s. His letters to his employer reveal a bewilderment in dealing with slaves. Occasionally one ran away, such as John, 'for no other cause than that he did not feel disposed to be governed by the same rules . . . that the others are governed by.' But this nonconformist, to the perturbation of the overseer, quietly returned and picked up his hoe.

Like Job, Cain never saw the end of trouble, and he writes his employer that 'Your negroes have a disease now among them that I am at a loss to know what to do. Two of them are down with venereal disease, Die and Sary. Dr. Jenkins has been attending Die four weeks . . .' Then ungallantly he adds: 'From what I can learn, Die got it from Sary.'

There was the woman called Darky. Once she so terrorized her fellows that Cain had to apply a 'modest correction.' But this, far from intimidating her, only led her to threaten to poison her housemates. Perplexed by Darky, who seems to have been possessed of the wrath of Medea wronged, the overseer, his spirit broken, poured out his heart to his employer: 'I believe her disposition as to temper is as bad as any in the whole world. I believe she is as unfaithful as any I have ever been acquainted with . . . I believe she has been more injury to you . . . than two such negroes would sell for.' Despondently he concludes: 'I have tryed and done all I could to get on with her . . . but I have been disappointed . . . I cannot hope for the better any longer.'

We do not know the ultimate fate of this temperamental woman, but Cain's troubles continued. Once he raised a slave to the rank of driver and several men decamped in protest. When he put three work gangs into the fields, 'So soon as I am absent . . . they are subject to quarrel and fight, or to idle time, or beat and abuse the mules; and when called to account each negro present when the misconduct took place will deny all about the same.'

Unless the overseer was carefully watched by the planter, it was almost inevitable that he would behave badly, for his advancement depended upon his ability to produce a large cotton crop. He was therefore strongly tempted to overwork Negroes, neglect the stock, and exhaust the land. His shortcomings were intensified by the desire of planters — especially absentee planters — for large present profits regardless of the future.

Something of the daily routine of the overseer may be gleaned from the instructions of a Louisiana planter: 'It is strictly required of the manager, that he rise at dawn . . . every morning; that he ring a bell for the assembling of the hands; require all hands to appear at a fixed place, in 20 minutes after ringing the bell, and there see that all are present . . . after which the hands will receive their orders.

'All sick negroes will be required to report to the manager at morning call either in person . . . or through others.

'Immediately after morning call, the manager will repair to the stable . . . and see to the proper feeding, cleaning and gearing of the horses . . .

'The manager will take his breakfast; and immediately after, he will visit and prescribe for the sick, and then repair to the fields to look after the hands, and he will remain with them as constantly as possible.'

Since slaves were valuable chattels, their health deeply concerned planters. One yellow-fever epidemic in Louisiana cost planters $4 million in lives lost, and a planter, after a series of pestilences, wrote: 'Oh, my losses almost make me crazy! God alone can help.'

Owners of lands in pestilential areas along the lower Mississippi hired Irishmen and Germans to dig ditches, and when Olmsted asked a planter why he did this, the reply was: 'It is dangerous work and the negro's life is too valuable to be risked at it.' Another planter, bemoaning the high wages he had to pay free labor for ditching, told W. H. Russell, the London *Times* correspondent: 'It was much better to have Irish do it who cost nothing to the planter if they die, than to use up good field hands in such severe employment.' Russell adds: 'Heaven knows how many poor Hibernians have been . . . buried in this Louisiana swamp leaving their earnings to the dram shopkeeper and results of their toil to the planter.'

Olmsted observed on the Alabama River that when cotton bales were being loaded onto a steamboat from a high bluff, Negroes stood at the top pushing the heavy bales down to Irish deck hands who tried to capture and stow them. The steamboat captain said: 'Niggers are worth too much to be risked here. If the Paddies are knocked overboard or get their backs broke nobody loses anything.'

Planters usually contracted with a physician at a stipulated annual salary to look after their slaves, and they issued precise instructions to overseers concerning slaves' health. Senator Hammond of South Carolina, a large landowner, ordained that 'No negro will be allowed to remain in his own house when sick, but must be confined to the hospital. Every reasonable complaint must be promptly attended to and with any marked or general sickness, however trivial, a negro may lie up a day or so . . . Remedies are to be chosen with the utmost discrimination . . . and the overseer must record in the prescription book every dose of medicine administered.'

In 1861, when W. H. Russell observed slave children on a plantation near New Orleans, he was reminded of the plight of English children then employed in textile mills, and he noted in *My Diary North and South*: 'Mr. Seal [the overseer] conducted me to a kind of forcing-house, where the young Negroes are kept in charge of certain old crones . . . while their parents are away . . . A host of children were . . . playing . . . very happily and noisily. I was glad to see the boys and girls of nine, ten, and eleven years of age were at this season, at all events, exempted from the cruel fate which befalls poor children of their age in the mining and manufacturing districts of England . . . The little ones came forward . . . babbling out, "Massa Seal," and evidently pleased to see him.'

Massa Seal was proud of the physical condition of the children, and he told Russell: 'The way to get them right is not to work the mothers too hard when they are near their time; to give them plenty to eat, and not to send them to the fields too soon.'

Large plantations conducted nurseries where children were fed well and nursing infants were often taken at regular intervals to their mothers in the fields or, if the distance was not too great, mothers came to the infants. They also had hospitals with separate wards for men and women.

Planters concerned themselves with prenatal and postnatal care of slave women. Pregnant women who were sick stayed in the hospital until delivery time. Attended by midwives, they were often permitted to refrain from work for four weeks after giving birth to a child. Precise instructions were given overseers, as in the following orders of Senator Hammond: "Sucklers . . . leave their

children at the children's house before going to the field. The
period of suckling is twelve months. Their work always lies within
one-half mile of the quarter . . . The amount of work done by a
suckler is about three-fifths of that done by a full hand . . . Pregnant women at five months are put in the suckler's gang. No plowing or lifting must be required of them . . . Plantation midwives
shall attend all women in confinement . . . The confined woman
lies up one month and the midwife remains in constant attendance
for seven days . . .'

The planter's self-interest dictated that slaves should be fed
well, sheltered, and clothed. Aside from issued rations such as
cornmeal, bacon, salt pork, and occasional extras including molasses, fish, buttermilk, rum, and coffee, many plantations permitted
slaves to use as much as two acres of land for a garden and till it
with plantation teams and implements. Negroes built their own
shelters. Sometimes they were rude huts. Sometimes they were of
such sound construction that many stand today in good condition.

As for clothing, we may note Senator Hammond's issue to his
slaves. In the fall each man got two cotton shirts, a pair of woolen
pants, and a woolen jacket. In the spring each received two cotton
shirts and two pairs of cotton pants. Every woman was given six
yards each of cotton and woolen cloth in the fall, and six yards
each of light and heavy cotton cloth in the spring plus needles,
thread, and buttons. Men and women received a pair of strong
shoes in the fall and a heavy blanket every third year, and there
were special clothing allowances for children.

Sanitary rules were strictly enforced on well-managed plantations. Overseers were required to see that slaves were clean about
their persons and houses. Their bedding was inspected and sometimes a Negro habitually unclean about his person was forcibly
scrubbed under the overseer's eyes.

A number of Southern states legally restricted the slave workday,
but generally slaves worked the same long hours as free laborers
in the United States that might extend to 15 or 16 hours a day in
busy periods, including intervals for eating and rest. Sunday was
universally a day of rest except in rush periods. Many planters gave
their Negroes a half-holiday on Saturdays, and from three days to
a week at Christmas.

Slave-management required skill and patience on the planter's part. Ullrich B. Phillips, an authority on United States slavery, says: 'The easygoing and plausible disposition of the blacks conspired with the heat of the climate to soften the resolution of the whites and make them patient. Severe and unyielding requirements would keep everyone on edge; concessions when accompanied with geniality and not indulged in so far as to cause demoralization would make plantation life not only tolerable but charming.'

The planter's life was not always a happy one. What with handling the stubborn and the fractious among the slaves — the aged, the infirm, men, women, and children — all with various wants and grievances and each requiring individual treatment, he was often a harassed man. Olmsted tells of visiting one planter for three hours. During this period he was constantly interrupted by Negroes seeking his personal direction or assistance, and was thrice required to leave the table. On the same subject Harriet Martineau wrote: 'Nothing struck me more than the patience of slave owners . . . with their slaves. When I consider how they love to be called "fiery Southerners" I could not but marvel at their forbearance under the hourly provocations to which they are liable in their homes.'

Some observers believed that only a man Southern-born was capable of the exercise of patience and forbearance essential to the status of the kindly, efficient slaveowner. Solon Robinson, the shrewd Northern agriculturist, said that Negroes plied their hoes 'at so low a rate, the motion would have given a quick-working Yankee convulsions.' Here we may listen again to Harriet Martineau who said: 'Persons from New England, France or England becoming slave owners are . . . the most severe masters, however good their tempers have always appeared previously. They cannot, like the native proprietor, sit waiting one-half hour for the second course or see everything done in the worst possible manner, their rooms dirty, their property wasted, their plans frustrated, their infants slighted — themselves deluded by artifices — they cannot like the native proprietor endure all of this unruffled.'

Slaveholding imposed heavy duties upon the planter's wife. Speaking of wives of middle-class planters, who lived at best in small comfortable houses or at worst in enlarged log cabins,

Hundley, a contemporary observer, said the labors of the wife of a middle-class planter were heavy, for 'besides the cares of a mother, the anxieties of a housekeeper, and the wants of a husband, she has to look after the wants of the blacks.' She superintended the making of slaves' clothing, daily went to the smokehouse with the cook to make certain that provisions were bountifully supplied, and visited the cabins of sick slaves. 'With her own delicate hands,' says Hundley, 'she administers . . . medicine . . . and when all medicines have alike become unavailing, sits down beside the lowly couch of the dying African and tenderly consoles his last moments.'

Let us watch Floride Calhoun, wife of John C. Calhoun, on their luxurious South Carolina plantation. In her *John C. Calhoun*, Margaret L. Coit writes: 'Not the least of the burdens of the plantation lay upon the women of the plantation . . . Men could sleep through . . . the night, when, at a terrified whisper . . . a woman roused herself, threw a tippet over her nightgown, and hurried . . . to the storerooms beyond, searching for medicine bottles in the flickering candlelight — or for a Bible. What did men know of that endless walk to the quarters . . . the rocks and ruts cutting into her slippers, and the trees looming up out of the darkness? And then the long hours of watching . . . the feverish sleep of a sick child, or a dying man. Men had the responsibility of slavery . . . but what did they know of the work of it?'

Floride knew, and for her the day was long.

After breakfast, Mrs. Calhoun 'might walk down to the quarters to see that the old woman in charge was not eating the children's supply of food.' At home again, 'A woman would report that one of the hands was "fevered and onrestless"; and Floride herself would again hurry to the storehouse to measure out . . . calomel, and to hold the head and slip the spoon in the sick man's mouth . . . Five minutes later, she might be running back to the quarters to attend a field hand who had gashed his foot with a hoe . . . First she would tie an apron over her dress; then . . . she would calmly examine the injured foot, dripping with blood and sweat, superintend a bath, prepare a healing application, and bind it on with her own hands.'

Even the author of *Uncle Tom's Cabin*, Harriet Beecher Stowe, spoke well of the plantation mistress: 'Many of them,' she wrote, 'surrounded by circumstances over which they can have no control, perplexed by domestic cares, of which women in free states can have very little conception, loaded down by duties and responsibilities which wear upon the very springs of life, still go on bravely and patiently from day to day . . . rescuing those who are dependent upon them from the evils of the system.'

The plantation was a complex organization. It was a homestead, a hierarchy, a conscript army, a factory, a pageant, a matrimonial bureau, a nursery, a divorce court. According to Phillips, it was filled with sound, movement, and color: 'The procession of plowmen at evening . . . the bonfire in the quarters with contests in clogs . . . the work songs in solo and refrain . . . the baptizing . . . the torch light pursuit of 'possum and 'coon, with full-voiced halloo to baying houn' dawg and yelping cur . . . the husking bee, the quilting party, the wedding, the cockfight, the crap game.' Here all was governed by rules and moved with orderly regimentation. It was the overseers' duty to enforce the rules and, to a large extent, the plantation prospered or failed as he was competent or incompetent.

He had 'drivers' chosen from among the better-trained slaves; men similar to the 'straw bosses' of today's plantations. Drivers — where the task system prevailed — allotted the day's tasks to slaves, and saw that the work was done. They had limited powers to punish the laggard or the refractory, and were charged with the duty of getting Negroes to bed on time at night and out of bed on time in the morning.

Large plantations also had other slave functionaries such as carpenters, blacksmiths, wheelwrights, and a key-carrying steward who doled out materials and provisions. These positions carried with them particular honors, exempted their holders from field work, and were eagerly sought.

Everybody worked except the disabled. Children carried water, looked after infants, drove stock, fed poultry, harnessed saddle horses, ran errands. From 10 to 16 years, boys often made nails, and girls engaged in spinning yarn. Above 16, they worked in the fields or learned a trade. Aged and infirm women cared for nursery children, sewed garments, spun and wove, and sometimes acted as assistant cooks or hospital nurses. Old men were gardeners, wagoners, or stock tenders.

By way of approach to what is now called scientific management, on many plantations there was a division of labor in field work; a distinction was made between hoe hands and plow hands and there was even a division or function in hoeing. On Governor McDuffie's South Carolina plantation, hands were divided into three classes at planting time: 'First, the best hands embracing those of good judgment and quick motion. Second, those of the weakest and most inefficient class. Third, the second class of hoe hands . . . Those classified as first class would run ahead and open a small hole about 7 to 10 inches apart into which the second class dropped from 4 to 5 cotton seeds and the third class follow and cover with a rake.'

Upon the basis of fitness for labor, slaves were classified as fullhand, three-quarter-hand, half-hand, and quarter-hand, ratings usually being made annually. Negroes could ask for a temporary or permanent reduction in rating, and masters found it a good policy to respect their wishes in this case whenever possible.

Some plantations were operated on the task system; others on the gang system. Under the former, each slave was assigned his individual plot every morning and the work was supervised throughout the day. In the evening, or the next day, the planter could check the results obtained by overseer and slaves. Under this system, when the slave finished his task, he could take off the remainder of the day.

'I find it a good plan,' said a South Carolina planter in 1854, 'as every overseer will find it to be, to separate his hands when he cannot be with them all day by stepping the ground they have to hoe over . . . and set the tasks by that for the day, and place each hand a day's work apart; then the overseer can see each hand's work separately, and be at no trouble to find his indifferent hand's work.'

A task unit was usually a plot of ground 150 feet square. 'Tasking' was applied to hoeing, picking cotton, and pulling corn, but it was not applied to plowing. Experience enabled planters to make nearly exact estimates of a fair day's work even where tasks were not rigidly standardized, and Thomas Jefferson concluded that 'A laborer will weed 500 corn hills a day.'

Under the gang system Negroes worked in groups controlled by a driver who set the pace, and they worked all day except for meal and rest intervals. This system, however, often led to abuse as the driver drove Negroes on with the lash.

It is notable that on small plantations where there was less division of labor than on large plantations, Negroes often toiled diligently. On a small Mississippi plantation, says Olmsted, 'I asked our host if he had a foreman or driver for his negroes. He did not . . . They needed no driving.

' "If I ever noticed one of 'em getting a little slack I just talked to him, telling him he must get out of the grass and I want to hev him stir himself a little more, and then maybe I would slip a dollar into his hand and when he gits in the field he would go ahead, and the rest seeing him, won't let themselves be outdistanced by him. My negroes never want no lookin' arter. They take more interest in the crop than I do myself . . ." '

Every large plantation had police regulations to govern the behavior of its slaves. Something of their nature appears in the rules of a large Georgia plantation just before 1861:

> No Negro could marry a person off the plantation, or one not belonging to it, without the owner's consent, nor could any slave marry a free Negro.
>
> If a man's wife was on another plantation he might visit her once a week.
>
> A strict curfew was imposed. Any Negro found out of his quarters 'after the last bell,' was subject to punishment.
>
> No Negro could receive the visit of a stranger Negro without the owner's permission.
>
> None but the plantation's own preachers was permitted to preach. They had to preach on Sundays 'during the daylight,' or quit.
>
> Instant obedience was expected of every Negro and 'If a

Negro resists when corrected, every other Negro man present must assist in arresting him.'

The use of or possession of liquor was strictly forbidden slaves.

It might be thought that since the multiplication of slaves enriched the planter he would be indifferent to their sexual relations. Yet the plantation whose regulations we have been observing provided that adultery and fornication must be 'invariably punished,' along with stealing, lying, using profane language, fighting, and quarreling.

No Negro could leave the plantation without written permission of the overseer or owner, and under the patrol system slaves were required to have tickets when away from the plantation. Leave, however, was commonly granted Negroes to visit other plantations on Sundays.

It was required that Negroes be punished for 'abusing the stock, losing their implements . . . leaving gates open,' or injuring plantation property. 'By rigidly adhering to this rule, they will soon be careful . . .' It was particularly enjoined upon overseers not to permit Negroes 'to have barrels, ashes, chicken-coops, trash or filth of any kind under or about their houses. The quarters must be cleaned every week.' Implements were marked 'with the first letter of the name of the negro to whom they had been assigned.' Slaves could thus be made responsible for their tools.

The severity or leniency of slave regulations varied from plantation to plantation. Although the lash was often used, and fear of it was generally thought to facilitate discipline, many planters employed other forms of punishment for infractions of rules. They denied offenders holidays, gave them extra labor, or confined them on a small diet. In time, public opinion came to oppose the use of the lash altogether. Few planters could ignore society's sentiments, especially when good management dictated that they should try to have satisfied labor. The sullen or desperate slave was a genius at shirking the task and at sabotaging the enterprise. He could constantly annoy his master and as a last resort he might run away.

Some planters not only were liberal in their regulations governing slaves, but also encouraged them to earn money for themselves. This was true of Joseph and Jefferson Davis on their plantations, Hurricane and Brierfield, in Warren County, Mississippi.
They also charged their slaves with maintaining discipline through
slave courts that had formal methods of judicial process and enforced their decrees by Negro constables, subject only to the planter's power of pardon. The system worked well and lasted until
the area was invaded by Federal troops.

In the plantation system methodical severity seems to have been
often counterbalanced by methodical leniency. The planter could
compel slaves. But self-interest dictated that he seek their co-
operation.

There can be little question that from the early colonial period
until the Civil War there was a steady improvement in the treatment of slaves. It reflected the increase in slave values, the smaller
proportion of slaves freshly come from Africa, and the progress of
the slave himself in civilization, efficiency, tractability, and decency.

Gray, after he had finished a comprehensive survey of United
States slavery, concluded that because the slave was ignorant of
any other condition, was free from responsibility, and had his
simple physical needs well provided for, he 'was frequently a veri-
table child of the sun. There was unquestionably some truth in the
claims of Southern apologists that there was more misery in the
factory towns of England and of New England than on the majority of Southern plantations . . . There were large possibilities in
slavery as a system for educating barbarians in the rudimentary
elements of civilization, but it offered no promise of higher development to the black man. "So far shalt thou go and no farther,"
was deeply engraved on the cornerstone of slavery in America.'

There was a great difference between the laws on paper and
the system that existed in reality. The laws were not strictly applied. Slaves *were* taught to read and write. They *did* go abroad in
a manner contrary to law. They *did* congregate despite laws
forbidding their assembling. The real emphasis of slave codes was
more upon the social problem arising from the presence of large
numbers of Negroes than upon their estate as property.

J. G. Randall holds that slavery was 'so involved in con-

troversy and so productive of emotional reaction that the . . .
scholar finds it no easy task to reach . . . unbiased conclusions
. . . Sectional differentiation between the right and wrong of
Negro bondage is not as clear-cut as has been supposed.' About
the slave codes he remarks: 'It could not be said that either the
laws themselves or the actual practices of the institution were
primarily motivated by any intention to treat the Negroes harshly.'

But the internal slave trade was inevitably marked by brutality.
It brought great suffering to thousands of hapless Negroes who
were driven along the highway in coffles, herded in pens, torn
from their families, and sold at auction. Often they were taken
from districts where slavery was vanishing into other districts where
it was flourishing, where tasks were harder, and their bonds became heavier and more permanent.

The most brutal aspects of slavery had to do with slave crimes,
especially insurrection and running away. There were relatively few slave uprisings but the fear of them — especially after
the Nat Turner Rebellion of 1831 in Southampton County, Virginia — haunted the Southern mind and led to harsh laws. Yet
slaves were generally unprotestingly submissive. Along with the
stories of brutality and torture that are told about the capture
and punishment of runaway slaves, it should also be remembered
that they ran away for many reasons other than mistreatment.
Many masters did redress slave grievances, and the number of
runaways was small. There were millions of slaves but only a few
thousand fugitives.

The fierce, proud American Indian fought the white man against
overwhelming odds and was nearly exterminated. But the Negro
almost cheerfully adapted himself to bondage and did the work of
the South as he loyally served those who held him in chains. In
the process he lost his memories of Africa and became Amer-
icanized. Even in the matter of folklore, as Professor Phillips shows,
'Bre'r Rabbit superseded his jungle prototype.'

Slavery, however unintended or unanticipated the result, effected
a profound transformation in the life and heritage of the slave
population. Wharton, in *The Negro in Mississippi 1865–1890*,
writes: 'Slavery was for the Negro an effective civilizing influence.
With or without conscious effort on his part, he absorbed the

basic materials of western culture. His education was weak in many essentials, but there is no other example in recent history in which so large a mass of people was brought so far out of barbarism in so short a time.'

In 1861, thousands of farmers and planters went to war, leaving their old men, women, and children among multitudes of Negroes who held the whites' lives and living in their hands. There were difficulties between whites and Negroes, innumerable 'incidents,' occasional killings of whites, and frequent pillagings by Negroes. But the farms and plantations, in the midst of a titanic upheaval, were relatively calm, whether because of slave pliancy, fear, the existence of good relations between master and slave in the past, or because Negroes remained in a state of equilibrium until the issue of the war had been decided. In any case it is clear that masters confidently left their homes and families in the care of slaves and there was almost universal justification for their confidence. Perhaps this constitutes an illuminating commentary on the reasonableness and tolerance that generally characterized the relationship of the two classes.

The size of individual slaveholdings has been exaggerated by postwar romanticists. Just as many White Russian refugees dowered themselves with titles and estates upon coming here, although they might have been beekeepers or droshky-drivers at home, so many Southerners have endowed their ancestors with slave-swarming plantations. The fantasy bears little relation to fact, as the following compilation by Professor J. G. Randall shows.

More than 75 per cent of the white population owned no slaves at all. In 1850 only 347,825 white families, of a white population of six million, owned slaves and they owned them in these proportions:

Holders of	1	slave each	68,820
"	" 2–4	slaves each	105,683
"	" 5–9	" "	80,765
"	" 10–19	" "	54,595
"	" 20–49	" "	29,733
"	" 50–99	" "	6,196
"	" 100–199	" "	1,479
"	" 300–499	" "	56
"	" 500 or more	" "	11

Middle-class planters — whether they are defined as owners of 10 to 50 slaves or 20 to 50 slaves — resided on their own lands, usually ran their plantations without overseers, lived simply, and worked hard. Gray says that 'The middle-class planters were frequently forcible, hard-fisted, self-made men. They were not idealistic, and they did not cultivate the graces. They were humdrum, honest, pious, substantial. Frequently they were well informed on politics and practical matters . . . Many, however, were innocent of "book learning . . ." Some . . . were reckless gamblers and hard drinkers, but after the pioneer period a large majority were religious, taking their religion seriously and uncritically. Although without the social graces, the women were not lacking in refinement . . .'

Below this group were men owning less than 10 slaves. Ignorant, slovenly about farming, often living in squalor, they nonetheless led cheerful, carefree lives. Olmsted calculated the income of the farmer owning one slave family of five at not more than $125 a year. 'I have seen many a workman's lodge at the North,' he wrote, 'where there was double the luxury that I ever saw in a regular cotton-planter's house on plantations of three [slave] families.'

An establishment of this kind is vividly described by Huckleberry Finn: 'Phelps's was one of those little one-horse cotton plantations and they all look alike. A rail fence around a two-acre yard; a stile made out of logs . . . to climb over the fence with and for the women to stand on when they are going to jump on a horse; some sickly grass patches in the big yard . . . big double house for the white folks — hewed logs with the chinks stopped up with mud or mortar . . . round-log kitchen with a big broad . . . passage joining it to the house; log smokehouse back of the kitchen; three little nigger cabins in a row t'other side the smokehouse; one little hut . . . down against the back fence, and some outbuildings down a piece the other side; ash-hopper and big kettle to bile soap in by the little hut; bench by the kitchen door, with bucket of water and a gourd; hound asleep there in the sun . . . some currant bushes and gooseberry bushes in one place by the fence; outside of the fence a garden and a watermelon patch; then the cotton-fields begin and after the fields the woods.'

Poor men growing rich overnight is a old American tale so often told that the 'success story' has long been a staple of our mental fare, the core of our 'inspirational literature,' and the stuff of folklore. Quick wealth has been created by discoveries of oil, gold, copper, silver, iron; by furs and by wars. It has also been created by cotton-growing and by speculation in land and slaves. There arose a prewar group of newly rich planters of whom a contemporary wrote: 'Who has not heard of Mississippi fortunes that sprang up like Jonah's gourd in a single night? The bulk of the plantations were held by adventurers who had gotten tired of the dull routine of their daily business and by young men . . . who had the gift of the time, nerve for anything.'

Such men flaunted their wealth. We see some of them in a frozen moment as they appeared to an observer in the St. Charles Hotel in New Orleans just before the War: 'When all the cotton widows and cotton girls had bought their new dresses . . . they displayed them at once in the St. Charles parlor. You hear it whispered that the dress . . . worn by that young belle standing there before you cost Papa $2,000 and that lady by her side from Red River flames with $20,000 worth of jewelry.'

At the other extreme were some well-to-do planters who scraped, pinched, and drove their slaves unmercifully. Locally they were called 'Southern Yankees.'

There were also Negroes, chiefly Louisiana Negroes, who had been freed and, with their former master's aid, had become slave-holding planters. Frequently they were women — former mistresses of planters — who had been freed in the wills of their masters and left considerable property. Members of this group, like their masters in 'French' Louisiana, were French-speaking and communicants of the Roman Catholic faith. In 1851 a former slave, Cyprian Ricard, bought at a sheriff's sale in Iberville Parish (county) an estate with its 91 slaves for $250,000, the equivalent perhaps of a million dollars today. Marie Metoyer of Natchitoches Parish died in 1840, leaving 58 slaves and more than 2,000 acres of land. At his death in 1854, Charles Roques, of the same parish, left 47 slaves and 1,000 acres of land.

New Orleans Negroes who owned slaves were among the firmest

defenders of slavery as an institution, and were bitterly opposed
to any suggestions that slaves be set free. In 1860, among the
360 Negro taxpayers of Charleston, 130 were listed as possessing
390 slaves.

Fairly early in the nineteenth century it became clear that
the development of the nation was to proceed along Hamiltonian
rather than Jeffersonian lines. Agriculture and commerce were to
be dominated by industry and finance. But the prewar South
remained largely agricultural.

Southerners had a marked distaste for the mechanic arts, pos-
sibly because of the heritage of an English gentry ideal. Con-
sequently those who might have become successful industrialists
devoted themselves to farming. The ambitions and aspirations of
Southerners differed from those of Northerners, and each section
bore a different face because of slavery in the South and its absence
from the North. A farmer became a planter by acquiring extensive
lands and numerous slaves, and he sent his sons to the universities.
From this group sprang the majority of the large-scale planters of
Virginia, Georgia, and the two Carolinas. Margaret L. Coit says
of them: 'Slaves meant money and money meant education, and
education and the tastes of a gentleman were all that the aristocrats of Charleston and Savannah had had a few generations
before . . .

'What the planters did embody was the fulfillment of the
common ideal. The Southern society was a society of gentlemen,
not because the gentlemen were in the majority, but because the
majority aspired to be gentlemen . . .'

This is perhaps one clue to the transcendent influence of a tiny
minority of planters over the huge majority of yeoman farmers
and other people. South Carolina, for example, had always been
controlled before 1865 by aristocratic planters. Of 63 South
Carolinians who had held the office of governor or United States
congressman between 1778 and 1865 only two appear to have been
of humble birth. Nearly all of them were communicants of the
Episcopal Church, although the Baptist and Methodist churches
were the churches of the white masses.

'It may be doubted,' writes W. E. Dodd in *The Cotton Kingdom*, 'whether there were twenty thousand Episcopalians in all the region from Charleston to Galveston at the outbreak of the Civil War, yet members of "the church" were almost invariably found in the seats of . . . governors, congressmen, and magistrates. St. Michael's Church in Charleston was the Westminster of the cotton country; and to be buried in the sacred soil of that parish was almost as good as to be alive in less favored provinces . . .'

Thus a few thousand planters achieved the remarkable feat of creating the image of the Old South that still lingers in men's minds, while imposing their views, prejudices, and desires upon a whole region. Whatever their vices or virtues, whether they were right or wrong, they dominated the majority of the people in the only way they could have dominated them — by strength of character and force of conviction. For the men dominated, far from being servile, were proud, touchy frontiersmen, born Jeffersonians with a fierce sense of personal freedom. Yet they enthusiastically accepted the leadership of an oligarchy.

V

'And Live and Die for Dixie!'

So SANG STEPHEN VINCENT BENÉT in *John Brown's Body*, the poet's ear hearing long silent voices, his spirit re-creating a vanished mood:

> *But something so dim it must be holy.*
> *A voice, a fragrance, a taste of wine,*
> *A face half-seen in candleshine,*
> *A yellow river, a blowing dust,*
> *Something beyond you that you must trust,*
> *Something shrouded it must be great,*
> *The dead men building the living State*
> *From 'simmon-seed on a sandy bottom,*
> *The woman South in her rivers laving*
> *That body whiter than new-blown cotton*
> *And savage and sweet as wild-orange-blossom,*
> *The dark hair streams on the barbarous bosom,*
> *If there has ever been a land worth saving* —
> In Dixie land, I'll take my stand,
> And live and die for Dixie . . !

The period 1830–60 was marked by sharp gyrations in the cotton economy. If these had produced purely economic effects, they would be of only antiquarian interest. But they were also symptomatic of a critical political situation. This was the time when the South revealed a determination to retain its cotton-slavery system, the time when its leaders, moving from one course to another, frenziedly beat their wings but were always held by the cage of their world.

In the 1820s there were more antislavery societies in the slave states than in the free states. Slavery was not on its way out. But the South was looking squarely at its evils, as is demonstrated by the debate over emancipation in the Virginia legislature in 1831 and 1832. There the effort to abolish slavery failed but nonetheless it was formally denounced by the representatives of a slave-holding people. Within a few years, however, scarcely a Southern voice was to be lifted in defense of emancipation.

'By 1837,' writes C. Vann Woodward, 'there was not one anti-slavery society in the South . . . Opponents changed their opinions or held their tongues. Loyalty to the South came to be defined in terms of conformative thought regarding one of its institutions . . . and the recency with which one had denounced Northern abolitionism became a matter of public concern . . . The institution that had so recently been blamed for a multitude of the region's ills was now pictured as the secret of its superiority and the reason for its fancied perfection.'

If today we often cannot separate politics from economics (or vice versa) this was not less true in the United States of 'the house divided.' Two essentially antithetical systems existed upon the same soil. The one was a retrogressive, primitive, agricultural, cotton-slavery regime. The other was a relatively progressive industrial-farming community based upon free labor constantly augmented by European immigration.

Cotton culture involved the South in irreconcilable political-economic contradictions and forced it into impossible positions. We shall relate some of these to the cotton economy of the three decades before the Civil War, occasionally dealing with statistics of the case. But they are not, in the given circumstances, merely ghostly digits of a long dead society. They are the stuff of which grand tragedy was made, abstract numerals marching to the bugle through a ruined and bleeding land.

As the cotton kingdom expanded production rose with extraordinary rapidity, going from about 150,000 bales in 1815 to more than 4.5 million bales in 1859. This is a prodigious increase of production. Within this brief period, output doubled between 1815 and 1820, doubled again by 1826, and again between 1830 and 1837. By 1851 the crop was twice that of 1837. By 1859, it was double the size of that of 1849.

For all that, the cotton economy was shaky, disturbed, and fearful of the future. In 1858, a planters' convention — one of a long line of such gatherings — met at Macon, Georgia. Significantly, its agenda suggested *political* rather than economic considerations: 'The First, the Cotton Power; 2nd, The Cotton Power as an American Power; 3rd, The Cotton Power as a Union Power; 4th, The Cotton Power as an Anti-Abolition Power.'

Here were intimations of dread things to come; of guns sounding at Fort Sumter within three years after the meeting of this convention.

In the two decades before the War, Southern leaders became increasingly aware of some disquieting facts. Agriculturally, industrially, and financially, the South was lagging behind the North. Even though the South was overwhelmingly agricultural — and Southern leaders found this especially galling — the North exceeded in land values, conservation practices, crop productivity, and thriftiness. Nor was the North marred by the appearance of ruin, decay, and slovenliness that characterized much of the South. The North also led the South in commerce, industry, railroad building, wealth, and population. Southerners were deeply upset because the disparity between the sections in these respects was the product of little more than two generations.

The ever-growing lead of the North over the South in most of the indices of progress was regarded by Southern statesmen as dangerous in the event of civil conflict. Planters and many ordinary men, however, saw it simply as proof of the victimization of their section by the North. What was little recognized by the South was that while it had gone a dreamy, agrarian way, almost cotton-intoxicated, the North had developed an asset of the greatest value: a tribe of tough, aggressive, farsighted, ingenious businessmen. It was almost the eve of the Civil War before the South developed even a small group of able, driving business leaders. In the context of the North's commercial preoccupations and the South's obsession with cotton, we may consider the famous 'Cotton Triangle.'

During the early nineteenth century, New Orleans, strategically located near the mouth of the Mississippi, was the link between South and West. Shipping center for the grain-rich Northwest and the Mississippi Valley, and distributing center to these areas for imports going up river, it gave promise of becoming America's greatest seaport. It was a promise the more potent after the Louisiana Purchase of 1803 brought an empire to the nation. New Orleans prospered. But by 1825 the Erie Canal was in operation. New Yorkers used it to take the Northwest grain trade from New Orleans and bring it to New York via the cheap shipping route of the Great Lakes and the Erie Canal.

Although its grain trade diminished, New Orleans had still another opportunity. Between 1820 and 1860 there was a rising export demand for cotton, and what port was better situated to handle it than New Orleans? Cotton might have been taken in Southern-owned ships sailing from New Orleans and other Gulf ports to Liverpool and Le Havre without touching at New York, and the same vessels could have returned with European goods.

Now entered the 'Cotton Triangle.' Its corners were composed of the Southern port where cotton was lifted, the European port to which it was delivered, and the port of New York. Northern-owned ships sailed from Southern ports carrying cotton to Europe. They returned to New York with cargo or immigrants. Then they went south with cargo or in ballast to lift cotton. These activities enriched Northern middlemen, shipowners, insurers, warehousemen, and bankers.

There was an even more profitable form of operation along the Triangle than this. New Yorkers assured their commercial success by coastal packet lines that brought cargo from the South for ships sailing from New York directly to Europe. The coastal vessels delivered domestic and foreign merchandise to Southern ports, lifted cotton there, and at New York transferred it to transatlantic vessels. Thus they had a profitable outward cotton cargo, and a profitable inward cargo, on returning to New York, of

European goods; a balance of cargo that would have been impossible without cotton.

New Orleans was one of the greatest exporting cities of the country, but her bank deposits were insignificant. Less than a third of the returns on the cotton that annually left her docks ever found place in her banks. And what was true of New Orleans was true of other leading Southern cities. They annually exported four times as much as they imported. But New York, Philadelphia, and Boston imported more than they exported. The cotton South was buying the bulk of its goods in the North and selling the whole of its output either to Europe or to the North at prices fixed in Liverpool, the world market. From this commerce the merchants of New York, Boston, and Philadelphia made huge profits.

By 1851 cotton constituted 40 per cent of America's exports. Then Southern leaders dolefully realized that New York was getting 40 cents of every dollar Europe paid for cotton.

In those days, the pickings rich, Yankee accents were heard in Charleston, Savannah, and New Orleans as shrewd traders sought their share of the lucrative trade. But Jeremiah Thompson spoke with the accent of Yorkshire. A Quaker, he had come to New York from England about 1815. Some ten years later he was the world's largest cotton trader.

The greater part of the proceeds of cotton was left in the hands of those who supplied the South with goods of all kinds. Tariffs, freights, insurance, commissions, and profits which Southerners had to pay consumed the earnings of the plantations. 'Thus while the planters monopolized the cotton industry, drew to themselves the surplus of slaves, and apparently increased their wealth enormously, they were really but custodians of these returns, administrators of the wealth of Northern men who really ultimately received the profits of Southern plantations and Southern slavery.'

What of Southern businessmen as they noted all this? In February 1846, the editor of *De Bow's Review* wrote on 'The Origin, Progress, and Influence of Commerce.' But he extolled commerce in an overblown way that must have astonished hardheaded Northern businessmen. The editor said: 'We are to speak of Venice and Genoa, who were to modern ages what Tyre and

Carthage were to those which have been numbered before the Christian Era. Inspired with the recollections of the past, and full of the holy associations of the moment, Byron, standing on the "Bridge of Sighs" reviewing the ruins of Italian glory . . . with full heart and impassioned eloquence, lamented over the mistress of the Adriatic, her "dead doges," her perished commerce.'

These purple sentiments, however, neither launched ships nor provided cargoes. About a decade later, De Bow got down to business in extolling business. This time he said: 'The doctrine that Cotton is King is taught to the South . . . That Cotton *might* be King may be true, if Commerce could be made Queen. As matters stand, they form different dynasties . . . The total exports of the country (in 1857) were $340,000,000, of which the South supplied one-half . . . But the ships of the North convey our products to the North . . . New York City has become the great medium of exchange for the country.'

In the tough world of affairs, the planter suffered a self-imposed disability. It would endure so long as he planted cotton almost exclusively and constantly expanded an essentially speculative venture. In the circumstances, it was perhaps inevitable that he should be victimized by his factor-banker because commercial banks regarded him as too high a risk, as indeed he generally was. He was victimized by the markets, since he had no control of the marketing apparatus and there were not even reliable sources of information about markets. Usually short of cash, the planter often had to sell his cotton at unfavorable moments to the enrichment of British and American middlemen.

But he was also victimized by his illusions. The stronger and more prosperous the North grew, the more his (and the region's) influence in the nation's councils declined. Many planters refused to see this, although Calhoun knew that a primarily agricultural section would remain a permanent minority, and slaveowners would be condemned by non-slaveowners.

Political power was moving from the Old South to the New South of the Gulf states. Cotton grew luxuriantly in the fecund earth of that warm, wet region where both men and vegetation tended to the excessive. The sudden growth of Gulf plantations, the arrogant self-confidence of Gulf oligarchs who came to Con-

gress, their romantic propensity for creating an aristocratic philosophy, and, finally, their defense of slavery — not as an evil to
be gradually uprooted, but as a positive good to be perpetuated
— all these, as the nineteenth century passed the halfway mark,
contributed to the hostility whose end was civil war.

By 1850 the wealth of the cotton states had been rapidly
concentrated into the hands of three or four thousand families.
They lived on the best lands and received three-fourths of the
returns from the yearly exports. Two-thirds of the Southern white
people possessed no slaves and received little of the community
production.

Many Lower South planters had made quick fortunes. If this
was not good for them, if it was perhaps disturbing to the soul's
repose, it was worse to see them look down upon the Northern
businessman buying and selling in the market place as a boor and
vulgarian. And quite naturally, the contempt of the planter was
returned. The businessman did not feel humble or guiltily money-
minded in the presence of the planter. For this was the man —
the aristocrat, if you please — who came to believe not only that
slavery was good, but that it was noble and justified of the Lord,
the moment he found that it had again become profitable.

The planter refused to search out the root of his (and the
region's) dilemma. He went on beguiling himself by repeating
that he was being done in by the North. A Richmond convention
of 1857 stated that belief, while reiterating Southern determination
to preserve slavery: 'Nearly a quarter of a century ago it first began
to manifest itself to the Southern states, that, although they
embraced in proportion to population the wealthiest producing
region in the world, they were contributing . . . to the commercial opulence of other sections of the nation.' The convention's
aims were plainly and forcefully stated. They were 'to secure to
the Southern States the utmost amount of prosperity as an integral
part of the Federal Union or enable them to maintain their
rights and institutions in any event.'

There was no doubt that the cotton South had made a huge
contribution to 'commercial opulence.' The value of cotton exports
alone had risen nearly five times from $42,767,000 in 1846 to
$191,806,000 in 1860. At home, cotton had become the basis of

a large industry, for in the period 1840–60 domestic mill consumption of cotton had risen from 252,000 to 846,000 bales.

Cotton had indeed a phenomenal place in the whole American economy; a dominance never since attained by any single American product of field or factory. Long before the Civil War, cotton had become the leading American export commodity. On the eve of conflict, in 1860, it accounted for more than half the nation's total exports of $400 million. These cotton exports played a powerful role in the emerging industrial United States because they helped pay for imported machinery, raw materials, and the service of the nation's foreign loans — all essential to the North's rising industrial apparatus.

In the period 1815–60 the United States' foreign trade grew rapidly. But the country's internal trade grew even faster, and before 1860 surpassed its foreign commerce. The 'American system' was now being created as demand increased for home manufactures and home markets needed farm crops. Populous cities already existed and soon most producers were to be generally free from dependence upon the export market. But the sole great exception was the cotton planter. His bonnie 'lay over the ocean.'

By the middle of the nineteenth century, certain great changes were making themselves manifest on the face of this continent. Urban-industrial forces were gaining dominance over rural-agricultural forces. The age of finance and industrial capitalism was dawning. And it was clear that the North's rapid growth in wealth and population was to continue. It was the region of the industrial revolution where manufacturing and commerce predominated, and it was also the region, not of commercial, one-crop agriculture as in the cotton South, but of general farming.

The South remained almost exclusively a primitive agricultural economy occupying a colonial or semi-colonial position in its relationships with the North. The North supplied manufactures. Northern merchants granted long-term credits to their Southern customers, just as British merchants had once granted similar credits to their colonial American customers. Lacking such credits, little business could have been done with the cotton South because it was chronically short of cash. Yet the system bound the region even closer to a one-crop economy and inhibited Southern manufacturing.

The South might have partially avoided all this by importing European goods, in spite of the tariff hurdle. But this could scarcely have been done because would-be Southern importers did not have the capital to enable them to extend credits to planters who constituted the larger part of their market. And the South at best was a shaky market. Widely fluctuating cotton prices made purchasing power extremely unstable, beside the fact that the 'normal' purchasing power of the whole community, heavily weighted with slaves, was extremely low. Nor was this all. The trade of Southern seaports was dominated by Northern merchants — men, the South complained, who had little interest in the section or sense of identification with it.

In their more morbid moments of frustration and anger, Southern leaders not only complained of what they regarded as 'tribute' exacted from their region by Northern suppliers, but also estimated what it had cost. The 'exaction' for the period 1800–1860 they put at $3 billion. The leaders, however, with a high capacity for self-hypnosis, ignored factors in the system itself that ran against them. Single-cropping exhausted the soil and required frequent removal to new lands where the process was repeated: a situation calling for constant expansion of the cotton kingdom. The plantation system, because it employed extensive rather than intensive cultivation methods, demanded large investments in slaves and therefore extensive credits that could only be furnished by local factors and Northern merchants. But in the last three decades before the War, there arose a disquietingly wide gap between cotton prices and cotton costs; a matter that was interminably discussed throughout the cotton country, especially in the 1840s and 1850s.

The cotton kingdom shifted its center from the Upper South to the new, fertile lands of the Gulf states as the soil of the older areas wore out. A report of the South Carolina legislature in 1843 merely confirmed what men already knew: 'These lands [in the Gulf states] produce an average of 2,500 pounds per hand, while the lands in Carolina yield but 1,200 pounds.'

During the 1840s and the 1850s, a great horde of men poured into the rich alluvial lands along the Gulf, the Mississippi River, and its western tributaries. These migrant groups were composed of planters from the older areas, their younger sons, and Negroes. Such great numbers departed from South Carolina, Virginia, Kentucky, Maryland, and Missouri, along with their slaves, that they filled up Mississippi, Alabama, Louisiana, and some counties of eastern Texas and Arkansas.

By 1850, according to Professor Carman, there were 388,000 Virginians and 128,000 Marylanders living in other states. Alabama and Mississippi grew prodigiously. In 1810 their combined population was only 40,000, but in 1860 it was 1,660,000.

These people had come to a new home to raise cotton. In 1826 more than half the crop was still being raised in the Old South. In 1859, however, its production was less than one-fourth of the total. Alabama was the leading cotton producer in seven of the years preceding the war. In 1859 Mississippi's crop alone was as great as that of four states of the Old South.

The effects of the shift of cotton production from the older areas of the Piedmont to the Gulf states were political as well as economic, and important decisions were coming more and more to be influenced by New South voices. In this area of little political discipline, all was new. Consider, for example, Mississippi. The home of Jefferson Davis, whose parents had migrated there from Kentucky, was representative of the new cotton South. For not a single leader was a native-born Mississippian and half the leaders were Northern immigrants.

All might have been well had it not been for that ole devil — costs. The investigations of Phillips show that slave prices had fluctuated rather sharply, upward and downward, from colonial days until 1845. Then prices rose steadily until the coming of the War so that by 1860 the average price of a prime field hand was $1,500. The reason for the high price was scarcity.

Big planters of the rich Gulf plains were not seriously damaged by this increase. Their productivity, it has been estimated, was two to four times as great as farms of the Old South. Since they operated on the gang system, they could increase their productivity, and because they could reproduce their slave supply they were not, so to speak, slaves of the slave market. It was the small farmers who felt the impact of higher slave prices. Their small slave establishments were often without women and children. Sometimes they had to hire slave labor in rush seasons, paying the increased costs of hire, and they had to buy slaves when their Negroes were no longer productive. So, too, because they worked in the fields with their Negroes, they could not increase productivity through the gang system. Yet this is an incomplete list of their disabilities. They usually occupied the poorer lands, were at great distances from markets, and paid high prices for inadequate credits. Discontent burned steadily among them.

Their spokesmen became the non-compromisers and firebrands of the 1850s, and they sought relief at the point where they were 'hurting' the most: the cost of slaves. They were for reducing the cost by reopening the African slave trade. It did not matter that the price might be secession, and from the mid-'fifties until Fort Sumter, every commercial convention heard this dangerous question heatedly argued.

In 1860, a Georgian told the Democratic National Convention that Southerners ought to ask their Northern friends, including Democrats, to 'take off the ruthless restrictions which cut off the supply of slaves from foreign lands.' He then said that he thought the state of Virginia was 'more immoral' than the African slave trade, and more unchristian. This because, as he explained, when he had gone into that state 'to buy a few darkies,' he had to 'pay from $1,000 to $2,000 a head, when I could go to Africa and buy better slaves for $50.' Naturally, a state guilty of overcharging for slaves was 'unchristian.'

Other costs rose too, and everywhere the North was middleman to the South. It was merchant, wholesaler, banker, insurer, and in each of its capacities took its toll for services rendered. Southern leaders clamored, therefore, for 'direct trade' that would bypass New York en route to Europe. They sought lower freight rates, reduced tariffs, elimination of middlemen, and lower interest charges. But all this, however rational, was attended with a fatal flaw. The South was caught, so to speak, in the moving stairway of politico-economic evolution and hung there, suspended on a cotton cord, while its leaders sought to dislodge it by means that, in the circumstances, were fanciful or ineffectual.

Thus, over and over, the region's need for industrial independence was repeated. Typically, the Sumter (South Carolina) *Banner* in 1849 urged the necessity of 'bringing up the rising generation to mechanical business,' thereby freeing the South of 'Northern foes.' The newspaper plaintively asked: 'In what part of the South can be found engineers, carpenters, painters, engine builders, masons and architects, but are Northerners?' Then it urged the South to abandon the foolish notion 'that the mechanic is no gentleman — that it is degrading.'

As the South's wealth and power steadily diminished by comparison with the wealth and power of the North, Southern leaders moved to the advocacy of a kind of industrial isolationism as the remedy for the region's troubles. Impossible of achievement, it was indicative of the presence of the malady that modern psychologists call 'retreat to the womb.' Thus in 1850 James De Bow suggested that the South construct her own ships, carry her own goods, manufacture cotton at home, diversify industries, and build roads and railroads. Beyond this, he urged that Southern people stop 'summering' up North, stop sending children to be educated in the North and educate them instead at home, and encourage the creation of a Southern literature. 'Light up,' he said, 'the torches [of industry] on every hilltop, by the side of every stream, from the shores of the Delaware to the furthest extremes of the Rio Grande — from the Ohio to the capes of Florida.'

As sectional bitterness increased, so did the volume of Southern preachments for economic independence. In 1855 the New Orleans *Crescent* complained that the South imported all its machinery, clothing fashions, domestic utensils, hats, printing machinery, steamboats, and road-making materials from the North. Then it concluded, as did so many other contemporary editorials, with an exhortation: 'The *vis inertiae* that has been so long and so justly charged against Southern character must give way to a new impulse and we must manufacture as well as produce.'

At almost the same moment, Albert Pike, attending the New

Orleans Commercial Convention of 1855, addressed himself to the
same subject in more homely manner, saying: 'From the rattle
with which the nurse tickles the ear of the child born in the
South to the shroud that covers the cold form of the dead,
everything comes to us from the North . . . We eat from Northern plates and dishes, our rooms are swept with Northern brooms;
our gardens dug with Northern spades, and our bread kneaded
in trays or dishes of Northern wood or tin . . .'

The longed-for agricultural-industrial diversification of the region
was impeded by massive difficulties which yielded neither to exhortation or denunciation. The South was bound to, and bound
by, its cotton-slavery system. It imposed upon the region not
only what one might call powerful economic 'sanctions,' but
behavioristic sanctions scarcely less powerful. Few Southerners
were equipped by skill or experience for industrial management.
The ablest managerial minds were in agriculture, not only because
it seemed to offer good opportunities but also because employment
in it accorded with sectional values.

If there were few actual or potential managers in the cotton-
slavery regime, there were few artisans and fewer apprentices.
White labor was abundant. Yet it would have been difficult to
lure whites of small means into factories and make docile workers
of them. Poor they may have been, but they were fiercely independent, difficult to discipline, careless, intractable. (They were
to retain these qualities and yet become volunteer soldiers of one
of the finest fighting forces men have known — the Confederate
Army.) They had elbow room on the uncrowded frontier. They
felt themselves to be untrammeled Americans. Their material
needs were small. Fish in the streams and game in the woods and
a little earth gave sustenance for body and soul in the form of
cornbread and whiskey. Why, then, enter the prison cell of a
factory and surrender the wild, free life of the woods?

There was also Negro labor. Slaves had become competent
carpenters, masons, cobblers, and weavers. There had even been
complaints that Negroes were depriving whites of jobs. They had
worked from the beginning in tobacco factories and were employed almost exclusively at the famous Tredegar Iron Works in
Richmond. In 1851 a New York *H~~ld* correspondent visited

the cotton mill at Saluda, South Carolina, and reported: 'The Saluda factory employs 98 operatives . . . they are all slaves . . . the superintendent is decidedly of the opinion that slave labor is cheaper for cotton manufacture than white labor . . . The mill has been operated by slave labor with one white overseer for about two years.' But there was no surplus of Negro labor upon which a rising Southern industry might rely. The constant expansion of the cotton kingdom called for more and more slave labor, and its system of extensive cultivation demanded a large amount of labor to produce a relatively small output. Nor, as we have seen, was there any appreciable flow of European immigrants to the South.

The region was married indissolubly to an institution from which it would be parted only by death.

In the absence of adequate railroads, cotton was transported on river vessels ranging from great Mississippi River steamboats — the finest vessels on inland western waters — to small craft that plied lesser streams. Here is a contemporary account (1859) of 'A Cotton Landing on the Chattahoochee [Georgia]': 'When you arrive at one of these landings . . . sudden is the awakening . . . Freight, perhaps passengers, are to be conveyed on shore; cotton, provisions, fuel are to be brought on board. Laborers set to work . . . the Negroes invariably accompanying their movements with as much action and loquacity as would suffice in loading half a dozen steamers.'

The steamboat's arrival draws the people of the countryside to the landing: 'A planter or two and their overseers stand looking on; two or three negresses with white turbans and black babies on the bank above, and some sprawling urchins at various elevations, are sure to enliven the scene. Some young ladies, too, have driven several miles from a neighboring plantation to enjoy the not too frequent excitement.'

But this is no river-boat show: 'You bid adieu to tranquillity for the next hour. What with hauling cotton bales on board, and stowing away incredible numbers of them . . . what with "wooding-up" and what with jolting and bumping . . . you would think the boat was going to pieces there and then.'

Southern leaders were aware that the section greatly needed railroads, and construction of the first was undertaken in 1833. By 1860 there were approximately 10,000 miles of trackage. These railroads opened up the interior for settlement and provided somewhat better trade channels than had existed before. Yet the South, on the eve of '61, was largely rural with a sparse, scattered population. It had few industries, and always there were the old, stubborn obstacles to industrialization. But nonetheless, in the period 1850–60, the value of Southern manufactures was double that of the preceding decade.

Still it lagged industrially behind the nation. In 1860 its manufacturing capital was less than 16 per cent of the nation's total and much of that was concentrated in the border states. The invested manufacturing capital of the cotton-growing Lower South was only about $43 million, Mississippi employing $4 million industrially. This was approximately half the value of its 229,000 horses and mules. In New England, 1 out of every 8 people was a factory worker; in the Middle States, 1 out of 15. But in the South only 1 of every 82 was industrially employed.

The field of cotton-textile manufacturing had shown significant progress. Yet it involved the South in a politico-economic contradiction with which it still wrestles. The cotton farmer, needing export outlets for his crop, favors low tariffs. The cotton-textile manufacturer, seeking to protect his home market, favors high tariffs. When, therefore, builders of a cotton mill near Athens, Georgia, in 1827, plumped for high tariffs, the local newspaper editor, aware of the conflict of interests between cotton manufacturer and cotton grower, said: 'A sense of safety and a feeling of independence combined with an expectation of profit have urged gentlemen to an undertaking with which their political convictions are at war. And we are authorized to state that these sentiments have, by no means, undergone a change; that their project is certainly not to give countenance to a system that they have always denounced, but is to be regarded as a measure unquestionably defensive.'

South Carolina violently expressed its low tariff sentiments by declaring null and void the 'tariff of abominations' of 1828, the nullification ordinance to become effective as of 1 February 1833.

This tariff bill, the highest yet, led to the emergence of clear sectional differences in regard to protection; the differences, roughly, between the interests of a raw cotton community and those of a manufacturing community. President Andrew Jackson was moved to monumental wrath, and showed his hand to his Vice-President John Calhoun. Facing him at a large dinner, Jackson proposed the toast: 'Our Union, it must be preserved.' Thus he answered the threat of secession implied by nullification. Calhoun responded with the toast: 'To our Union, next to our liberties, most dear.'

Jackson strongly defended the Constitution when it suited him to do so, and it now suited him to argue that the states had no power to veto acts of the federal government. But while he thundered and threatened, he advised Congress to modify the law that had caused the trouble and Henry Clay rushed a compromise tariff bill through Congress that combined conciliation with a measure of protection. Secession, as a method of protecting minority interests, was therefore postponed until 1861.

South Carolina's stand received widespread support because of the growing distrust of the influence of capital in business and politics. Household industries were declining under the impact of the factory, and in 1832 Senator Wallace of New Hampshire said: 'Now the farmers' daughters are obliged to herd together . . . in the manufacturing establishments; or if they remain at home, no longer find that profitable and wholesome employment which was so highly beneficial to the prosperity and to the morals of the whole community.'

At about the same time the Alabama legislature made a formal declaration whose essence was repeated time after time until voices shouting to be heard were lost in the loud alarms of Civil War artillery. The legislature declared that 'The sponge of monopoly has absorbed nearly the whole wealth of the nation . . . Of 21,000,000 people, less than 300,000 are said to own the whole of the immense public debt and nearly the whole of the landed property.'

As time passed, the South's leaders were to insist that the opposition, first of the Whigs and then of the Republicans, was simply a combination of interests intent upon plundering the country; that in their rapacity lay the dissensions that were dividing the nation. It was a case of the Interests against Agriculture, and Reuben Davis of Mississippi stated it in 1860: 'There is not a pursuit in which man is engaged (agriculture excepted) which is not demanding legislative aid to enable it to enlarge its profits and all at the expense of . . . agriculture . . . Those interests . . . have united . . . to use the government as the instrument of their operation . . . This combined host of interests stands arrayed against the agricultural states; and this is the reason of the conflict which . . . is shaking our political fabric to its foundation.' Slavery had nothing to do with the case, Davis insisted. The furor over it was feigned to cover the aims of the plunderers. 'Relentless avarice,' he said, 'stands firm with its iron heel upon the Constitution.'

If the planters were losing the fight against the census returns, as the phrase of the day had it, if the growth of the foreign and domestic trade of the North, its manufactures and finance and roads and railroads and population and wealth was running far ahead of those of the South, the planters nonetheless still had a powerful voice in the nation's councils. W. H. Seward of New York said that the slaveholding class of 347,000 persons 'has become the chief governing power in each of the slaveholding states and it practically chooses thirty of the sixty-two members of the Senate, ninety of the two hundred and thirty-three members of the House of Representatives, and one hundred and five of the two hundred and ninety-five electors of the President . . . of the United States.' He argued that 'Two antagonistic systems' were being brought into closer contact and — words of fatefully true prophecy — 'irrepressible conflict.'

While partisans of sectional economics had their heated say, and the nation's attention was focused upon the dramatic conflict between Andrew Jackson and the Bank of the United States, Southern industrialists were slowly building cotton mills. By 1840 their investment was about 12 per cent of the total capital of American cotton textile industry. By 1860 they had nearly doubled it. William Gregg's South Carolina mill had so prospered that in 1859 his mill village had a population of 900 and his capital was $400,000. In North Carolina, Edwin Holt, producer of the famous 'Alamance plaids,' pioneered the making of colored cotton cloth

in the South. He built houses for his employees, sold them supplies, and — like many of his New England counterparts — interested himself in their religious lives.

Agriculture was also progressing, especially in the Southeast
cotton belt. The Dickson brothers brought better methods of
cultivation to Georgia and taught various farming skills to slaves.
Richard S. Hardwicke led the way in hillside ditching and soil
conservation, and he pioneered horizontal plowing in the Lower
South. Charles W. Howard argued that it was senseless to employ
valuable slave labor on the less valuable lands, and introduced
grasses fruitful for rotation purposes. Progress was made on many
fronts in the prewar South. Yet men suffered alternating shifts of
mood as cotton prices rose or fell. The depression of the fifth
decade increased their discontent with their economic system.
But the prosperity of the 'fifties cheered them and renewed their
confidence in their institutions.

Returning cotton prosperity, moreover, enormously increased
the material values at stake and slaveowners' determination to
defend them. And the argument rang loud that if the South's
labor supply were adequate to the potentially cultivable cotton
acres, its wealth would enormously increase.

The cotton economy was now faced with the profound problem
of mounting costs. Prices rose in the 1850s as a result of California
gold discoveries. The costs of short-term capital were high. The
prices of prime field hands were rising alarmingly. But the cotton
market was unpredictable and uncontrollable, and the North was
sinking deeper and ever deeper roots in the American economy.
Crisis faced the South. It had to rejuvenate its economy. This
required, at the minimum, that it take the following steps:

> Slave costs had to be reduced even if this meant re-
> opening the African slave trade.
>
> Free, or at least freer, trade had to be established so
> that the American market might be opened wider to the
> manufacturers of the cotton South's best customer — Great
> Britain.
>
> The South had to become independent of the North
> for shipping, brokerage, insurance, and credit. This could

be brought about by enabling the English to sell more goods and services to the South. Then English capital could go South for developing railroads, shipping, and opening banks.

The South must oppose the growing economic alliance between New York and New England capital and Western enterprise. Hence the region must oppose the use of public moneys to build Northwestern railroads, to open Western public lands to homesteaders, and to permit unrestricted immigration.

And, imperatively, the movement into the Western lands must be checked in order to prevent the political power of the free states from growing greater.

If this program could not be realized, was there a possible alternative? Whatever men may then have thought, and there were many varying and conflicting opinions, we know in retrospect that secession and political independence constituted the inevitable alternative.

In the decades that have passed since '61, innumerable historians have earnestly discussed the 'cause' of the Civil War, giving various interpretations of the issue in its moral, political, social, and economic aspects. It is not within the purposes of our inquiry to weigh these interpretations. Yet, whatever the 'cause' of the War, cotton culture was certainly central to the decade of debates that preceded it. Perhaps the most famous utterance on the subject was the speech delivered in the Senate in 1858 by Senator Hammond of South Carolina. Challenging the North and Europe, and attributing almost the power of deity to cotton, he said: 'Without firing a gun, without drawing a sword, should they make war on us we could bring the whole world to our feet. The South is perfectly competent to go on, one, two, or even three years without planting a seed of cotton. I believe that if she were to plant but half her cotton, for three years to come it would be an immense advantage to her . . . What would happen if no cotton were furnished for three years? I will not stop to depict what anyone can imagine, but this is certain: England would topple headlong and carry the whole civilized world with her save the South.

'No, you dare not make war on cotton. No power on earth dares to make war upon it. Cotton is king!'

But if the North should 'dare' to make war upon cotton? The balance militarily would be against the South because she had kept her capital in slaves and cotton lands and did not have the factories or the railroads for modern war. And the balance would be against her morally because, in order to produce cotton, she had abandoned the Jeffersonian view that slavery was an evil which must be brought to the earliest possible end.

In 1860 cotton growing had become the greatest single interest in the United States. Negro slavery seemed to cotton growers the only available form of labor. It was natural, therefore, that they should equate prosperity and progress with the preservation and expansion of the slavery system. It was also natural that cotton growers, who bought great quantities of Northern manufactures and borrowed heavily from Northern bankers, were able to affect favorably a powerful section of Northern opinion, and at the same time their purchases of corn and pork gave them a strong influence in the Northwest.

The planters had a dominant place in Congress; seemingly an all-powerful place in the last years before the War. It was not only that the House of Representatives was Democratic, and the Senate was overwhelmingly Democratic. It was also that, as Professor Dodd says, 'The President and Cabinet were in full sympathy with the Southern Democratic leaders; and seven of the nine justices of the Supreme Court were either owners of plantations or proslavery in attitude. The chairmen of all the great committees of Congress were owners of slaves and ready to initiate legislation in the interest of the lower South. Why should not the planters, experts in government, direct the policy of the United States?'

The answer was various. It was that by the end of the 1840s New York had replaced New Orleans as the outlet to the West, and the railroad construction program of the 1850s made its place even more secure. It was also that the West was filling up with people, and with the boom of the 1850s, Eastern capital poured into lumbering and mining, building railroads, building cities. Now the promoters and the commission men and the agents looked to Chicago, New York, and Boston for their sources of capital and trade rather than to St. Louis, New Orleans, and Mobile.

In the wake of the capitalists and speculators came a great movement of settlers from the Middle states and from northern Europe, and there also came shopkeepers, merchants, and manufacturers from Germany. Between 1856 and 1860, according to Professor Dodd, nearly half a million newcomers came to Illinois alone, many of them drawn by the new lands opened up by the Illinois Central Railroad, and Chicago's population increased twentyfold during the '50s. 'The people who came to the state at this time,' wrote Dodd, 'were Germans, English, Scotch, and New Englanders, and they brought with them opinions and ideas hostile to slavery and the South.'

By this time Pittsburgh was prospering and New England had dozens of busy industrial towns. But the South was constantly growing weaker by comparison. In 1860 Southerners owed Northern capitalists $400 million. Yet the crux of the matter and the essential source of economic disparity between the sections was this: the South tilled the land, and the North ran the machine.

The youth, chivalry, and great mass of yeoman farmers — the strength of the South — had romantically come to believe that bravery, the high heart, and adventurousness can (or certainly should) conquer all. And it followed that the planters who had always regarded Northern businessmen as money-grubbing vulgarians should think of them as potentially poor soldiers. 'Men like Ruffin believed,' says Miriam Beard, 'that material advantages counted for little against martial prowess . . . Business men, they thought, had ever been poor fighters . . . The Southern agrarians thought they could defeat the North, viewed by them as a degenerate commercial Carthage, too greedy for profit "to waste millions of dollars and men to gratify the abolitionists . . ." They did not realize how warfare had changed in 2,000 years, and how helpless even Scipio Africanus would be in the nineteenth century if he lacked a train to take him to the front.'

In April 1861, when President Lincoln decided to send an

expedition to provision beleaguered Fort Sumter in Charleston harbor, civil war was imminent. A talented woman, Mrs. Chesnut, wife of a South Carolina Senator and Confederate officer, in her *Diary from Dixie* conveys the agonizing feel of approaching tragedy: 'April 8th. 1861 — Tried to read . . . but could not. The air too full of war news and we are all so restless.

'Went to see Miss Pinckney . . . Governor Manning walked in, bowed gravely, seated himself by me . . . and said: "Madam, your country is invaded." I asked, "What does he mean?" He meant this: There are six men-of-war outside the harbor . . . Hostilities are about to begin . . . The agony was so stifling I could hardly see or hear . . . I crept silently to my room, where I sat down for a good cry.'

Four days later, Mrs. Chesnut attended the 'maddest dinner we have had yet . . . We had an unspoken foreboding that it was to be our last pleasant evening.'

At home after dinner, she could not sleep. She knew that if Major Anderson, U.S.A., did not surrender Fort Sumter by four in the morning, the orders were that it should be fired upon. Feverishly awake, she heard St. Michael's bells chime out. 'I count four and begin to hope.' But at half-past four there came the 'heavy booming of a cannon. I sprang out of bed, and on my knees prostrate prayed as I never prayed before.'

The diplomacy of compromise between the sections had not prevented war. The North had 'dared' to make war on cotton. Now there was to come into play a strange 'Cotton Diplomacy.' It was designed by Confederate leaders to win the war for the Confederacy in the chancelleries of European powers.

VI

The March of Cotton

A DYNAMIC, SUSTAINED EFFORT by cotton growers took cotton from Virginia to Texas within 60 years. Men might flame with malaria and die of yellow fever. They might encounter virgin, vine-entangled forests that had to be removed with fire and ax; great swamps and dangerous flooding rivers. Their families might have to live in clearings amid lonely wilderness. They might lack labor and capital; endure where there were few roads and no railroads. It did not matter. Cotton marched on.

Its rapid advance across the face of an empire was a prodigious achievement, the more remarkable because cotton demands immense amounts of hand labor and the latter was in short supply. Millions of acres were hand-planted, as if they were a flower garden. Billions of plants were individually thinned and kept free of grasses. Then, at harvest time, sun hot or air frosty, the cotton was picked by backbreaking labor, plant after plant, men going over the fields two, three, four times.

Men have long known that cotton flourishes only under certain soil and climatic conditions. But, says Gray, it was early believed that 'cotton country began in the southern counties of

New Jersey and in the northern counties of Delaware, Maryland, Virginia. The southern line of Pennsylvania continued eastward seems to be the northern boundary for what may be called the cotton region of the United States.' Even as this was being said, pioneers were moving into the region between the Appalachians and the Mississippi River where they grew cotton for household use and shipped some of it as a money crop. By 1810 Tennessee — then the West — was producing 6,000 bales of cotton. Before 1815 cotton culture rapidly developed in upper South Carolina and east central Georgia, making these states the nation's leading cotton producers that, in 1811, grew two-thirds of the total crop of 160,000 bales.

Cotton culture was a disrupting or radically transforming element wherever it appeared. And so it was when it came to South Carolina and Georgia. Slave populations increased. Agriculture became commercialized. Diversified farming and handicraft economy gave way to commercial plantations. Small towns grew smaller, their growth stunted. Industry languished. Grain and stock raising lost importance. As household manufactures declined, store-bought goods took their place. The pioneer's cabin was succeeded by the planter's comfortable house, or sometimes his mansion. Roads were opened to the coast, river navigation was improved, and a formerly backwoods region came into closer relations with older, settled coastal regions.

Cotton's march may be measured by the growth of the slave population in areas where it went. Thus in four South Carolina cotton counties, slaves increased from 14.4 per cent of the population in 1790 to 61.1 per cent in 1860, and this was not untypical of other areas.

Far to the south, in Louisiana and the Mississippi Territory, before the Louisiana Purchase, in an area where two civilizations — Latin and Anglo-Saxon — touched but did not merge, where French and Spanish were more commonly spoken than English, cotton early made its way. In 1801 Governor Claiborne of the Mississippi Territory estimated the value of its crop at $700,000 or about 10,000 bales. In the year of the Purchase (1803) cotton plantations were being developed along the Mississippi in the vicinity of Baton Rouge, Louisiana, and were extending back from the

river, and by 1809, cotton had become the principal product of the
Red River Valley and the Opelousas (Louisiana) district.

Cotton production was extremely profitable in the lower Mississippi region. Its lands were within reach of men of modest means.
In the beginning rich alluvial lands in Louisiana, with water communications to New Orleans, sold for $2 to $4 an acre. In many
areas there was no problem of land clearing so that favorable
weather and high cotton prices made it possible for men to lay
quickly the foundations of a fortune. The larger plantations were
above New Orleans, but there were many small planters — mainly
of French extraction — living on the fertile lands of the Lafourche
and the Atchafalaya.

Trial and error, as we have described, marked early cotton cultivation. Thus production reached its peak in Virginia in 1826 and
thereafter declined. Men learned that middle Tennessee was not
suited to profitable cotton cultivation, and a contemporary writer
tells us what happened there: 'From this date [1802] until 1812
but little difficulty was experienced in the culture of Cotton — the
seasons were mild — its growth seldom impeded by cold in the
Spring or injured by early frost in the Fall. But from the date of
that gloomy season . . . commonly termed "the shakes" there
appeared to be an evident change in the seasons — and the culture
of Cotton was for several years almost an entire failure. In 1824
fine crops of Cotton were again released in Tennessee, but this
success was of short duration . . . the culture of Cotton in middle
Tennessee had been precarious since 1812 and by no means a
source to be relied on.'

The area of cotton expansion was constantly enlarged but the
rate of expansion was uneven, depending on the fluctuating prices
of the staple. In general the expansion was so rapid that, excepting
Texas, the principal outlines of the cotton belt were formed in
the period 1825–50, and even in Texas cotton production made
considerable progress during this time.

In some regions the growth of the cotton kingdom was impeded
by the presence of Indians. This was true of Alabama, Mississippi,
Arkansas — territories mainly held by Indians before the War of
1812. In 1823 Robert Crittenden, Acting Governor of the Arkansas
Territory, wrote to John C. Calhoun, Secretary of War, saying:

'Mr. Bates [an Indian agent] tells me he has had frequent conversations with you, on the subject of the extinction of the Quapaw claim . . . They are a poor, indolent, miserable remnant of a nation, insignificant and inconsiderable.'

Obviously such Indian wretches should not own rich cotton lands that ought to belong to deserving whites. The Governor pointed out that Indians held 'the south side of the Arkansas from the first high land to the Little Rock, the seat of Government, a distance . . . of Two hundred and fifty miles. The staple production of the Arkansas as high up as Little Rock is cotton . . . The south side is high, rich and immensely valuable . . . Here the culture of cotton will reward the laborer as richly as in any part of the unsettled States, and the River through the whole extent of the Quapaw claim, is navigable for Steam Boats 9 months in the year . . .'

This would not do: rich cotton lands on navigable streams in the hands of heathen Indians; lands that ought to be owned by God-fearin', church-going, white men. Hence, according to God's will, Indians throughout the Lower South were deprived of their lands by wars, phony treaties, and sundry ingenious chicaneries devised by the good and the just. Just before Jackson became President, the state of Georgia, rebelling against the outrageous proposition that red Indians ought to be left in possession of even those lands that had been ceded them by federal treaties, tore up the treaties and dislodged the inhabitants. Mississippi and Alabama, no less sensitive to moral disharmonies than Georgia, stole the lands of the Choctaws and Chickasaws.

Indians, being Indians, ought to have accepted all this. But the Creeks acted 'uppity.' They had the nerve to talk about the Constitution and hired a lawyer to make the point that it is unconstitutional for a state to annul a federal contract. Such duplicity on the part of ungrateful Indians enraged Jackson. He told them that it would be indefensible of them to hold to their rights. Many chiefs saw the logic of his argument that even if the courts should uphold them, the whites would nonetheless take their lands, and the choice seemed to be plain robbery or robbery with murder.

The Creeks and Choctaws bowed to the white man's wisdom. They abandoned 17 million acres of land in Mississippi and Alabama, and moved west across the Mississippi River. But the Cherokees moved to the Supreme Court. The Court told the state of Georgia to leave them alone. Georgia ignored the Court. So did the President of the United States, Andrew Jackson.

Once when Henry Clay spoke for the Indians in Congress, Harriet Martineau, a visitor that day, described the scene. 'As many as could crowd into the gallery leaned over the balustrade, and the lower circle was thronged with ladies and gentlemen, in the centre of whom stood a group of Cherokee chiefs, listening immovably. I never saw so deep a moral impression produced by a speech . . . I saw tears of which I am sure he [Clay] was wholly unconscious falling on his papers as he vividly described the woes and injuries of the aborigines. I saw Webster draw his hand across his eyes; I saw every one vividly moved except the vice-president, who yawned somewhat ostentatiously, and the Georgia Senator who was busy brewing his storm.'

In 1832, the Supreme Court again held that Georgia was without authority over the Indians, and again Georgia ignored the Court. Then Jackson is alleged to have said, 'John Marshall has made his decision, now let him enforce it.' This is doubtful, but there is no doubt that Jackson wrote: 'The decision of the Court has fell still born, and they find they cannot coerce Georgia to yield.'

As Indians moved out, white men moved in. They moved so rapidly that by 1837 uncleared Alabama lands were bringing $35 an acre and clearing costs were an additional $15 an acre. The southern Alabama cotton crop increased from 11,000 bales in 1820 to 195,000 bales in 1836.

The seizure of Indian lands profoundly influenced the South's future. In 1826, despite slavery, it was almost entirely a yeoman society. Such men as Andrew Jackson and John C. Calhoun were born members of poor families in the South Carolina uplands, and Abraham Lincoln and Jefferson Davis belonged to plain Kentucky families. Yeoman farmers seemed more in tune with the times and the future than tidewater planters of Virginia and South Carolina whose lands were approaching exhaustion, and who had to feed slaves multiplying faster than work could be found for them.

Slaveowners would not abandon their property and emigrate. But where, in any event, could they go? The country north of the Ohio was closed to them. The Appalachian uplands were not suitable for the plantation economy of numerous slaves and large land holdings; neither were the Kentucky and Tennessee valleys. Yet even as planters surveyed the bleak prospect, they were being ground between the diminishing fertility of their lands and the increasing number of slave mouths to feed. This combination, they must have recalled, had financially ruined Jefferson, Madison, and Monroe. It was the same combination that moved the mordant John Randolph of Roanoke to comment acidly that the time would come when Southern masters would run away from their slaves and slaves would advertise for return to their masters.

It did not seem unlikely that the South would become a land of small farms and medium-sized plantations, and although slavery might not vanish overnight, it would become moribund. Men novelly began to conserve the soil. They even planned small-scale industries and diversification of the region's economy. But in the 1820s and 1830s, as the Indian lands were stolen, the whole course of events was changed. The failing plantation system found itself revived by being able to acquire huge acreages of new land in districts that lent themselves admirably to large-scale cotton production.

Soil conservation became less interesting. Diversification of the economy was postponed because surplus capital could be profitably employed in expanding the kingdom of cotton. (It did not occur to anyone that the South was taking the wrong path; that the failure to diversify its economy was to be fatal in 1861–5.) So, too, Negroes were suddenly transformed from a liability into an immense asset. Their market price rose and the more they multiplied the better, for they could be sold on a rising market. All this postponed further consideration of the Negro problem and soon Southern leaders denied that there was such a problem. The evolution of the South toward an egalitarian farming and small-business economy was stopped. By the 1840s and 1850s the trend was toward a class-conscious oligarchy.

The theft of the Indian lands, then, altered the South's politico-economic destiny. The once hardpressed tidewater planters now found that instead of having to live on half rations, they could emigrate to the West with their slaves and hope to become rich almost overnight.

Immigrants bring many things wherever they come: written laws and unwritten codes of behavior, cookery, architecture, religion, folklore, manners, prejudices — the infinitely varied items that make up the complex we call civilization. Cotton culture helped establish a Protestant, Anglo-Saxon dominance in the South. Newcomers from Europe did not usually go South to live because they disliked slavery. And immigrants from the Eastern colonies seldom ventured into the French settlements on the west side of the Mississippi River. But, themselves of Anglo-Saxon stock, men went early to the British settlements of the Natchez region which became the first sector of extensive Anglo-Saxon colonization along the lower Mississippi.

The Southern white population continued to be overwhelmingly Anglo-Saxon, and today constitutes the largest racially homogeneous bloc in the country. This is not the place to describe the effects on the region of its almost exclusive Anglo-Saxon colonization beyond noting that this made it largely Protestant of faith. The 16 million Negroes in the United States today, through the efforts of Protestant missionaries among their slave forefathers, are also predominantly Protestant.

A decade before Mississippi entered the Union in 1816, the plantation system had already been introduced. The countryside was still harshly primitive and a man contemplating a horseback journey from Natchez to Nashville over the Natchez Trace would first make his will before setting out on the dangerous trip. Yet, such was the rapid growth of cotton culture in the area that planters had already begun to build comfortable houses and, by the 1840s, Natchez was one of the richest of American towns.

The cotton frontier also moved elsewhere at an astonishing rate. In the 1830s the bottom lands of the Arkansas were as they had been when the world was young. But before 1860 they had a well-defined plantation system. The growth of cotton culture in the great rich alluvial region known as the Yazoo-Mississippi Delta, however, was retarded by floods, and it was not until the eve of the

Civil War that Yazoo planters built levees that made them fairly secure against the rivers.

In the Gulf plains, lands were rich, streams numerous and navigable, and in 1816 when steamboats came to the Mississippi River, a huge region witnessed a brilliant flowering. The period 1830–60 was the golden age of Mississippi River trade with its fleets of palatial and pedestrian steamboats which carried passengers, cotton, flour, grain, and all manner of goods up and down the river.

Sales of manufactures and foods by Northern manufacturers and farmers to Southern cotton growers grew steadily during this entire period. Much of the early trade was carried on by flatboats, one of which brought to the lower Mississippi an obscure, ungainly flatboatman named Abraham Lincoln. Levi Woodbury, writing in 1833 of a trip down the Mississippi, said: 'At every village we find from ten to twenty flatbottom boats, which besides corn on the ear, pork, bacon, flour, whiskey, cattle, and fowls, have a great assortment of notions from Cincinnati and elsewhere. Among them are brooms, cabinet-furniture, cider, plows, apples, cordage . . . They remain in one place until all is sold out, if the demand be brisk; if not, they move farther down. After all is sold they dispose of their boat and return with the crews by the steamers to their homes.'

As time passed and plantations grew larger, water-borne peddling vanished. Planters engaged agents at New Orleans to sell their cotton and buy their supplies, with the result that by 1856 flatboats were no longer listed in large numbers among the river arrivals at New Orleans. For a brief period the great river made New Orleans Queen of the West. The traffic on the Mississippi was so heavy that between 1830 and 1840 no American city kept pace with New Orleans' increase of wealth and trade, and its population grew from 46,310 in 1830 to 168,175 in 1860.

During the same years the value of the receipts of produce brought from the interior to New Orleans grew prodigiously — from approximately $22 million in 1830 to $185 million in 1860. The largest part of this great increase was in cotton, which in 1860 constituted 60 per cent of the value of all commodities entering the city. New Orleans had no rival as a cotton market, and in 1860 approximately $109 million worth of cotton was sold there.

The coming of railroads, slow though their construction was in the antebellum South, and the increased use of rivers sharply stimulated cotton culture. Railroads joined Nashville and Memphis with Chattanooga, Knoxville, and their eastern connections. The Mobile & Ohio was planned to connect Mobile with northeastern Mississippi and the Tennessee Valley, and ultimately to furnish a continuous route to St. Louis and Chicago by way of the Illinois Central. Louisville was connected by the building of the Louisville and Nashville. A railroad joined Vicksburg with Brandon, Mississippi, and Selma, Alabama, furnishing a direct link between the Mississippi River and the Eastern seaboard. A line connected Memphis with Little Rock, and other lines were constructed in the Carolinas and Georgia. Wherever tracks were laid, cotton culture was stimulated, and production nearly doubled in the decade 1849–59.

At the end of this period Mississippi led the nation in cotton production with a crop (round numbers) of 1.2 million bales. It was closely followed by Alabama with a million bales. Then came Louisiana, Georgia, Texas, Arkansas, South Carolina, Tennessee, and North Carolina. There was a small output in Florida, Missouri, Virginia, and Illinois.

Texas has long been our principal cotton state. But it had a relatively late start in cotton culture because American immigration into the area was slow before the Texas Revolution. Slaveholders were uncertain of the status of slavery, which was indeed illegal under Mexican law, and marketing facilities were poor. Texas planters, moreover, had to pay duty on cotton shipped to New Orleans and as late as 1835 they grew only three or four thousand bales a year.

In the 1830s there were few Negroes in Texas and pioneers preferred the Mexican economy of herding and self-subsistence farming to cotton and the plantation system. This point of view was expressed by a young man to whom Olmsted talked in the late 1850s. 'The young man probably owned many hundred acres of the range . . . and a large herd of cattle. He did not fancy taking care of a plantation. He was a regular Texan, he boasted, and was not going to slave himself, looking after niggers. Any man who had been brought up in Texas, he said, could live as well as he wanted to without working more than one month in the year. For about a month . . . he had to work hard, driving his cattle into the pens and roping and marking the calves. This was always done in a kind of frolic in the Spring — the neighboring herdsmen assisting each other. During the rest of the year he hadn't anything to do . . . When he wanted to buy anything he could always sell some cattle . . .'

Texas was not to become a great cotton region until after 1865; a movement accelerated by the coming of railroads.

Cotton culture dragged with it everywhere that it went the heavyweight of its credit system. If the slave was in thrall to the planter, the planter was often in thrall to the banker, called the factor or commission merchant, who was a combination moneylender and buying-selling agent. These men owned no lands or slaves. They planted no cotton. They limited their risks. And they grew rich, building great houses in Memphis, New Orleans, Charleston, Savannah, and other cotton capitals. Many of them were Shylocks in frock coats. Yet whether at the christening of a child, in the state legislature, or in their counting houses, there hovered about them an air of High-Church respectability and the heady aroma compounded of impeccable solvency and financial power.

The factorage system was an imported product. British factors had acted as bankers and agents for colonial clients. Recalling them, a writer in De Bow's Review said: 'The principals of the mercantile houses resided in Great Britain, and junior partners conducted the business in Virginia. Some of these concerns branched out, like polypi, to the villages and court-houses and, some of them, also like polypi, consumed the substance of all that came within their grasp . . .'

How did the Virginia planter fare under factorage? One student of the system concluded that 'no civilized people has been so badly paid for their labor as the planters of Virginia during the entire colonial era and for long years afterward.'

When commercial cotton production began in the United States, planters at first used existing marketing organizations that dealt in the older staples of rice and tobacco. Commission merchants for these commodities now bought cotton outright or consigned it to London and so became cotton-marketing specialists. They lived in the seaport cities of Charleston and Savannah, but others soon began to do business in Mobile and New Orleans. These cities became large-scale marketing centers. Thus, in 1851, Mobile could store 310,000 bales of cotton and its compresses had a capacity of 7,000 bales daily.

The planter shipped his cotton to the factor who sold it for a commission of 2.5 per cent. But since the cotton was in his possession and prices often fluctuated widely, he often abused his agency relation to the planter by becoming buyer-seller. In 1858 *Farmer and Planter* spoke out against this sharp practice: 'Many cotton Factors are also cotton *Speculators*, having an interest directly opposed to the interest of the planters and interior shippers. It behooves the latter to scan with a suspicious eye singular and improbable statements of estimates of the supply of cotton put forth by the former.'

Because the planter lived far from the city and transportation was slow and difficult, the factor, a city resident, performed many services for him. He bought things needed for the plantation and the planter's household: hardware, cloth, groceries, wines, and so forth. The factor charged such purchases to the planter at prices higher than market prices, and then added his commission of 2.5 per cent. But this did not exhaust his category of profit possibilities. He also took a bite out of the farmer for moneys laid out by him to defray costs of transportation of cotton, storage, insurance, drayage, weighing, sampling, and repairing bales.

The factor was, above all, the planter's banker. The plantation system was a credit-capitalist enterprise strongly touched with the speculative. It depended to a large extent upon 'boughten' goods, often even food for men and beasts. The system's expansion, calling for more and more lands and slaves, frequently acquired at high prices, made more and more credit necessary to it so that in the circumstances there came to be both a wide use and abuse of credit.

Banks did not usually grant the credits. The antebellum South was not rich in banks, and its banks were not rich. They were usually located, moreover, not in the interior where cotton was grown, but in the seaports where cotton was marketed. They engaged primarily in commercial banking rather than in financing cotton growers. Their onetime effort in this field had proved disastrous, so they financed planters only indirectly through the factorage system.

It was the factors, then, who did the financing, securing themselves in numerous ways. One method was the taking of what amounted to liens on the crops, although the lien system did not come to full fruition until after 1865. Generally they charged what the traffic would bear, interest rates running from 8 to 30 per cent per annum. It was natural, therefore, that planters should seek legislation for 'cheap money' and just as natural that factors should oppose it. The planters lost this battle, but it is one that has been fought for years by farmers who in recent times have finally won something of a permanent victory.

The factor who made large profits from cotton — the almost imperishable fiber that could always be turned into money — granted credit to the planter on the condition that he grow nothing but cotton. Thus the factorage system, aside from the burdens that it laid upon the planter, had a profound societal result. It bound the planter to a one-crop agriculture and held him in a form of cotton-slavery.

A lesser result was that factor-marketing hampered the growth of interior markets and led to the concentration of wealth, power, and population in a few cities. Yet before the coming of railroads some cotton was marketed inland at towns accessible to river navigation. Memphis, which is located on the Mississippi River in the center of a huge cotton region, became the largest of the interior markets, an eminence it still retains. In 1860 it handled nearly 400,000 bales of cotton.

The burdens of factorage, the dislike of commercial banks for cotton-financing, the rapid expansion of cotton culture often accompanied by the making of quick fortunes, together with a speculative lust that has often marked the cotton economy, led that economy more than once into a wild speculative spree. One of the most spectacular came in the 1830s when the new cotton areas were being overwhelmed by an influx of men from the older areas. Some were bankrupts. Some had exhausted their lands. Some were younger sons who arrived with a few slaves to get rich quickly in a new country. Others were planters who stayed home but established new plantations to be run by overseers or relatives.

The principal instrument of their financing was state banks. Essentially devices for land and slave speculation, they had the privilege of issuing notes and performing the functions of commercial banking. Louisiana established the first in 1821. Twenty years later all of them, scattered over much of the cotton South, had gone broke.

The most grandiose in conception was the Union Bank of Mississippi. It had eight branch offices scattered throughout the state, and a home office in the capital city of Jackson. Chartered in January 1837 with a capital stock of $15.5 million, the bank was permitted to do business when $500,000 was subscribed. After the state's faith for the whole capital and interest was pledged, the state issued $15.5 million in 5 per cent gold bonds, payable to the Union Bank. Unfortunately, however, the bank opened just at the start of the disastrous depression of 1837, and shares could not be sold to local investors. Whereupon the legislature ordered the Governor to take $5 million of shares for the state. Bonds used for payment were sent by three commissioners to Eastern markets, and Mississippi anxiously awaited word from them. Finally it came. Nicholas Biddle, president of the United States Bank at Philadelphia, had bought the whole series. The bonds were to be redeemed in five equal installments of $1 million.

The news from Philadelphia caused an explosion of joy in the rude frontier town of Jackson. Bonfires were kindled. Guns were shot off. There was general rejoicing when the money finally arrived at Jackson in the form of British gold. It had come to New Orleans by steamship. Then a river steamboat had brought it up the Mississippi to Vicksburg where a heavily guarded wagon train had taken possession of it and hauled it over bad roads to Jackson. All along the road men had gathered to stare at the golden train and dream their golden dreams.

The bank made loans to speculators and indulged in fantastic banking practices. By 1840 it was broke. In 1842, by vote of the people, the bank's bonds were repudiated. Those who had bought them in good faith, relying on the pledge of the state of Mississippi, got nothing. Neither they nor their descendants were ever to get anything.

State banks in other parts of the South went broke in much the same manner as the Union Bank. A contemporary diarist, W. H. Willis of North Carolina, tells us something of these days: 'Speculation, speculation, has been making poor men rich and rich men princes. Men of no capital in three years have become wealthy and those of some have grown to hundreds of thousands. But as great as all the resources of Miss. and as valuable her lands, yet there were limits to both and these limits have been passed, lost sight of and forgotten as things having no existence.

'A revulsion has taken place and Miss. is ruined. Her rich men are poor and her poor men beggars. Millions and millions have been speculated on and gambled away by banking, by luxuries and too much prosperity, until of all the states in the Union, she has become much the worst.

'We have seen hard times in North Carolina, hard times in the East, hard times everywhere, but Miss. exceeds them all. Some of the finest lands . . . may now be had for comparatively nothing. Those that once commanded from $20 to $50 an acre, may now be bought for $3 or $5 . . . while many that have been sold at sheriff's sales for 50¢ were considered worth $15 to $20 . . . So great is the panic and so dreadful the distress that there are a great many farms prepared to receive crops and some of them planted and yet deserted, not a human being to be found upon them.'

But nothing could stop the march of cotton, including occasional spectacular collapses of the economy. By 1850 the cotton kingdom extended for more than a thousand miles from South Carolina to the region near San Antonio. The breadth of the kingdom, from north to south, ranged from 200 miles in Carolina and Texas to 600 or 700 miles in the Mississippi Valley. The area where cotton could be easily grown measured 400,000 square miles.

In 1850 the Lower South had a population of 2,137,000 white people and 1,841,000 Negroes, nearly all of whom were slaves. The great majority of the whites lived in areas where slavery was non-existent or of little influence. But nearly all the slaves lived in the cotton belt.

The upbuilding of this region had been accomplished with great speed. It was the work of only 30 years. Great forests vanished before fire and ax, the destruction decreed by men who seemed to flame with a passion for growing cotton. Hardly had land been cleared and a crop planted when slaves were set to felling trees and burning logs, preparing 'new ground' to take the place of the newly made clearings that would soon be abandoned.

The vast horizons of the country, the fertility of the soil, and the thousands of square miles of good cotton soil within easy reach of navigable rivers made men heady, restless, suffused them with the feeling that the country belongs to him who can exploit it, and gave them a sense of illimitable opportunity. All this influenced not only the South but the whole course of American history. There are times in men's lives when they feel that they can do anything. In the last three decades before the Civil War the driving, ambitious men of the cotton country must have felt that almost anything was possible to them.

They were hell-bent to grow cotton. But let us now turn to the role of cotton in the great national tragedy that loomed ahead for cotton growers and the whole nation.

VII

'Lord Russell Presents His Compliments . . .'

THE NEW ORLEANS *Crescent* was in accord with Confederate policy and public opinion when it urged planters to destroy their cotton 'rather than let it fall in the hands of the Yankees.' And now on an April day of 1862, cotton was being destroyed. A Union fleet had forced the entrance of the Mississippi and captured New Orleans. Sarah Morgan Dawson, a young Louisiana girl, watched the destruction and describes it in *A Confederate Girl's Diary.* 'We went this morning to see the cotton burning . . . Wagons . . . were loaded with bales . . . to be burned. Negroes were running around, cutting them open, piling them up and setting them afire . . . Later Charlie sent for us to come . . . and see him fire a flatboat loaded with the precious material . . . Negroes were rolling it down to the brink of the river where they would set the bales afire and push them in to float burning down the tide . . .

'The flatboat was loaded with as many bales as it could hold without sinking. Most of them were cut open, while Negroes staved in barrels of whiskey, alcohol, etc., and dashed bucketsful over the cotton . . . There, piled the length of the whole levee or burning in the river, lay the work of thousands of Negroes for more than a year past . . . Men stood by who owned the cotton . . . They either helped or looked on cheerfully . . . A single

118

barrel of whiskey that was thrown on the cotton cost the man who gave it $125 . . . An incredible amount of property has been destroyed today, but no one begrudges it.'

There was no cotton in the blood of Christopher Gustavus Memminger, Secretary of the Treasury of the Confederacy. Born in Germany where his father was a casualty of the Napoleonic wars, he was brought up in a Charleston orphanage, his mother having died shortly after arriving in the United States. A precocious student at the University of South Carolina, he became a brilliant lawyer, and a drearily earnest man with a passion for detail and statistics. Now he sat in the headquarters of the Confederate Treasury in Montgomery. It consisted of one hastily furnished room, and there was a single employee — Henry D. Capers, who became Memminger's biographer. Soon an officer appeared with an order from President Davis instructing the Treasury to provide money for fitting out a hundred men.

Capers pulled some Federal currency notes from his pocket, and said there was no other money available, but Memminger arranged a credit at a local bank on his personal guarantee. 'At the beginning,' he later said, 'the Confederacy did not have enough money to buy the desk on which the Secretary wrote.'

It never did have much money. During four war years, the Confederacy scraped together only $25 million in hard cash. Upon this sum, tiny in relation to its needs, it maintained an army of hundreds of thousands of men, employed a lesser army of civil servants, and provided the circulating medium for the economic life of nine million people. It spent hard money at the rate of about $6,250,000 a year. This was only twice what the Federal Government was spending in a single day.

There was also paper money, floods of it. Even paper stock had to be found at home because the South had manufactured little or no paper in its reliance on the North for nearly everything, and bank notes and bonds had been engraved before the war by the National Bank Note Company and the American Bank Note Company in what was now the enemy city of New York. But, nonetheless, nearly everybody printed money sometime during the War: states, counties, cities, towns, banks, railroads, and industries.

Barbers, bartenders, and small tradesmen issued paper tokens valued at 5 to 50 cents. And all this brought joy to counterfeiters whose task was made easy by the crudity of the currency.

Yet all the while, the hard-pressed Confederacy possessed a huge source of real wealth to which it did not turn. In the fall of 1861, cotton planters held millions of bales of cotton for which they had no market. They would gladly have accepted Confederate bonds for their cotton. Then the Treasury could have shipped it to Europe and established great cash balances to rely on for its fiscal security. Benjamin Franklin had made a precedent of this principle. When he went to Paris in 1776 on a diplomatic mission, the ship that carried him also carried a cargo of American tobacco. Franklin was expected to sell the tobacco and use the proceeds for the expenses of his mission.

But this simple scheme met no approval in the Confederate Cabinet. At the first Cabinet meeting, says Leroy P. Walker, who for a brief period filled the war office, 'there was only one man there who had any sense and this man was Benjamin [Judah P. Benjamin, former United States Senator from Louisiana, who ultimately became Secretary of State in the Confederate Cabinet]. Mr. Benjamin proposed that the Government purchase as much cotton as it could hold, at least 100,000 bales, and ship it at once to England. With the proceeds of a part of it he advised the immediate purchase of at least 150,000 stands of arms . . . The residue of the cotton to be held as a basis for credit. For, said Benjamin, we are entering on a contest that may be long and costly. All the rest of us fairly ridiculed the idea of a serious war. Well, you know what happened.'

The amount suggested by Benjamin — 100,000 bales — would have brought the Confederacy approximately $50 million, a resource that would have given it great strength in the early, critical months of the war. Professor Frank L. Owsley estimates that in 1861 the Confederacy could have shipped two million bales if it had chosen to.

Christopher G. Memminger, Secretary of the Treasury, ridiculed the proposal to ship cotton to Europe, and regarded the concept as unconstitutional and economically unsound. He called it 'soup house legislation,' because it would have brought relief to planters who had no market for their cotton.

But the fact is that the Confederacy kept its most powerful economic weapon under lock and key because it did not want to use it. This was in accord with the prevailing King Cotton theory that had been put almost on a par with the states-rights doctrine. 'King Cotton,' says Owsley, 'became a cardinal principle upon which all the men who were to lead the South out of the Union and guide its destiny through the Civil War were almost unanimously agreed.' The Confederacy in 1861–2 not only shipped no cotton but took every measure to see that no one else did either. When the Union started its naval blockade of the South, Confederate leaders, obsessed by the notion that cotton is king, welcomed it almost as a godsend. President Jefferson Davis, according to his contemporary Southern biographer, Edward A. Pollard, 'actually welcomed the blockade and vaunted it as a blessing in disguise.'

The notion that cotton was paramount internationally had been argued by David King in *Cotton Is King: or Slavery in the Light of Political Economy*. Published in 1855, the phrase 'Cotton is King' was soon on every Southern tongue and it became gospel by repetition.

The Confederacy turned away from the real wealth of its cotton supply and launched its King Cotton diplomacy with the objective of bringing Britain and France to intervene in the war. Regarding themselves as struggling for independence in the manner of their ancestors of 1776, Confederate leaders remembered that the colonies might have lost without French aid. If Britain were to intervene in the Civil War, France would follow, and the Confederacy would triumph. Its leaders based their hopes upon a number of assumptions.

First of all, they felt that they would have the support of the British upper classes whose attitudes were nearer to those of the South than of the equalitarian North. They believed, moreover, that Britain would delight to see two nations established on American soil, for the United States was potentially a powerful economic rival and its democratic system could threaten the British social system. Southerners also assumed that Britain would be lured by an agricultural, new Southern nation that could offer her exporters large economic opportunities through free, or at least freer, trade. And British merchants, dealing directly with the South instead of through Northern middlemen, could earn greatly increased profits.

But if these factors failed to provoke Britain's intervention in the war, there was the final, overwhelming consideration that would force her hand — King Cotton. Britain's greatest industry was cotton manufacturing. Four million of her twenty-one million people derived their living from it.

This huge trade seemed at the mercy of its American supplier of raw material, for three-fourths of its cotton came from the South. Britain had long sought an alternative cotton supply in India, but to no avail. From 1800 to 1860 her cotton demands rose 1,000 per cent, but India's cotton supply rose only 20 per cent. Hence Southern leaders assumed that Britain's greatest industry, the support of millions of her people, the mainstay of her export trade, and a source of large profits for her businessmen, was at their mercy. *Blackwood's Magazine* had grumbled that this placed the subsistence of 'millions in every manufacturing country of Europe within the power of an oligarchy of planters.' France was in a somewhat similar plight. Her cotton-manufacturing industry was second to that of Great Britain and most of its supply was drawn from the South.

Certainly Confederate leaders devoutly believed that 'Cotton is King,' and the theme was reiterated by Jefferson Davis at Montgomery in 1861. The President of the provisional Confederate Government said: 'An agricultural people — whose chief interest is the export of a commodity required in every manufacturing community, our true policy is peace and the freest trade which necessities will permit. It is alike our interest, and that of all those to whom we would sell and from whom we would buy, that there should be the fewest practicable restrictions upon the interchange of commodities. This common interest of the producer and consumer can only be interrupted by an exterior force, which should obstruct its transmission to foreign markets — a course of conduct which would be as unjust toward us as it would be detrimental to the manufacturing and commercial interests abroad.'

Davis used cautious, circumlocutory diplomatic language because he spoke, not to the Confederacy, but to England. He was promising her, in the event of Confederate triumph, the boon of free (or freer) trade with the new Southern nation. And he was reminding her of the damage she might suffer through a cotton shortage. In other words: Cotton is King!

Many Southerners believed not simply that cotton was king, but that it was an absolute monarch, so deeply were they under its spell. W. H. Russell, the famous London *Times* war correspondent, visited New Orleans ('which now feels the pressure of the blockade') and recorded dreams of its leaders. 'Through the present gloom come the rays of a glorious future . . . with the entire control of the Mississippi and a monopoly of the great staples on which so much of the manufacture . . . of England and France depend. They believe themselves . . . to be masters of the destiny of the world. Cotton is king — not alone king, but czar . . .'

This was the firm, almost fanatical conviction of many Southern leaders. Because of it they attempted the strange task of forcing great powers to intervene in a dangerous foreign war by withholding from them supplies of cotton. Yet this seemed rational to men of the times and, writing from Montgomery, Russell said: 'They [Confederate leaders] firmly believe the war will not last a year. They believe in the irresistible power of cotton, in the natural alliance between manufacturing England and France and the cotton-producing slave states . . .'

As Montgomery, so Charleston. A merchant pointed to cotton bales on a wharf and exclaimed to Russell: 'Look out there! There's the key will open all our ports, and put us into John Bull's strongbox as well!' The influential Charlestonian, Barnwell Rhett, held an even more extreme point of view, and Russell drily said of him: 'Rhett is persuaded that the Lord Chancellor sits on a cotton bale.'

Cotton seems to have cast a wizard's spell not only over political leaders, firebrands, and fiscally innocent merchants, but also over hardheaded businessmen and economists. For here is De Bow, economist and editor, saying: 'Let us teach our children to hold the cotton plant in one hand and the sword in the other, ever ready to defend it as the source of commercial power abroad, and, through that, of independence at home.'

Slavery was the cornerstone of the Confederacy and cotton was its foundation. King Cotton diplomacy stemmed naturally, therefore, from the minds of men whose power and privilege derived directly or indirectly from cotton; men who believed that their 'king' was as important to everybody else as to them.

In April 1861, the Union formally began a blockade of the Confederate coast from the Chesapeake Bay to the Rio Grande. For a long time it was a paper blockade. The tiny Union navy was inadequate to the huge task of effectively patrolling 3,500 miles of coast, a dozen great ports, and almost 200 minor ports. But the Confederacy refrained from trying to ship cotton through the sieve-blockade, and deliberately withheld cotton from shipment. This policy was supported by the planters, the press, and the people. On 14 September 1861, the New Orleans *Price Current* said: 'The planters appear to be firm in their determination to withhold crops until the blockade should be removed.' At the same time, warehousemen and insurance men warned planters that if they forwarded cotton to New Orleans, no one would receive it. So, too, state legislatures favored the embargo and obstructed would-be cotton shippers.

The embargo dealt with baled cotton — cotton in being. But two considerations persuaded the Confederacy to restrict further production. The first was that the South must grow more food for herself. The second was — men reasoned — that when Britain realized she was being condemned to long-term cotton starvation, she would recognize the Confederacy.

The Confederate Congress, dominated by states'-rights concepts, usually left the task of restricting cotton production to the states. Thus Arkansas limited the planting of cotton to two acres per field hand, and Georgia placed a tax of ten cents a pound on all cotton produced on a farm in excess of 2,500 pounds. The combined effects of labor shortages, farm disorganization, and legislative restriction of production were astonishing. The cotton crop fell from 4,500,000 bales in 1859 to approximately 300,000 bales in 1864.

In addition to reducing cotton plantings, the Confederate Congress required owners to destroy all cotton that might fall into the hands of the enemy and we have observed, through a girl's eyes, the burning of cotton at New Orleans. In the Upper South, when Port Royal, South Carolina, was taken by the Federals, the Charleston *Courier* said: 'At eleven o'clock last night the heavens towards the southwest were brilliantly illuminated with the patriotic flames ascending from burning cotton. As the spectators witnessed it they involuntarily burst forth with cheer after cheer, and each heart was warmed as with a new pulse . . . We learn . . . that the patriotic planters on the seaboard are applying the torch to their cotton . . . Thirteen cotton-houses have been burnt on Port Royal Island, one on Paris, and one on St. Helena, since the Yankee occupation.'

The *Courier* did not report that men, whether from an excess of zeal or in panic, sometimes burned cotton gins along with cotton; nor does it record the anguish of those who saw their sole treasure incinerated. When Confederate cavalry burned cotton near Columbia, Tennessee, a farmer who owned part of it wrote: 'It was a sad thing to see a body of armed men roll out a man's whole dependence for money and the support of his family before his eyes . . . and stick fire into it and he dare not open his mouth.'

The Confederacy's cotton-burning policy was noted in the report of the Boston Board of Trade for 1863. It had, said the Board, defeated Federal plans for supplying Europe with seized cotton: 'The Confederates have guarded this article with unusual vigilance, burning . . . all likely to fall into our hands, knowing that the "Cotton Famine" of Europe was their most active agent in bringing about a recognition of their confederacy.' An estimated 2.5 million bales of cotton were destroyed by their owners or by the Confederate armies.

Because of the cotton burning and severe restrictions on its production, it became Union policy to grow cotton on seized plantations and we shall consider this effort before returning to the blockade and King Cotton diplomacy.

In 1863 the *American Agriculturist* observed: 'There is a field opened for Northern enterprise . . . upon which pioneers have entered with a fair promise of success. A large part of the country along both banks of the Mississippi, from Memphis to New Orleans, is now in the hands of the government, having been abandoned by its owners.'

Three Commissioners of Plantations, appointed to lease seized plantations, met at Vicksburg every few weeks to pass upon applications. Lessees paid the Federal Government a tax of $4 a bale, and had the privilege of buying supplies from quartermasters at military posts within the region. *The American Agriculturist* made the potent announcement that 'Those who engaged in the business last year are said to have made money.'

Liberated plantation slaves were put to work on the same plantations under new, Northern masters who had leased the lands. The Federal Government prescribed regulations for their treatment and some lessees abided by them, but the majority abused Negro labor for the sake of quick profits. Lessees often bribed provost marshals, and a New York cavalryman who was once quartered on a Louisiana plantation wrote: 'The provost marshals and lessees are linked together in the scheme to defraud the Negro . . . The plantation manager agreed to pay the Negroes . . . $5 a month . . . When paying them off the other day, he would say to this one that he had not hoed his cotton well, and to another that he was not quick enough in getting out in the morning . . . and so on through the whole list of hands, giving to some 50 cents, others $1, and so on up to $3 . . .'

But the cheating lessees had their own troubles and sometimes wailed so piteously that we can almost feel sorry for them, scoundrels though they were. One complained that he had been much put upon by wayward nature, 'Rebel' raiders, and U.S. Treasury agents, and he poured out his heart in a letter to the *Wisconsin State Journal*: 'Who hath woe, who hath sorrow? He that raiseth cotton on a Government plantation. Who hath much greenbacks and expecteth more? The official that letteth the plantation . . . ! Who hath honesty undefiled? He that hath hair growing in the palm of his hand!'

The lessee, obviously feeling sorry for himself, continued his catalogue of woes: 'Men from the North came down,' he said, 'stocked the plantations and started a crop with the promise of military protection. The thing was going off beautiful, when lo!

the guerilla came and swept off all those Yankee assets like a whirl-
wind.' Whereupon many lessees returned home. Others, un-
daunted, restocked the plantations and made a fresh start. But
then appeared Massachusetts recruiting officers who 'raided every
plantation . . . enlisting every able-bodied he-nigger in the country.' They were followed by another plague: Union officers with
orders to take the planters' horses and mules.

'These trials,' said the correspondent, 'were borne with com-
mendable fortitude but unfortunately not a Christian spirit. So
Divine Providence took a hand . . . and appointed the army
worm as the receiver of the crop . . . The army worm is so called
from its resemblance to the army officers who always appropriate
to their use at least $\frac{9}{10}$ of all cotton that passes through their
hands.' Then, head bowed, the doleful lessee-correspondent concludes: 'so mote it be.'

Some of the seized plantations were run by high-minded men
who attempted to be missionaries to the Negroes and plantation
superintendents. They also had troubles; troubles of the spirit.
When their charges blandly lied and thieved, they attributed these
faults to the slave system, and were forgiving. Yet as time passed
their mood became one of embittered disillusionment. For example, the missionary-superintendent who assumed his duties on a
sea-island plantation just after leaving Harvard, was eager for the
improvement of the 'degraded' blacks. But after two years of work
among them he wrote: 'The untrustworthiness of these people is
more . . . troublesome than ever . . . Their skill in lying . . .
their habit of shielding one another (generally by silence), their
invariable habit of taking a rod when you . . . have been induced
to grant an inch . . . joined with amazing impudence in making
claims — these are the traits which try us continually in our deal-
ings with them and sometimes make us almost despair of their
improvement — at least in the present generation.'

Many planters continued to operate their plantations within
occupied territory, their former slaves working as freedmen. They
were better off than those employed by Northern lessees. The
planters were not trying to get rich quick. They were primarily
concerned with holding their property and earning a living until
the return of peace and civil government. They also felt a solici-

tude for the Negroes because of past associations and knew that they would have to rely upon their labor in the future.

None of this was lost upon Thomas W. Conway, superintendent of Negro labor for the Department of the Gulf. An antislavery Yankee, he reported to General Hurlbut in 1864: 'Of the men who are known as the "old planters" of the country, so far as dealing fairly with freedmen is concerned in the matter of wages . . . as a rule, they have paid them more promptly, more justly, and apparently with more willingness than have the new lessees from other parts of the country.'

In June 1862, Union troops occupied the great inland cotton market of Memphis, and immediately a huge trade sprang up between Southern civilians and Yankee troops as the former exchanged cotton for a wide variety of supplies. The Congressional Committee on the Conduct of the War estimated that within two years from $20 to $30 million worth of supplies reached the Confederacy through Memphis. The pressure to trade seemed to reach the bursting point early in 1863 when cotton reached the undreamed-of price of $1 a pound. Charles A. Dana, then on a special mission in Memphis, tells us what happened: 'The mania for sudden fortunes in cotton raging in a vast population of Yankees scattered throughout the country and in this town has to a large extent corrupted and demoralized the army. Every colonel, captain, and quartermaster is in secret partnership with some operator in cotton; while every soldier dreams of adding a bale of cotton to his pay. I had no conception of the extent of the evil until I came and saw for myself . . .' The cotton-barter traffic between the enemies became so great, and Union leaders were so concerned by it, that Senator Collamer suggested the Union withdraw its army and enlist a force of 'Yankee peddlers . . . to go down there and trade them all out.'

In New Orleans, the brother of the city's military commander, Ben Butler, grew rich from illegal trade in cotton with Southerners, while James Lusk Alcorn, who remained on his plantation throughout the war, sold hundreds of bales of cotton for 'greenbacks,' gold, and manufactured goods.

General Sherman said that Cincinnati furnished more goods to the Confederacy than Charleston, and a judge advocate of the Union fleet blockading the North Atlantic commented: 'The munitions of war were furnished [Confederates] in large quantities . . . by citizens of the United States . . . Horace Greeley used to say that the ideas and vital aims of the South were more "generally cherished" in New York than in South Carolina.'

Large numbers of ships ran the Union naval blockade, some owned by the Confederacy and its state governments, others by individuals or groups of speculators, and a fourth category composed of foreign vessels. The latter generally belonged to enterprising Englishmen and Scotsmen who had the ships and capital necessary for the potentially profitable but risky venture. At first Nassau was their base, but yellow fever and the Union fleet caused them to shift to Bermuda, only 600 miles from the cotton port of Wilmington, North Carolina.

One of the most famous of the blockade-runners was the Confederate-owned *Robert E. Lee*. A Clyde-built iron steamer, reputed to be the fastest afloat, she ran the blockade 21 times — mostly out of Wilmington, North Carolina — before she was captured. Commanded by John Wilkinson, a former United States naval officer, he once burned part of his cargo of cotton under the boilers to increase his speed away from a pursuing warship.

Since blockade-running was usually a private venture conducted by men who took large risks for the sake of potentially large profits, it was conducted with an eye not to Confederate needs, but to owners' profits. They soon found that it was more profitable to carry luxury goods than such utilitarian items as iron rails. Hence they brought to Southern ports champagne, laces, perfumes, and women's apparel. 'When Captain Hobart Pasha of the *Venus*,' writes Clement Eaton, 'asked a Southern woman in England what was most needed in the Confederacy, she unhesitatingly replied "corsets . . ." Southern ladies made heroic sacrifices for . . . the Confederacy . . . but they would have corsets . . . The blockade runners would return from the Confederate ports laden with cotton that they sold . . . in Europe [for] five times its prewar value . . .'

The luxury trade did not end until 1864. Then the Confederate government required that every blockade-runner have a permit and allot at least half the cargo to military items. It is estimated that the chances of capture were only one in ten in 1861, and one in eight in 1862. But they were one in three by 1864, and when Wilmington was captured in January 1865, blockade-running practically ceased.

Altogether more than 600 blockade-runners violated the blockade some 8,000 times. They brought in over 600,000 small arms, 550,000 pairs of shoes, and large quantities of meat, coffee, saltpeter, lead, and other supplies. They also took to Europe approximately 1,250,000 bales of cotton.

The blockade was a decisive factor in Union victory. This is not to say that without it the Confederacy would have won the War, but there is little doubt that if there had been no blockade the War would have been greatly prolonged and might have ended in a stalemate. But Britain, contrary to Confederate hopes, did not violate it. Let us turn now from the bleeding South, from its cotton pyres and deserted fields and blockade-runners, to Victorian London and inquire how King Cotton diplomacy was faring there.

Confederate leaders had accurately estimated cotton's role in the British economy. Arnold, in *The History of the Cotton Famine* (published in London in 1864) wrote: 'Had not French, American and Russian wars — had not railways and telegraphs their part . . . in this century, surely it would be known as the Cotton Age. This year 1860 was the *"annus mirabilis"* of King Cotton . . . His dependents were most numerous, and his throne most wide. There was no Daniel to interpret to him the handwriting on the wall, which within twelve months should be read by all who ran in letters of blood. What cared he? An argosy of ships bore him across every sea . . . He drank of the fulness of his power, and was satisfied; for he was great.'

This chronicler of the cotton famine joyfully noted the giant proportions of Britain's cotton-manufacturing industry. 'If figures can ever be magnificent,' he writes, 'if naked totals ever reach to the sublime, surely the British cotton trade in 1860 compels our admiration.' Its output was then valued at 'nearly six millions [pounds sterling] more than the gross revenues of the kingdom for the same period.' The very weight of this trade might have seemed to assure the triumph of King Cotton diplomacy. But the architects of the policy had failed in the all-important matter of timing. Indeed they could scarcely have chosen a more unfavorable moment.

Britain went into the beginning of the Civil War period with great stocks of raw cotton and manufactured cotton goods. She had bought heavily of the American crops of 1859 and 1860, and before May 1861 had received 1,650,000 bales of cotton. These were added to the stock of nearly 600,000 bales that she had at the end of 1860, to say nothing of her large inventory of Asian cottons. The War itself reduced Britain's cotton consumption as her once large export market to the United States shrank, while simultaneously her great cotton-goods markets in India and China were overstocked and 'troubled with indigestion and loss of appetite for two years.'

The outbreak of the War did not, therefore, put pressure on British mill owners to seek government intervention in the conflict. On the contrary, a rise in the price of cotton and cotton goods was to the advantage of mill owners as the anticipated cotton scarcity gave them large 'inventory profits.' In place of hard times, they had a shower of riches.

But as surpluses declined, and cotton stocks went unreplenished, there were forebodings in England, and on 27 December 1861, the London *Times* said: 'Christmas comes this year . . . on a people oppressed with a national loss and threatened with a formidable war. Already closed mills and short time have given some of our people an earnest of what they may hereafter expect . . . and the somber appearance of our churches and chapels last Sunday portends a bad season next spring.'

By midsummer of 1862, half of Lancashire's spindles were idle, and the *Saturday Review* said: 'The cotton famine is the saddest thing that has befallen this country for many a year . . . In the worst of our calamities there has seldom been so pitiable a sight as the manufacturing districts present at this time.'

During the first six months of 1862 Britain received only 11,500 bales of cotton compared to 1.5 million bales in the corresponding period of 1861. More than two million people were unemployed, millions more were on half time, and alms for the suffering trickled in from Australia, India, Canada, and even China. The London *Times* now said: 'The memory of the year which ends this day will hereafter be closely associated with the American war . . . No crisis in modern times has been so anxiously watched, nor has any European war or revolution so seriously threatened the interests of England.'

How was it then among textile workers? Of the 14,000 people of Glossop, 5,300 had been employed in its cotton mills. By the autumn of 1862, 40 per cent of the town's population was living on alms and distress was visible in long rows of shut-up houses, in frequent bankruptcies, and in the knots of unemployed standing on street corners.

A correspondent of the London *Times* visited the hard-hit cotton-textile town of Blackburn. He found one street occupied by cotton workers whose mill had been closed for more than a year. 'Every family had passed through the last winter without wages and were entirely dependent on relief . . . Some of them were lying four and five in a bed, others on a bundle of straw . . . In one house I saw . . . a little child, not more than two months old, whose mother, a lodger in the house, had died just after its birth. The mistress of the house — an old woman who got her living by hawking hearthstones — had taken on herself the responsibility of bringing it up . . .'

The destitution of cotton workers became so great that the Union sent them food. At the height of the cotton famine, John Bright, an active friend of the North, wrote to Senator Sumner of Massachusetts and suggested that 'If a few cargoes of flour could come . . . as a gift from persons in your Northern states to Lancashire working men, it would have a prodigious effect in your favour here.' Shortly thereafter three ships took cargoes of meat and flour from New York to Liverpool.

Across the channel in France, destitution among cotton-textile workers was perhaps even more acute than in England and, says Owsley, 'For a while people lived upon bran, water and herbs while half-naked children infested the countryside begging food.'

As for cotton to relieve the famine, in 1864 Britain received some Indian (surat) cotton, a rather dubious blessing. Short-fibered, brittle, wasteful in the working, operatives who processed it got one-third less than going wages. The word 'surat' became an odious epithet in Lancashire and when a firm of brewers was called 'surat brewers,' it sued for libel. John Bright told the story of the cotton-mill hand who, when the preacher was praying for more cotton, loudly groaned, 'Amen, O Lord! *but not shoorat!*' Nevertheless, surat cotton gave employment to 135,000 workers.

The destitution among cotton-mill operatives which Confederate leaders had counted on to bring British intervention in the War was now an accomplished fact. But how was it together with King Cotton diplomacy regarded in the foreign offices of Britain and France, in the great houses of English aristocrats, in the editorial offices of English newspapers, in the White House where President Lincoln brooded, and in the minds and souls of the suffering people of Lancashire?

The Union blockade of the Confederacy was, at the outset, little more than a paper blockade and therefore not binding by international law, since a blockade must be effective to be binding. Yet Great Britain did not take the position that there was no legal blockade because this might have involved her in war and Britain wanted no war. Further, by virtue of her position as the world's greatest maritime power, she was dependent upon blockading as an instrument of war, so did not want to compel a strict interpretation that might seriously hurt her in the future. Britain, therefore, accepted the blockade from its beginning.

The Civil War, however, sharply divided British classes as they had not been divided over a foreign struggle since the French Revolution. Generally speaking, the upper classes were pro-Confederate, the middle and lower classes pro-Union. The upper classes regarded the American Republic, with its strongly democratic bias, as a menace to the continuance of their power. Tories, still remembering 1776, joyfully anticipated the break-up of the United States, and the aristocracy hailed secession in 1861. Their sentiments were expressed by *Blackwood's Magazine* which said that this 'vaunted democracy' had dragged from 'his proper obscurity an ex-rail splitter' and put 'its liberties at his august disposal.' But Charles Francis Adams, American Minister to the Court of St. James's, said that educated Englishmen cared nothing for the South. 'Their true motive,' he wrote, 'is the fear of the spread of democratic feeling at home in the event of our success.'

Economic interests — specifically cotton interests — were also involved. Two decades before '61, these interests had shown their hand in Texas. Eager to escape dependence upon United States cotton and seeking new markets along with new cotton sources, Britain had offered financial aid and protection to Texas to encourage her independence. In 1843, Lord Brougham and Lord Aberdeen admitted that it was Britain's intention to foster abolition along with Texas independence. This brought a strange outburst from John C. Calhoun, then Secretary of State. The South certainly did not want as a next-door neighbor an independent, free-labor, cotton-growing country that would be a refuge for fugitive slaves and a menace to its social system. Hence Calhoun, linking the issue of Texas annexation with a defense of slavery, told Britain that she was trying to destroy in Texas an institution essential to the peace, safety, and prosperity of the United States!

As the War continued, British upper-class sympathies remained with the South, and on Christmas Day 1862, the American Minister wrote: 'The great body of aristocracy and the wealthy commercial class are anxious to see the United States go to pieces . . . The middle and lower classes sympathize with us.' Seven months later he remarked: 'The privileged classes all over England rejoice in the thoughts of the ruin of the great experiment in popular government.' Yet the ruin could be accomplished only by arms, and Henry Adams, son and secretary of the American Minister, said: 'Confederate victories brought rejoicing to Britain's aristocracy but Vicksburg's fall brought tears.'

The London *Morning Post*, regarded as the mouthpiece of Lord Palmerston, the Prime Minister, said in February 1862 that if the Union should win the war 'democracy will have achieved its greatest triumph since the world began . . . and who can doubt that democracy will be more arrogant, more aggressive, more leveling and vulgarizing . . . than it has ever been before?'

Nearly all the great English newspapers and magazines expressed sympathy for the South and hostility to the North, and with them stood the aristocracy, the Established Church, and seemingly the universities. English intellectuals were sharply divided. Benjamin Jowett, the Oxford translator of Plato, Robert Browning, Goldwin Smith, Leslie Stephen, Sir Charles Lyell, and John Stuart Mill were pro-Union. They saw the war as a struggle to free the Negro. But the most influential spokesmen for the Union were liberal statesmen and publicists such as John Bright, Richard Cobden, and W. E. Forster, men who believed that the triumph of the Union would hasten the spread of democracy in Britain. Yet many intellectuals were pro-Southern; among them Acton. For him the American war was a chapter in man's long struggle for freedom, and the South the protagonist of self-determination.

Henry Adams notes that Thackeray and Carlyle were bitter opponents of the Union, and he tells us that with regard to Lincoln and Seward 'English society seemed demented . . . The belief in poor Mr. Lincoln's brutality and Seward's ferocity became a dogma of popular faith . . .'

The last time Adams saw Thackeray, 'before his sudden death at Christmas in 1863,' the novelist 'was entering the house of Sir Henry Holland for an evening reception. Thackeray was pulling on his coat downstairs, laughing because, in his usual blind way, he had stumbled into the wrong house and not found it out till he shook hands with old Sir Henry, whom he knew very well, but who was not the host he expected. Then his tone changed as he spoke of his — and Adams's — friend, Mrs. Frank Hampton, of South Carolina, whom he had loved as Sally Baxter and painted as Ethel Newcome. Though he had never quite forgiven her marriage, his warmth of feeling revived when he heard that she had died of consumption at Columbia while her parents and sister were refused permission to pass through the lines to see her. In speaking of it, Thackeray's voice trembled and his eyes filled with tears. The coarse cruelty of Lincoln and his hirelings was notorious. He never doubted that the Federals made a business of harrowing the tenderest feelings of women . . . in order to punish their opponents . . . He burst into violent reproach. Had Adams carried in his pocket the proofs that the reproach was unjust, he would have gained nothing by showing them. At that moment

Thackeray, and all London society with him, needed the nervous relief of expressing emotion; for if Mr. Lincoln was not what they said he was — what were they?'

Adams considers Carlyle in the following passage:

'For like reason, the members of the [American] Legation kept silence . . . under the boorish Scotch jibes of Carlyle . . . If Carlyle was wrong, his diatribes would give his true measure, and this measure would be a low one . . . The proof that a philosopher does not know what he is talking about is apt to sadden his followers before it reacts on himself. Demolition of one's idols is painful, and Carlyle had been an idol. Doubts cast on his stature spread far into general darkness like shadows of a setting sun. Not merely the idols fell, but also the habit of faith. If Carlyle, too, was a fraud, what were his scholars and school?'

The English working classes and middle classes were pro-Northern. They regarded the American war as one for the vindication of democracy. After the Emancipation Proclamation they thought of it as a struggle for freedom. The Confederacy's able propagandist in London, Henry Hotze, therefore urged that extreme caution be used in advocating the Confederate cause among Lancashire cotton-mill workers. He wrote Judah P. Benjamin, Confederate Secretary of State, that they are 'actively inimical to us . . . The astonishing fortitude and patience with which they endure their miseries is mainly due to a consciousness that by any other course they would promote our interests . . .'

As North and South fought for British intervention or neutrality in the Civil War, the British Government's attitudes, though correct, were affected by the American military situation. From their point of view the autumn of 1862 seemed to justify an offer of mediation in the conflict. On the Peninsula, McClellan had been defeated. Pope had lost to Lee at Second Bull Run, and as the leaves were turning color, Lee's victorious armies invaded the North with good prospects of success. At the same time, Napoleon III was increasing his pressures upon London for mediation. A correspondence, appearing to favor mediation, passed between the Prime Minister, Viscount Palmerston, and the Foreign Secretary, Lord John Russell. But before the issue could be decided news came of Antietam — a Union victory. A sobered Palmerston postponed mediation and his Government never moved to bring it about.

In the next month, however, came the great surprise of the diplomatic battle. On 7 October 1862, the cotton famine being severe, William Gladstone, Chancellor of the Exchequer, made a sensational speech at Newcastle. This influential man, who had once proclaimed himself an 'out and out in-equalitarian,' said: 'Jefferson Davis and other leaders of the South have made an army; they are making . . . a navy; and they have . . . made a nation. We may anticipate with certainty the success of the Southern states so far as regards their separation from the North . . .'

This speech was made without ministerial approval and a few days later the Home Secretary, Sir George Cornwall Lewis, said that the Government did not contemplate any change of policy, thereby repudiating Gladstone.

Union leaders were anxious to win British public opinion, believing this to be the best method of keeping Britain out of the war. Many Englishmen had been confused, for although they were opposed to slavery, it had not been made clear to them whether the North was fighting for union or for emancipation, and Lincoln's statements had been to the effect that the war was being fought not to free the slaves, but to save the Union. In August 1862 he had written his famous letter to Horace Greeley: 'My paramount object in this struggle is to save the Union and is not either to save or destroy slavery . . .' But in the month following the writing of this letter, Lincoln issued the Emancipation Proclamation. This made it clear to the ordinary Englishman that the American war was no longer one for union alone. It was also a war for the liberation of slaves and freedom for all. Henry Adams wrote: 'The Emancipation Proclamation has done more for us here [London] than all our former victories and all our diplomacy.'

The greater part of the British press received the Proclamation with a blast of hostility. But 'If, as seems clear,' writes Herbert Agar in *The Price of Union*, 'Lincoln believed that to help the cause he must keep the workingmen of England friendly, his . . . Proclamation . . . succeeded. And the workingmen of Man-

chester sent him a noble address in which they welcomed the
hardships they had endured because of the blockade on Southern
cotton . . .'

At a great mass meeting of the workingmen of Manchester,
they addressed a letter to Lincoln imploring him 'for your own
honor and welfare, not to faint in your providential mission. While
your enthusiasm is aflame, and the tide of events runs high, let
the work be finished effectually . . . our interests . . . are identi-
fied with yours. We are truly one people, though locally separate.
And if you have any ill-wishers here, be assured they are chiefly
those who oppose liberty at home, and that they will be powerless
to stir up quarrels between us, from the very day in which your
country becomes, undeniably and without exception, the home of
the free!'

Lincoln, in one of his most felicitous efforts, replied: 'I know
and deeply deplore the sufferings which the working-men at
Manchester . . . are called to endure in this crisis . . . It has
been often . . . represented that the attempt to overthrow this
government, which was built upon the foundation of human
rights, and to substitute for it one which should rest exclusively
on the basis of human slavery, was likely to obtain the favor of
Europe . . . Through the action of our disloyal citizens, the
workingmen of Europe have been subjected to severe trials, for the
purpose of forcing their sanction to that attempt. Under the circumstances, I cannot but regard your decisive utterances upon
the question as an instance of sublime Christian heroism which
has not been surpassed in any age or in any country . . .'

The Manchester meeting, the Emancipation Proclamation, and
Lincoln's letter had a powerful effect on British public opinion
and politicians. Cobden wrote Senator Sumner: 'If an attempt
were made by the Government to commit us to the South, a
spirit would be instantly aroused which would drive that Government from power.'

As the Civil War dragged on, ultimate victory became more
and more a matter of staying power. Here the weaker Confederacy
was at a disadvantage. But if Confederate forces should threaten
Washington and other cities, its government might be able to

propose an honorable peace and, as General Lee wrote President Davis, 'would conclusively show to the world that our sole object is the establishment of our independence and the attainment of an honorable peace.' 'Showing the world' was plainly designed to bring about the recognition of the Confederacy by European powers.

But as Lee moved to 'show the world,' to convince the Union of the futility of further struggle, and to demonstrate to Europe that the Confederacy was unbeatable, he moved toward the debacle of Gettysburg. When news of it reached London, the British Cabinet accepted the prospect of ultimate Union victory. Confederate representatives in London of King Cotton diplomacy must have realized the failure of their mission when they received this message from Her Majesty's Secretary for Foreign Affairs: 'Lord Russell presents his compliments to Mr. Yancey, Mr. Rost and Mr. Mann . . . In the present state of affairs he must decline to enter into any official communication with them.'

The strange venture of King Cotton diplomacy had failed. Because the Confederacy made the mistake of withholding cotton from export, that government was soon a ruined financial structure, lacking adequate credit abroad and struggling at home under an ocean of paper — its brave soldiers walking barefoot, its supplies scarce, its civilians often hungry, and its whole territory plunged into poverty. But all the while it wasted the resources of cotton that might have secured food, clothing, and munitions, and prevented the sufferings endured by its soldiers and civilians for the lack of them.

A prisoner in Fortress Monroe, Jefferson Davis lamented this fatal mistake. If, said the reminiscent president, three million bales of cotton had been shipped to Europe before the Union blockade became effective, they would have brought a billion dollars in gold. 'Such a sum,' Dr. John Joseph Craven quotes Davis as estimating, 'would have sufficed . . . for a war of twice the actual duration; and this evidence of southern prosperity and ability could not but have acted powerfully upon the minds and securities and the avarice of the New England rulers of the North . . .'

Mr. Davis thought that no one could have foreseen the course of events, for when the wisdom of shipping cotton to Europe became apparent, it was 'too late.' The blockade had become too stringent, and planters had lost faith in Confederate currency. 'When we might have put silver in the purse,' he said, 'we did not put it there. When we had only silver on the tongue, our promises were forced to become excessive.'

King Cotton diplomacy was a failure, yet it was profoundly important among the great events of its time. In 1900, Charles Francis Adams, son of the American Minister to London during the Civil War, published a biography of his father. Its preparation had led him to a careful study of King Cotton diplomacy, and he wrote: 'The European cotton famine of 1861–1863, at the time a very momentous affair, is now forgotten: yet upon it hung the fate of the American Union . . . Simply ignored by the standard historians, it was yet the Confederacy's fiercest fight, and its most decisive as well as far-reaching defeat . . .'

VIII

'Bury Contention
with the War'

It was perhaps the last great chivalrous act of the dying Age
of Chivalry.

General Grant, modestly and sympathetically, tells the moving
story of Lee's surrender of the Army of Northern Virginia on
9 April 1865 at Appomattox Courthouse, Virginia: 'I had known
General Lee in the old army,' Grant wrote, 'but did not suppose
. . . that he would remember me.

'What General Lee's feelings were I do not know . . . It was
impossible to say whether he felt inwardly glad that the end had
finally come or felt sad over the result and was too manly to
show it . . . My own feelings . . . were sad and depressed. I
felt like anything rather than rejoicing at the downfall of a foe
who had fought so long and valiantly . . .'

Lee had come to surrender, but, says Grant: 'We soon fell into
a pleasant conversation about old army times . . . our conversation grew so pleasant that I almost forgot the object of our
meeting . . . General Lee called my attention to the object of our
meeting . . .'

Grant's terms were simple, almost a gentleman's agreement.
The Confederates should lay down their arms and give their
word of honor not to take them up again against the United

States. Then they might return to their homes. Writing the surrender terms himself, Grant specified that Confederate officers should be permitted to retain their sidearms, 'important to them but of no value to us; also that it would be an unnecessary humiliation to call upon them to deliver their sidearms.'

General Lee said that 'in their army cavalrymen and artillerists owned their own horses.' Could they keep them? Grant's reply was: 'I said . . . I took it that most of the men . . . were small farmers. The whole country had been so raided by the two armies that it was doubtful whether they would be able to put in a crop to carry themselves and their families through the next winter without the horses they were then riding . . . I would, therefore, let every man in the Confederate army who owned a horse or mule take the animal home. Lee remarked again that this would have a happy effect.'

Lee himself was paroled as a prisoner of war. A few months later, in one of the noblest American utterances, he addressed himself to the South: 'The war being at an end, the Southern states having laid down their arms, and the questions at issue between them and the Northern states having been decided, I believe it to be the duty of every one to unite in the restoration of peace and harmony . . . I have too exalted an opinion of the American people to believe that they will consent to injustice, and it is only necessary, in my opinion, that truth should be known for the rights of every one to be secured. I know of no surer way of eliciting the truth than by burying contention with the war.'

But, as we know, 'contention' was not buried with the war.

Two-hundred-sixty thousand Confederate soldiers had died. One-fourth of the South's white men of productive age were dead or incapacitated. The South had suffered a staggering destruction of towns, roads, bridges, railroads, at the hands of an enemy who had fought most of the war on her soil. Two-thirds of the region's livestock was gone. Slave property worth $2 billion was lost.

What remained? The land, the warm sun, the abundant rains, the soil passionate for fruition, and — the Negro. Upon these the agricultural South began to build again.

What was it like 'back home' at war's ending?

Eliza Frances Andrews returned to the 'burnt country' of Georgia where Sherman's armies had passed, and in *The War-Time Journal of a Georgia Girl* she reports her findings: 'About three miles from Sparta we struck the "burnt country"... There was hardly a fence left standing ... The fields were trampled down and the road was lined with carcasses of hogs, horses, and cattle that the invader had wantonly shot down ... The stench in some places was unbearable ... The dwellings that were standing all showed signs of pillage, and on every plantation we saw the charred remains of the ginhouse ... while here and there lone chimney stacks ... told of homes laid in ashes.

'Hayricks and fodder stacks were demolished, corncribs were empty, and every bale of cotton ... burnt ... I saw no grain of any sort except little patches they had spilled when feeding their horses and which there was not even a chicken left in the country to eat. A bag of oats might have lain anywhere along the road without danger from the beasts of the field, though I cannot say it would have been safe from the assaults of hungry men.'

In a field where 'thirty thousand Yankees had camped hardly three weeks before,' the diarist saw the 'poor people of the neighborhood' wandering over it and 'even picking up grains of corn that were scattered around where the Yankees had fed their horses ... The place had been picked over so often ... that little remained except piles of half-rotted grain, tufts of loose cotton, and the carcasses of slaughtered animals ... *Some men were plowing in one part of the field, making ready for the next year's crops.*' (my italics)

What was it like at war's end in once proud South Carolina? From the pen of one of her poets, Henry Timrod, had come *Ethnogenesis — Written During the Meeting of the First Southern Congress, at Montgomery, February, 1861.* He, too, seems to have regarded cotton as the South's impregnable armor:

> *A yellow blossom as her fairy shield,*
> *June flings her azure banner to the wind,*
>   *While in the order of their birth*
> *Her sisters pass, and many an ample field*

Grows white beneath their steps, till now, behold,
  Its endless sheets unfold
THE SNOW OF SOUTHERN SUMMERS! *Let the earth*
Rejoice! beneath these fleeces soft and warm
    Our happy land shall sleep
    In a repose as deep
  As if we lay intrenched behind
Whole leagues of Russian ice and Arctic storm.

But at the end of the War, Sidney Andrews, a New England journalist, found Columbia, South Carolina, 'in the heart of Destruction . . . You can only get in through one of the roads built by Ruin . . . You can only get out over one of the roads walled by Desolation.'

Columbia was indeed a wilderness of ruins. Not a store, office, or shop had escaped total or partial destruction.

Timrod, as war approached, had sung of Charleston:

> *Calm as that second summer which precedes*
> *The first fall of the snow,*
> *In the broad sunlight of heroic deeds,*
> *The City bides the woe.*

Postwar Charleston, Andrews wrote, was 'a city of ruins, of desolation, of vacant houses, of widowed women, of rotting wharves, of deserted warehouses, of weed-wild gardens, of miles of grass-grown streets, of acres of pitiful barrenness . . .'

It is also clear that an era of social history had gone to come no more. Thus, J. S. Pike, a contemporary observer, writes that in a South Carolina community 'there lived a gentleman whose income, when the war broke out, was rated at $150,000 a year . . . Not a vestige of his whole vast property of millions remains today. Not far distant were the estates of a large proprietor and a well-known family, rich and distinguished for generations. The slaves are gone. The family is gone. A single scion of the house remains, and he peddles tea by the pound and molasses by the quart, on a corner of the old homestead, to the former slaves of the family, and thereby earns his livelihood.'

An English traveler, Robert Somers, reported that the Tennessee Valley 'consists for the most part of plantations in a state of semi-ruin . . . The trail of war is visible throughout the valley in burnt-up gin houses, ruined bridges, mills and factories . . . and in large tracts of once-cultivated land stripped of every vestige of fencing . . . Borne down by losses, debts, and accumulating taxes, many who were the richest among their fellows have disappeared from the scene . . .'

We may see some of the postwar planters through the eyes of Myrta Lockett Avary. In her *Dixie After the War*, she wrote: 'We did anything and everything we could do to make a living . . . A once-rich planter near Columbia made a living by selling flowers . . . General Stephen Elliott sold fish and oysters which he caught with his own hands . . . Men of high attainments, without capital, without any basis upon which to make a new start in life except "grit," did whatever they could find to do and made merry over it . . .'

When we last met Colonel Thomas Dabney he was living affluently on his Mississippi plantation. After the war he returned to a house that had been denuded of its belongings and to a plantation stripped of all but the means of cultivating a little of it. Of work stock and cattle, there remained a few mules and one cow. Dabney had nothing that could be turned into cash except five bales of cotton. But he had four children to educate.

General Sherman had said that he would like to bring every Southern woman to the washtub. Susan Dabney Smedes, in her *Memorials of a Southern Planter*, tells us what her father did. ' "He shall never bring my daughters to the washtub," Thomas Dabney said. "I will do the washing myself." And he did for two years. He was in his seventieth year when he began to do it.'

Although he had never performed manual labor, the proud old man cultivated a vegetable garden, hauling water up a long hill, and he supplied not only his table but sold a large surplus in New Orleans. He was proud of his potatoes — 'the best ever seen in the New Orleans market' — and he was proud of his skill at washing clothes, saying that he had 'never seen snowier ones.'

'Oh, thou heroic old man!' writes his daughter. 'Thou hast a right to thy pride in those exact strokes of the hoe and in those potatoes . . . and . . . those long lines of snowy drapery! But those to whom thou art showing these things are looking beyond them, at the man! They are gazing reverently . . . on the hands that have been in this world for threescore and ten years and are beginning today to support a houseful of children!'

But it was not just planters and plantations that had been ruined by the war. Thousands of small farmers returned from the Confederate forces to burned houses and barns and wrecked farms. They went to work and restored them with the indomitable persistence of those unfortunate European farmers whose houses and farms have lain so often in the paths of devouring armies.

These men worked with the only tools they had — the very simplest such as the ax, saw, drawing knife, hammer, and auger. They fashioned crude plows and hoes of old farm implements or bits of iron and steel. They constructed rude wagons, platted shucks into horsecollars, made harnesses from hickory saplings, and traces from old chains.

When there was a shortage of work stock, the few surviving animals were passed from neighbor to neighbor. But sometimes there was no work stock so men hitched themselves to the plow. By ingenuity, backbreaking toil, and cruel self-denial, thousands of Southern farmers survived Reconstruction and rescued the South from ruin. They suffered mutely. They received no aid from any source, nor any sympathy outside the region.

This occurred during the period called, with unconscious irony, Reconstruction. The word implies, if not a regime of sweetness and light, the healing of the wounds of war, rebuilding the nation, and returning to calm thinking. But Reconstruction was something else.

'The South,' writes J. G. Randall in *The Civil War and Reconstruction*, 'had been broken by the war. Lands were devastated. Proud plantations were now mere wrecks. Billions of economic value in slaves had been wiped away by emancipation measures without that compensation which Lincoln himself had admitted to be equitable. Difficult social problems presented themselves in the sudden elevation of a servile race to the status of free laborers and enfranchised citizens. Accumulated capital had disappeared. Banks were shattered; factories were dismantled; the structure of business intercourse had crumbled . . .'

The long-range political-economic effects of Reconstruction were more harmful to the cotton South than the repressive short-term measures of postwar military government. Before '61, Democrats of the agricultural South and West had prevented non-agrarian interests from using the federal government to advance their fortunes. But when the Southern delegation left Congress in 1860–61, political control fell into the hands of Republican agents of commerce, finance, and industry. They moved so swiftly that, writes Arthur Link in *The American Epoch*, 'The reconstruction of national politics that began in 1861 had fully accomplished its objectives by 1877. *The business classes had executed a bloodless revolution. They had . . . wrested control of the political institutions from the agrarian majority and changed the character, but not the forms, of representative government in the United States.*' (my italics)

Industrial capitalism was now in the saddle. Industrial capitalists, through their Republican spokesmen, had captured the state and they used it to strengthen their economic position. While the war was being waged on battlefields and through Negro emancipation, the victory had been made secure in Congress by the passage of legislation having to do with tariffs, banking, public lands, rail-roads, and labor.

Eastern industrialists, who were bent on reconstructing the country for their own benefit, wasted no time in moving to do so after the Southern delegation had left Congress. Their congressional representatives, to the ultimate detriment of the cotton economy, passed a series of tariff bills from 1861 to the middle of 1864, the rates always being pushed upward. The pretext was that new revenues were needed to meet war costs, and manufacturers had to be compensated for the heavy excises they were compelled to pay. But greed triumphed over even the appearance of decency in the Act of June 30, 1864. The House passed it in two days, and the Senate in one.

The industrialists had their way. The Northeast was to make colonial dependencies of the conquered Southern states. High tariffs were to bear especially hard on cotton farmers. At the end of the War the average rate on dutiable goods stood at 47 per cent as compared with 18.8 per cent in 1860.

The situation created by rising tariffs was described by a young, unknown French correspondent from the Paris newspaper *Le Temps*. Nearly 50 years later, he became world famous as Prime Minister Georges Clemenceau of France. He now wrote: 'Protectionism is rampant in this country. When an industry is interrupted for a couple of weeks, importation of foreign goods is given as the reason, and men . . . frame a new tariff . . . People have been made to pay ridiculous prices for articles of primary necessity . . . and a few big men in the East have grown exceedingly rich.'

Congressmen enacting the National Banking Act of 1863 did not have cotton farmers in mind. Thus, a minimum capital of $50,000 was fixed for banks in communities with less than 6,000 population, and $100,000 for larger communities. Where would the impoverished rural communities of the postwar South find so much money? In any event, 30 years after the passage of the Act, there was one bank to every 16,600 Americans, but only one bank to every 58,130 Southerners. In Georgia it was harder to find a banker than a doctor. Three decades after Appomattox, 123 counties had no bank.

In 1865, Congress imposed a 10 per cent tax on bank-note circulation. Most of the banks affected submitted themselves to federal control. But in the South, discriminated against by the Treasury, what happened? J. G. Randall writes that shortly after the War, 'Woonsocket, Rhode Island, had more national circulation than North and South Carolina, Mississippi and Arkansas; Waterville, Maine, had nearly as much as Alabama . . . Rhode Island had $77.16 for each inhabitant, Arkansas had 13 cents . . . Not a single Southern state had obtained by October 15, 1869, its legal share of the $150,000,000 which was to have been apportioned according to existing wealth, capital and resources . . .'

The battered and bankrupt postwar South was urgently in need of internal improvements. In the period 1865–73, the federal government spent approximately $103 million on public works. Of this the South received $9.5 million. New York and Massachusetts combined got $21 million. The pittance, however, of the cotton states of Arkansas and Mississippi was approximately $185,000.

Southern Redemptioners were to turn this to good account as the nation moved toward the end of Reconstruction and the Compromise of 1877 in the Hayes Administration. The Redeemers, bidding for the continued support of the poorer class of whites, offered them two things. One was White Supremacy. The other was Internal Improvements.

Under the Compromise, Southern whites secured political autonomy. And the North dropped the Negro. One of his former champions, *The Nation*, said: 'The Negro will disappear from the field of national politics. Henceforth the nation, as a nation, will have nothing to do with him.' Another of his former champions, the New York *Tribune*, declared: 'After ample opportunity to develop their own latent capacities,' Negroes had only proved that 'as a race they are idle, ignorant and vicious.'

The old order was not revived by the Compromise which did not give the South parity with other sections. Rather, it bestowed political autonomy on the dominant whites. They could do as they pleased in matters of race policy with the tacit consent of the powerful, predominantly white North. They were also promised a share in the benefits of the new economic order. And what did this deal cost?

C. Vann Woodward is a brilliant authority on the Compromise of 1877. In *Reunion and Reaction*, he tells us the price paid by the South for political autonomy and a promise of economic benefits to come. '. . . *the South became, in effect, a satellite of the dominant economic region.* So long as the Conservative Redeemers held control they scotched any tendency of the South to combine forces with internal enemies of the new economy— laborites, western agrarians, reformers. The South became a bulwark instead of a menace to the new order.' (my italics)

The prewar combination of Western and Southern farmers was now shattered. They could not again act together to defend their joint interests. The agrarian South had been delivered over to non-agrarian interests, and had become a satellite of the banking, industrial Northeast. And the already burdened cotton farmers were to bear heavier burdens in the future. They could complain in vain of tariffs that ran against them, of railroad rates that crippled them, of the gougings of trusts and combines operating in cottonseed oil, jute bagging, farm implements, and other adversities. They might work hard, live meanly, and die in poverty to pass on to their children and their children's children the apparently irrevocable estate of poverty. The while the complaints of the living died on the stillness of the air.

This is not to say, however, that they were the victims solely of the machinations of 'outsiders.' Many of those who made, and kept, the Compromise of 1877, were native-born carpetbaggers who joined with their alien colleagues to ransack an already ransacked section. Some were members of old families, men who had held high civilian or military offices during the War. Scoundrels in frock coats and string ties, they had about them always an air of High-Church respectability.

Even as these men went their plundering way, a succession of postwar happenings foreshadowed change in the cotton fields. In 1866, a patent for a mechanical cotton picker was issued to A. Tiensch of Memphis. The longed-for, and yet dreaded, machine was not perfected until 70 years later, at which time it sharply affected the lives of thousands of cotton workers.

In 1867, the Report of the Louisiana State Commissioner of Immigration, said: 'The quantity of this product [cotton] raised by exclusive white labor has been immensely greater than has been heretofore estimated. In every part of this state . . . we find not only white men, but boys and girls laboring in the fields.'

Men no longer believed, or affected to believe, that Negroes alone could bear the heat and toil of cotton culture. In time, whites outnumbered Negroes in the cotton fields.

In 1869, David Dickson of Georgia, who was perhaps the first cotton planter to use commercial fertilizers, formulated a 'compound' which he said had unfailingly produced good crops whatever the season.

Dickson, who owned a plantation of 20,000 acres near Sparta, Georgia, was remarkably successful and his farming views were widely respected. His attitude that land should be intelligently cultivated — that it cost little more to grow a bale to the acre than a quarter bale — was the more readily perceived by postbellum than by antebellum farmers. For while slave labor had never been 'free' to the master, men now realized that labor was costly and ought to be used intelligently on the land.

Dickson's pronouncements started a fertilizer craze; the notion grew that fertilizers almost alone would produce a bale of cotton to the acre, and soon advertisements began to appear such as: 'Labor Question Settled. Cultivate Much Less Land. Use One-Third the Labor. Raise Three Times the Crop.'

'The fertilizer craze,' writes E. M. Coulter, 'was soon tinged with humbuggery . . . Faked fertilizers made their appearance, and farmers were soon growing suspicious of all brands . . . Those who thought that the South was raising too much cotton complained that all ready money was used to buy fertilizer to raise more cotton . . . Commercial fertilizers . . . helped the South regain its prosperity; but commercial fertilizers also deadened the farmer's interest . . . in building up his soil by proper crop rotation . . .'

There were wild flurries of interest in labor-saving machinery, including a steam plow. Said to do the work of twenty horses, steam plows imported from England were not even able to do the work of one horse. In 1866 appeared Howe's cotton picker, guaranteed to replace five or six human pickers. It proved to be a fake, but yet another promoter advertised in 1870: 'Hundreds of inventors have puzzled their brains to invent a substitute for the fingers of Sambo — to perfect a machine that did not vote, go to circuses, barbecues, &c., just when it was needed in the field.' This was another fake.

The cotton South had long been beguiled by the prospect of new crops, and after the War came many ventures. It was believed that ramie would grow wherever cotton would grow, that it was better than flax, and would bring high prices in London. It was tried and abandoned. Then the idea took hold that China tea would flourish throughout the South, and in 1870 the editor of *The Southern Cultivator* served tea brewed from leaves he had grown to ladies attending the Horticultural and Floral Fair in Augusta. But China never suffered from Southern tea competition.

The region also tried, or wanted to try, its hand at growing cinchona for quinine, esparto grass for papermaking, jute, castor beans, and so forth. In the end, however, it put its greatest effort into growing cotton.

So grievously was the cotton South damaged by the War that it was 13 years after Appomattox before its crop equaled that of '59. It took Alabama 18 years to reach this point. She had lost 25,000 men, about 20 per cent of her white male population, and thousands of women and children had been left helpless amid the wreckage. In 1880, the value of the South's farm machinery was less than it had been in 1860. Property values dropped catastrophically. Between 1860 and 1866 the estimated true value of all Alabama property dropped from $725 million to $123 million. Other cotton states showed similar losses.

The plantation system had been shattered. The banking system was ruined. The railroads had been almost entirely destroyed. Freed slaves were taught to hate their former masters. The anguish of death hung over almost every Southern home. The maimed were everywhere. In 1866 Mississippi spent one-fifth of her revenues for artificial arms and legs. Georgia, 15 years after the War, was spending $35,000 annually for this purpose.

These were some of the 'natural' consequences of war that the South faced as it made a new start. Grave injuries were inflicted upon it by Reconstruction but we shall consider here only factors that immediately affected cotton culture. For cotton growing remained the principal occupation of the Southern people.

Although cotton diplomacy had not won the War for the South, the large supplies of cotton that remained afterward might have become an important source of the region's rehabilitation. Instead, United States Treasury agents, under the Captured Property Act, seized $30 million worth of cotton. How much they stole is beyond estimate. Authorized to seize 'rebel' cotton, agents often took everything movable including indispensable work stock. They received one-quarter to one-half of the proceeds of seizures, but this being insufficient to slake their greed, they defrauded the Treasury by selling cotton at high prices and remitting for it at low prices. In *The South During Reconstruction*, Professor E. M.

Coulter writes of 'The two greatest cotton thieves.' They were, he says, 'Simeon Draper . . . and William P. Mellen . . . They seized cotton indiscriminately and then allowed the owner to recover part for a quitclaim on the remainder. This method was called "tolling." Sometimes a planter would find his cotton had to be tolled two or three times before it reached market. "Plucking" was another one of their inventions. In grading cotton, generous samples from five or six bales would provide a bale of "pluckings." Draper . . . became a millionaire . . . William E. Chandler, Assistant Secretary of the Treasury in charge of cotton seizures . . . emerged worth hundreds of thousands of dollars.'

The federal government, not content merely to seize 'old' cotton of the conquered provinces — fiber presumably affected with retrospective guilt — levied a special tax on 'new' cotton that yielded $68 million. In 1867, when a bale of cotton brought $67, there was federal taxation of $12.50 on it.

Georges Clemenceau wrote to his newspaper in Paris about the tax: 'Another mistake is the tax on cotton. This product . . . cannot compete any longer in the English market with the cottons of India and Egypt, and the result has been to discourage the growers, cause stagnation in shipping, poverty and privation among the masses, and unheard-of wealth for a few men in high places.'

The postwar cotton South was faced with many heavy tasks, but none were more important to its survival than these. It had to reconstitute its labor supply and put it on another basis for, in a sense, much of that supply had vanished when the slaves became free. It also had to find a way to finance itself. How did it try to achieve these aims?

Thousands of whites left the postwar South to become homesteaders in the West. Many went to Texas. In 1875, 50,000 people left Georgia, many of them bound for Texas, leaving signs on the doors of their abandoned houses reading, 'G.T.T.' ('Gone to Texas').

Searching for labor, the cotton country embarked for a while on a strange course. Believing that Europeans would be better than its ex-slaves, the region sought immigrants by chartering immigration companies and sending agents to Europe to induce men to come South. Few came. The South had never had many foreign-born residents. But in 1880 the number was smaller than it had been in 1860.

Planters preferred Europeans but they would compromise, if they must, with Chinese. Northern groups, however, opposed Chinese immigration. It was feared that the South might use the immigrants politically so, to clinch the matter, it was suddenly proclaimed that the Chinese were a low order of humanity. Congress barred them from citizenship. This act riled the Columbus (Georgia) *Inquirer*. The most cultured Chinese, it said, could not become an American citizen. But 'the lowest specimen of the negro tribes of Africa might become an American citizen.'

In the great cotton-growing state of Mississippi, planters were obsessed with the notion of replacing Negroes with Chinese coolies. Rumors were widely circulated that low wages satisfied Chinese, that their food and clothing demands were of the simplest kind, that they would work for $4 a month, live on little, and clothe themselves. But perhaps more impressive, rumor endowed the coolies with a great virtue in the eyes of their prospective employers: 'Freedom from the evil habit of impudence.' Coolies, then, were allegedly hardworking, cheap, and so frugal in their habits that they cost little more to keep than a hummingbird. Men became convinced by their own stories, and a commercial agency offered to deliver coolies at $50 a head and place them on plantations under long contracts at wages of from $5 to $7 a month.

Time, however, dissipated these dreamy projects. It appeared that it would cost at least $100 to bring a Chinese from Cuba to Mississippi. Once arrived he would have to be paid not less than $12 for a 26-day month, plus rations far more substantial than those furnished Negroes. In addition, Chinese knew nothing of cotton culture and, to make things worse, the federal government was becoming obstinate about letting them into the country.

Yet rumors continued to circulate. On a June day of 1869, the people of Vicksburg were wildly excited when they were told that the next day the steamer *Great Republic* would arrive with 500 Chinese. The Vicksburg *Times* saw this as the beginning of a tide that would bring thousands of these hardy, industrious people to the area. The editor urged whites to go to the wharf to see the 'coming laborers.' He also urged 'ungrateful negroes' to view the men who were destined to push them off the plantations. But, alas! There was not a coolie on the steamboat, and by 1882 Mississippians in Congress were joining with their colleagues from other sections to exclude Chinese immigrants from our soil.

The cotton South had failed to secure European or Oriental labor. Its own white labor was not sufficient for the tasks ahead. It had, therefore, either to employ the freed Negro or leave much of its lands uncultivated; a particularly pressing problem in the Gulf states where plantations tended to be large, the Negro population large, and the white population sparse.

What of the freedman? He did not like to take orders; that smacked too much of slavery. But a disorderly plantation was a rural anarchy and the journalist Sidney Andrews told the North: 'The hardest work before the North now is to teach the Negro what constitutes his freedom.'

This was not as simple a task as it seemed. Cotton culture aroused reminiscences of slavery that put the freedman's back up. He did not, for example, want to be summoned to work by the plantation bell. He did not like to hear the word 'overseer.' Often he did not want to return to growing cotton. *The Nation* reported one Negro as saying: 'If the old massa want to grow cotton, let him plant it himself. I'se work for him dese twenty years, and done got nothin' but food and clothes, and dem mighty mean. Now I'se freedman, and I tell him I ain't going to work cotton nohow.'

Many Negroes drifted westward, and in 1879 there was a strange mass movement to Kansas. But the Negroes were coldly received and numbers of them returned South. In general, however, the Negro population showed little inclination to emigrate. Although the North was then engaged in great tasks of railroad and industrial building, it showed little interest in the huge pool of Negro labor available to it in the South. Industrial builders preferred native-born whites and immigrants from Ireland and southeastern Europe to recently freed Negroes.

They stayed in the South. They yearned for land. But the

government that gave 200 million acres to railroads made little effort to provide land for landless Negroes. Aware of their longing for land, tricksters sold them $5-certificates purporting to be deeds to parts of the plantations they had tilled as slaves. Sometimes they included with the gaudy documents they handed their illiterate dupes a so-called deed reading: 'Know all men by these presents, that a naught is a naught, and a figure is a figure; all for the white man and none for the nigure. And whereas Moses lifted up the serpent in the wilderness, so also have I lifted this damned ole nigger out of four dollars and six bits. Amen. Selah!'

Yet landless Negroes, whose only skill was farming, could not go on, in the absence of Elijah and his 'manners,' being choosey. They may have disliked the concept of the farm manager ('overseer'), the plantation bell, and even 'makin' cotton.' But they had to eat. This meant working for the white man who had the land. Nor could the farmer go on being choosey about labor. He might have wanted European peasants or Chinese coolies. But he had to take what he could get and of whatever color. Indeed black-belt farmers soon came to prefer Negroes to whites.

In April 1875, when the War had been over for a decade and men had had time to reflect, the Hinds County (Mississippi) *Gazette* commented on farm labor. After concluding that the postwar South had little to offer white immigrants, the newspaper said: 'In spite of his newly acquired ability to move about, the negro remained a cheap and relatively docile laborer . . . After the freedman was shorn of political power, the great mass of native whites found they liked negroes much better than they did "foreigners."

'It soon became apparent that freedmen . . . furnished a more satisfactory type of labor than could be obtained from white workers . . . and few would hesitate to reject whites when there was an opportunity to obtain negroes.'

Ten years later the Raymond (Mississippi) *Gazette* published a 'sensible communication' from a landowner. He said that he had once wanted to obtain 'good, intelligent, thrifty white labor' instead of Negroes, but after years of trial he had failed to find whites of this kind. Then he continued: 'I do not say this to decry white labor . . . but give me the nigger every time . . .

He will live on less and do more hard work, when properly managed, than any other class of people. We can boss him and that is what we Southern folks like.'

The transition, however, from the slave system to the free labor system was not easily made. Many landlords, adjusting themselves to a new world, adopted the unfamiliar wage system. But its adoption in the circumstances was premature, and it was satisfactory neither to planter nor freedman. The Negro did not like to wait until the end of the year for his wages and the planter, subject to the credit system, might find at year's end that returns from his crop were insufficient to enable him to pay the Negro after satisfying the claims of factor or merchant. Even if the planter could have found the money to pay weekly wages, he would not have, for the Negro who got his hands on money would not return to work until he had spent it. Frequently he refused to hire his services for more than two days a week. Indeed the Negro's dislike for steady work was the greatest drawback to the wage system. As a slave he had associated the idea of freedom with idleness, and the ease with which a bare susbsistence could be obtained in the South made it difficult to divest the freedman's mind of this idea.

In 1866, the Report of the Commissioner of Agriculture said: 'To be free was to hunt and fish and lounge about the country town; to the women it was to desert outdoor employment, and ape in a slight degree the fashions and habits of the more fortunate white race.'

In the early years of freedom, moreover, the tendency of freedmen to congregate in large groups for social, political, or religious purposes made itself strongly felt. This inclination was strengthened by the efforts of carpetbag politicians from the North who sought to further their own plans by getting the Negro vote. With threats of re-enslavement and extravagant promises they tried to draw freedmen from their old masters. Negroes often deserted the cotton fields when they most needed attention in order to attend political meetings, and many crops were left ungathered for want of laborers. The cotton crop actually harvested in 1866 was probably less than a million bales, and the crop of 1866–7 was hardly more than two million bales.

Losses caused by these failures fell entirely on the planters. They had furnished Negroes with their subsistence during the making of the crop, but when they broke their contracts before the harvest, the planter was left without any return for his outlay. For these reasons the wage system was generally abandoned after the first year's trial.

Its successor was sharecropping. This system has been used extensively throughout the ages and it seems to develop naturally in the presence of certain factors. They include the existence of landless workers, a shortage of capital or credit, and dependence upon a cash crop that requires a long growing season. These were, as we have seen, characteristics of cotton culture. Negroes, usually unable to rent land or finance themselves, came to prefer sharecropping to the close supervision of the wage system, and by 1890 it was difficult to hire them on any other basis.

Sharecropping especially pleased freedmen because it marked the break-up of the old slave quarters. Croppers were established in scattered cabins, each usually located on land tilled by the occupants. This 'segregation of the quarters' also pleased planters. They had lost their power over the behavior of their former slaves, but they found that scattering the cabins reduced the incidence of misconduct that often occurred among freedmen when they were herded together.

Under sharecropping the cropper, according to the age and size of his family, would 'take up' 15 to 25 acres. The farmer furnished land, seeds, tools, equipment, and workstock at no charge to the cropper, plus a cabin, water, and firewood to be cut by the cropper in the farmer's woods. Often the farmer also supplied the cropper with an acre or two where he could raise chickens and a pig or two, and grow vegetables. The farmer agreed to furnish the cropper with food and clothing worth stipulated sums of dollars from January to the following August when money began to come in. Medicines and medical services were also provided.

The cropper agreed to grow the crops and give half his cotton, cottonseed, and corn to the farmer, and keep the other half for himself. He also agreed to repay the farmer, with interest, the money advanced to him in the form of food, clothing, and so forth.

This, briefly, is the famous sharecropping system. If the cropper in time acquired his own mules, equipment, and wagons, he might give the farmer only one-third of the crops made by him. Or he might become a renter, leasing for money. Sharecropping varied widely and on the same plantation one might find croppers, renters, and wage hands, while the methods of operation on two plantations was hardly ever the same.

Sharecropping was born of necessity, but later some quarters professed to regard it as scarcely less evil than slavery. We shall describe its growth but we cannot here enter the involved controversy over its merits. The arguments, moreover, are beginning to take on aspects of the academic, for sharecropping has long been dying and is doomed to disappear with increasing farm mechanization. Before abandoning this subject matter, however, it is perhaps meet to ask: What was the position of Negro and planter when sharecropping was born?

The Negro was ignorant, propertyless and, in the true sense of the word, innocent. Herbert Agar, in *The Price of Union*, says: 'Abandoned by the best men, North and South, and corrupted by the worst, an ugly future was assured for him [the Negro] by the Congressmen who took orders from Thaddeus Stevens and . . . from Benjamin Butler . . . who according to Lincoln was "as full of poison gas as a dead dog."

'It was wicked to force the Negro to rule the disfranchised white man when everybody knew the position would be reversed as soon as Northerners grew sick of governing their fellow Americans with the sword. It was wicked to turn the Negro free . . . without a thought for his future except that he must be bullied or bought into voting Republican. It was extra wicked to commit both these cruelties at the same time . . . There is a limit beyond which only mad moralists and the truly corrupt will go. It was the fate of the Negro . . . to be sacrificed to an alliance between these two. He didn't want to run the South. He wanted to learn how to read . . . and he wanted a few acres of land . . . But his Northern friends wanted to prove their political theories, or they simply wanted his vote. The moralists thought he could eat freedom . . . the others didn't think at all, beyond the next election. But . . . he gave them his vote, since they asked for it. And the white South has not forgiven him in eighty years . . .'

No other ruling group in American history has ever found itself in such bleak circumstances as the cotton planters a decade after Appomattox. They had lost their inherited wealth and the great accretions of wealth represented by slaves, and their Confederate bonds and paper had been repudiated. The Washington government would not even entertain claims for war destruction inflicted by invaders, and confiscatory taxes of the national and state governments in hostilely vindictive hands drove an already hard-pressed group of men almost to the verge of extinction.

During Reconstruction, moreover, they were threatened with the seizure and distribution of their lands. Carl Schurz said: 'In the independent possession of landed property, many Negroes saw the consummation of their deliverance.' Otherwise they would have been 'liberated from domestic slavery, only to be remitted to slavery to skill and capital.' Rumors swept the South that every Negro might obtain 'fawty acres an' a mule' from the expropriation of his old master, and in Louisiana a Negro uprising was feared. It was squelched by General Fullerton of the local Freedman's Bureau. He warned the Negro that he was indeed free; free to work, but not to seize his employer's property. He told Negroes: 'The Government will not do more for you than for the white laborers who are your neighbors.'

Planters felt certain their lands would not be distributed to the landless by the national government. Their reasoning was impeccable. The North would not stand for it because such a revolutionary example might incite Northern workers to demand a similar division of industrial property.

Here, then, when a new start was to be made on the war-devastated farms and plantations, was the Negro. He had only the labor of his hands. And here was the planter. He had little more than his land. Neither could look for aid or comfort beyond his own horizon. Hence, perforce, the slave who had been freed into poverty and his almost impoverished former master leaned upon one another and slowly made their way together out of the dark wood. It was one of the strangest mass relationships known to man.

We have been discussing the more fortunate planters who could hold their lands after the War. But crop failures and the decline in land values that occurred steadily for a number of postwar years compelled many men to throw their lands on the market. 'Plantations that had brought from $100,000 to $150,000 before the war,' wrote Henry W. Grady in *Harper's Magazine*, 'were sold at $6,000 to $10,000 . . . The ruin seemed to be universal . . . and the old plantation system, it then seemed, had perished . . . forever.'

Attracted by the extraordinarily low prices of the lands, there appeared an unexpected group of purchasers from the ranks of the poor whites. They were moved by the perennial earth hunger of their class, and were affected by the mania for growing cotton which, despite repeated failures, had seized the imaginations of all Southerners. The willingness of planters to sell on any terms, and of merchants to give credit on prospective cotton crops, induced this class to purchase lands which owners were so willing to sell.

'Never perhaps,' wrote Grady, 'was there a rural movement, accomplished without revolution or exodus, that equaled in extent or swiftness the partition of the plantations of the ex-slaveholders into small farms . . .'

One of the remarkable features of this movement was the purchase by Negroes in Georgia alone of nearly 7,000 farms in three years. Within this short time, the land purchases by small farmers in Mississippi were so extensive that the number of small farms of the state increased by nearly 40,000, and since a somewhat similar process was going on throughout the South, there was a marked decline in the average size of cotton-belt farms. Between 1860 and 1870 the decline was from 401 acres to 229 acres.

The elevation of the poorer class of whites to the status of peasant proprietors brought many changes. The most noteworthy was the sharp increase in the number of whites in the cotton fields. Before 1860 it was supposed that the proportion of whites to Negroes engaged in cotton culture was about one to eight, and that this kind of work was unsuited to whites. But all this changed as the poorer class of whites bought lands. 'By 1876,' writes M. B. Hammond, 'nearly forty per cent of the laborers engaged in the cultivation of cotton were whites and in some states the whites in the cotton fields outnumbered the blacks.'

The postwar South had little money. In its desperate need the people of the region turned again to the thing they knew best: growing cotton. They did so passionately. Between 1875 and 1890 they doubled their production, and tripled it in the next decade. 'Makin' cottin' might yield only a po' livin'. But it was a livin' and cotton had certain unique virtues.

Almost imperishable, you could 'hold' it until prices rose, if you could afford to. But you could not do that with grain or vegetables. If you planted perishables you could not always get them to market over the poor roads and broken-down railroads and, for that matter, where were the Southern markets that could absorb large quantities of them? Hence when it was suggested to men that they grow fruits and vegetables, they demurred. Cotton, however, was a sure thing. Thus the issue was settled as men's stomachs, so to speak, plucked at their sleeves and drove them to the cotton fields.

Yet hard money was necessary in order to make a crop. Cotton is a long time a-growing in the months that stretch between planting-time and ginning-time. In the absence of adequate banks and a banking system, who was to finance big planters and small farmers tilling millions of cotton acres? It was the cotton factor who continued to finance the planter as before the War, and the supply merchant who 'carried' the small farmer.

We have hitherto observed the manner in which the factor operated and the charge he exacted for his services. Since Memphis, in the 1880s and 1890s, handled an annual cotton crop of 400,000 to 700,000 bales, and was situated in the midst of a vast cotton-growing area, let us go there to see how its cotton factors fared.

Bankers and brokers, the factors were also purveyors and wholesale grocers to planters, supplying them with the whiskey they drank, the sowbelly their Negroes ate, the shoes both whites and Negroes wore, and the gin that cleaned the planter's cotton. As presidents and directors of banks, factors were the money masters of the city. Nearly all of the cotton firms conducted a wholesale grocery business, and so large was this trade that in 1891, 41 of the factor-wholesalers sold $35 million of groceries alone.

One of the richest of this group was Napoleon Hill. He came to Memphis penniless shortly after the War, but 20 years later his firm was handling 100,000 bales of cotton a year and doing a business of $5.5 million. He lent planters money at high interest rates, furnished their supplies at high prices, and sold their cotton on commission. He built warehouses and charged planters to store their cotton, organized a fire insurance company to insure planters' cotton, and helped organize a bank where he borrowed cheaply and lent dearly to his planter clients. Out of his riches he built a great red-brick house, and Shields McIlwaine in *Memphis Down in Dixie* tells us something of the habitation of the cotton-factor king: ' "Only the best" was the rule of furnishing the house; magnificence, the scale. Mirrors twelve feet tall; a stone vase resting on the heads of life size gilded herons . . . At the Centennial Exposition . . . in Philadelphia, Napoleon and his wife asked if they might buy the bedroom suite which had won first prize . . . The bed was the glory of it all; a sofa built into the footpiece, a half canopy with red curtains draped against the headpiece, ten feet high; the upper edge of the side rails was quilted at the place where one might bark his shins on retiring . . . Were not the gorgeous beds of another Napoleon behind silk ropes in French museums for all to see . . . ?'

Credits were given to small farmers by supply merchants. The system had its vices, but it also had one overriding virtue: it lent money. All over the South men who could get some cash, or could persuade Northern merchants to extend them credit, became bankers and suppliers to farmers. By the 1880s nearly every crossroads village, every hamlet lost in malarial swamps or deep woods, had one or more banker-merchants, and towns had them by the dozen.

Neither sharecropping nor the lien system that underlay merchant credit was of planned design. They arose out of necessity. And if they proved to be something of a curse to cotton culture, they were the best systems that men could devise from the ruins of the old regime. Chaining men to the one-crop system, causing them to mine the soil, the lien system encompassed whites and Negroes in a dire slavery. All this illustrated the grim observation of Louis XIV: 'Credit supports agriculture, as cord supports the hanged.' Since the prewar South could not supply the principal capital for its cotton culture it was forced into a position of financial thralldom to the North. In 1860, when the value of the region's crops was $200 million, less than $30 million was in Southern banks.

Postbellum farmers had no choice. They could either starve or produce cotton under the lien system. How did it operate?

The farmer pledged the crop he had not yet planted for a loan at a rate of interest to be determined by the lender. Little cash figured in the loan. The borrower would 'take it out' in supplies delivered by the merchant-lender: sowbelly, cornmeal, clothing, molasses, plow points, harness, sometimes coffins, and so forth. These goods were often evaluated at 30 to 70 per cent more than their cash prices. On top of this was piled an interest rate that might be 40 per cent or higher.

The farmer could not benefit from competition among merchants because after giving one merchant a lien on his crop he had no other security to offer. When his cotton had been ginned, he could not store it to await higher prices or sell it in the market because he must first pay his debt to the merchant, the man who held him in a species of serfdom. And who often stepped in as buyer of the farmer-debtor's cotton? None other than the merchant who put a price on the cotton favorable to himself. At the end of a year of toil and worry, the farmer was fortunate to find himself holding a 'clear receipt,' showing that his indebtedness to the merchant had been discharged, and able to buy a bottle of 'Chrismus whiskey' and a few shells for rabbit hunting. But his troubles were not over. He not only needed credit for the next season, but his contract bound him to renew the lien to the same merchant for the next crop.

M. B. Hammond, in *Cotton Industry*, writes: 'When one of these mortgages has been recorded against the Southern farmer, he has usually passed into a state of helpless peonage . . . With

the surrender of this evidence of indebtedness he has also surrendered his freedom of action and his industrial autonomy . . .
Until he has paid the last dollar of his indebtedness, he is
subject to the constant . . . direction of the merchant. Every
mouthful of food he purchases, every implement . . . his mules,
cattle, the clothing for himself and his family, the fertilizers for
his land, must be bought of the merchant who holds the crop
lien, and in such amounts as the latter is willing to allow.'

Lordly antebellum factors, as we have seen, lent money to the
planter on condition that he grow cotton only. The postbellum
supply merchant exacted the same condition. Cotton was almost
as 'good' as money for it was readily marketable, imperishable,
comparatively easy to handle, and it could not be consumed by
the producer as could corn or hogs. The merchant, therefore,
compelled his debtors to plant nothing but cotton and objected
if they wanted to raise corn, wheat, or potatoes. Hence the farmer
complied, and when he went to the store bought 'a bale of
Indiana prairie hay, a sack of Milwaukee flour, and a side of
Chicago bacon. Even cabbages shipped from Germany and Irish
potatoes from Scotland were among items charged on one farmer's
bill.' It was the danger of losing this business that set the
merchant against crop diversification and caused him to limit
his farmer-debtor to cotton-growing. Under this system the latter
had to buy all his consumer's goods from the merchant at
exorbitant prices.

Similarly, if the farmer should pasture land or plant soil-building
crops, the merchant's lucrative trade in fertilizers might suffer.
The use of commercial fertilizers, especially in the older cotton
states, had come to be regarded as essential and trade in fertilizers
rose to such large proportions that from 12 to 33 per cent of the
total value of the cotton crop was consumed in this way. In
the case of the tenant farmer, fertilizer was used not to improve
the soil permanently, but merely to stimulate growth of the season's
crop. The one-crop system created a steady, permanent market for
commercial fertilizers.

But, says Hicks in The Populist Revolt, 'Cotton was the crop
the Southern farmer knew best how to raise . . . The ignorance
of the Southern farmer was so complete that most of the propa-

ganda for diversification . . . was utterly unintelligibile to him, if it reached him at all. There was rarely any resentment among farmers against the merchant's demand that cotton be the exclusive crop. Content with his own ignorance, the Southern farmer made little effort to raise food crops that would have made him independent, and he remained all too willing to buy costly fertilizers in order that he might cultivate his traditional crop of cotton on worn-out ground year after year.'

Fire-breathing 'Pitchfork Ben' Tillman, Governor of South Carolina and later a Senator, believed that the farmers of his state suffered because of their ignorance of farming and so he sought to establish agricultural schools for them. Yet Tillman himself, a farmer before he became a politician, illustrated a weakness of the more ambitious group of cotton farmers.

Tillman wrote: 'I had cleared money [growing cotton] up to 1881, and bought land and mules right along. In that year I ran 30 plows, bought guano, rations, etc., as usual, amounting to $2,000, all on credit . . . To have been entirely free of debt would have made me feel like "a kite without a tail." Uninterrupted success had made me a fool . . .'

Then came a series of crop failures for three years. Tillman bought provisions from supply merchants at 'sickening prices,' his pocketbook flattened 'like Bill Arp's when a elephant had trod upon it,' and he lost much of his land at forced sales.

Tillman, like thousands of farmers then and now, was the victim of his own overspeculation. And as most farmers who overspeculate, he was a bad loser. The businessman usually takes his speculative losses quietly. But the speculating farmer who gets caught is more likely to blame heaven and hell for his troubles and run wailing to Congress for 'relief' from the devils who had tempted him to ruin.

Thirty years after the War, the cotton South was farther from being self-sustaining than it had been in 1860. Cotton culture had enormously increased but, said Otken in The Ills of the South, 'From 1865 to 1890, cotton planting has been a mania. The neglected corn field with all its consequences is a part of Southern history.' (my italics)

Eroding people on eroding lands is pictured by the Report of the Commissioner of Agriculture for 1886. It noted that a large proportion of cotton farmers are in debt for 'current supplies,' and these debts absorb all or nearly all of the profits of production. The while, said the Report, 'The soil is wearing away, with the lives of the cultivators, for the benefit of the commercial class.'

A Mississippi supply merchant told Otken that his firm sold 300,000 pounds of bacon a year and bought between 2,500 and 3,000 bales of cotton. The bacon price was generally higher than the cotton price, and 'it is fair to believe that one-third of the cotton delivered to this firm paid for bacon.'

In the 30-year period after the War, the human and work stock population of Mississippi sharply increased. Yet the state's food products, noted Otken, 'were less in 1870, less in 1880, less in 1890, and less in 1892, than in 1860.'

The more that men were gripped by cotton mania, the deeper they sank into the slough of debt and despair. As they concentrated labor and capital upon the task of producing one commercial crop, they increased it beyond the world's demands, lowered the price, and then bought western corn and hay at prices higher than they received for their cotton. All this was done on credit, and Hammond estimated that 'three-fourths of the cotton planters and their tenants . . . "buy on time," and pay usury to factors, merchants or others.'

Freedmen, once they had comfortably settled into their new status, showed an especially strong liking for cotton growing. They were more familiar with its cultivation than with that of other staples. But, more important, cotton growing permitted, sometimes even demanded, the presence of gangs of folks working together in the fields, and this appealed to the Negro's social instincts, which impelled him to work with others rather than alone.

Often the farmer's account with the supply merchant became hopelessly depleted because of bad crops, low prices, and so forth. He gave the merchant a mortgage on his farm, and frequently in the end was compelled to 'assign' it. Then he left the neighborhood with his family to join the tens of thousands of poor, obscure sharecroppers of the cotton country. Large numbers of men, trying to rise amid the ruins of military defeat and pillage, dragged out bleak lives of toil and deprivation. But so long as they lived they continued to grow cotton and thus never escaped the compulsion of the lien-credit system that held them in thrall. Even though cotton prices declined steadily for nearly two decades after the War, cotton production steadily increased. The crop of 1873 — a 'panic year' — brought 14 cents a pound. In 1894, 24 million acres yielded a record output. But selling at less than 5 cents a pound, it brought less than the 1873 crop gathered from only 9 million acres.

The supply merchant was not, of course, responsible for all the ills of the cotton South. Nor was he, for all the garments of villainy in which he has been clothed, simply a coldblooded rural schemer. He, too, was the victim of the 'system,' and liens had the approval of state legislatures because there was no other way to finance thousands of small farmers. The merchant charged high rates of interest on loans and high prices for things he sold. Yet he paid dearly for money lent him by a factor. And the factor paid dearly for money borrowed from a bank that in turn had borrowed from the ultimate lender: some shadowy, never-to-be-seen figure immured in a metropolis tower. The merchant also ran the risks of crop failures and widely fluctuating prices; elements that might bankrupt him. Cotton's price fell so low in 1894 that merchants would not grant further credit to their customers and so compelled a reduction of cotton acreage for the 1895 crop.

There were other risks. Hammond tartly observes that 'Honesty is a virtue which is little regarded by many people . . . of the South, especially by freedmen, who are nearly all recorded on the books of the merchants as credit purchasers. The danger of losses involved by doing business with this class of purchasers has been the prime cause of the great difference between cash and "time" prices, while the frequent failures of advancing merchants . . . do not furnish proof to the statement that, "the road to wealth in the South . . . is merchandising." '

Sixteen years after the Compromise of 1877, a Congressional committee found that 'cotton cannot . . . be raised profitably at less than eight cents a pound, nor without loss under seven cents.' For the seven years preceding this finding, the farm price of cotton had been less than seven cents a pound. This drove farmers to grow larger quantities of cotton to compensate for its low price. Of course the effect was to depress prices further and, as prices fell, farmer's debts, in terms of baled cotton, almost doubled.

In their despair farmers blamed the national currency, saying that it was being manipulated for private gain. Their outcries seem to have penetrated the remote recesses of Congress, for a Senate Committee on Agriculture, although it did nothing to help, at least expressed the Senate's awareness of the farmers' existence by a peevish commentary on them. It said there was 'widespread discontent among cotton producers and a disposition to discredit their old time conservative methods and to induce a too ready acceptance of plausible theories for relief.'

Naturally, it was wicked of farmers to accept even 'plausible theories of relief.' But no one offered actual relief. Forty years were to pass from the day of the publication of the Committee's report to the time when a frightened Congress moved to help distressed cotton farmers.

From 1866 on, with the exception of brief periods of high prices for farm products, farmers complained of their lot and appealed vainly to Washington for help. They did not seem to realize one stark fact of their life. It was that long ago, during the crisis of the Union, there had been a shift in the balance of power in Washington and many of the state capitals away from farming interests to such non-agrarian interests as banks, railroads, and industrial corporations. And the pendulum — obedient to the new physics — was to continue to swing only one way: toward the non-agrarian interests.

The South went on year after year producing great wealth in the form of cotton and cottonseed products and eating the bitter bread of poverty. Each June the fields were starred with billions of cotton blossoms, cream-white, soft-red, shell-pink. They vanished after a brief day under the fierce eye of the sun, giving way to bolls; hard tight little globes of green containing the embryo of cotton. For three months they grew in sun and rain until suddenly in August the cotton began to burst its confining walls. Then bits of white here and there flecked the sea of green. As the days passed the whiteness spread rapidly and more rapidly until it undulated in

waves and rolled in billows, drowning the land beneath its soft-
ness. Now came men, women, and children, white and Negro, to
gather the harvest, long coarse canvas sacks slung over their shoulders, trailing the ground as they walked. They endured the backbreaking labor of cotton picking from sunup until sundown, day
after day in the hot sun or frost, until only stalks remained to become brown and withered and to rattle forlornly in the winds of
winter until they were plowed under in the spring. Then men
again followed their mules down the endless turnrows as they prepared the land for the new crop, and so through the days and so
through the years until men and mules were one with the dust
they plowed.

The cotton South plowed and planted and picked and endured
in backwardness and poverty, land and men eroding together and
washed together anonymously into the gullies of time. All the
while the region's poor whites and poor Negroes, struggling over
already gnawed bones, hated each other, for when there is not
enough to go around, the quality of mercy often sickens and dies.
Sometimes the whites, in an explosion of their own misery and
hopelessness and helplessness, would hang a Negro to a tall tree, a
hard-eyed god looking down from a pale and pitiless sky.

IX

Cotton Is a Frontier Crop

COTTON IS A FRONTIER CROP restlessly seeking new horizons, and new soil and climate that are favorable to it. It made the long march from Virginia to Texas before the Civil War. Recently it has moved on, ever westward, across the mountains to New Mexico, Arizona, and California where frontiers have been opened to it in semi-arid lands. There men cause the onetime desert to blow white with cotton as they sink deep wells and pump water through a dry land.

The progress of cotton culture in the Far West has been swift and on a huge scale; a phenomenon of American agriculture. If this were merely another 'success story' in a prodigal country where success stories are a dime a dozen, it would be meaningful only to those who have participated in it. But its meaning transcends the region.

Transmountain cotton culture demonstrates that the American pioneer spirit is still vigorously alive, and it also shows that the Malthusian horror is not inevitable. An expanding, technologically alert agriculture can keep pace with — or even outpace — the needs of an expanding population.

The nation's geographical frontier — the fabled frontier of song and story and motion picture — was closed by fiat some 60 years ago when, in 1890, the Bureau of the Census said that it was closed. Much of American history up to that point had been a history of the ever-moving frontier, and an important school of historians had 'explained' the United States in terms of it. Many men mournfully concluded when the frontier was 'closed' that thereafter we should merely be consolidating our gains; that we had passed from a dynamic to a static society and thus were approaching the position of the older European nations. But this was to reckon without the rapid growth of an extraordinary technology of agriculture as well as of industry, or the persistence of the resourcefulness and energy that had enabled Americans almost within the span of a single century to bring to a high pitch of development a huge, hitherto undeveloped, continent.

While men were saying that cotton was a dying crop, Westerners were bringing great acreages into production; once empty acres whose yield was greater than that of the older Southeast cotton areas. While other men were saying that the United States economy had become 'mature' — a lament first lifted when the first President took office — Western cotton growers invested large sums in cotton culture and, unconscious of intimations that 'it couldn't be done,' did it. Within 35 years the California cotton crop moved from insignificance to a place that puts it among the nation's leading producers and in one recent year (1951) gave it second rank among cotton states.

By 1910 the Old South had been growing cotton for a century. During most of this time California produced no cotton, or so little that even the all-seeing eye of the Bureau of the Census did not take it into account. At the end of the second decade of the twentieth century, the Bureau reported it, but the crop was scarcely a drop in the ocean of American cotton. Six thousand bales had come from the hot, humid, below-sea-level Imperial Valley. Cotton's stay there, however, was short. In 1920 the Valley abandoned it for other things.

The abandonment of cotton there illustrates the flexibility of American agriculture. Farmers, calculating complex factors of soil, climate, price, supply and demand, often turn — on the basis of comparative advantage — from one crop to another. Hence the Valley substituted for cotton more profitable melons and vegetables. Maturing early in the year, flowering luxuriantly in the Valley's soil, there was a great demand for them at good prices in the Eastern states and in the rapidly growing California home market.

Cotton, then, after a life of only ten years in the Valley, vanished from its soil. But soon the vigor of its new life in another California area astonished the cotton trade.

Cotton moved to the San Joaquin Valley. The largest and most fertile Valley in the Far West, magnificent to the eye, it lies in the broad trough between the towering Sierra Nevada and the lower Coast Ranges. Given water, almost any crop will flourish there and 200 high-yield crops are produced on its more than four million acres of farmland. Here is a new, regional cotton kingdom capable of still further expansion if more water could be brought to it. Yet only 75 years ago this prodigally rich area was a desert. Semi-arid, treeless, inhospitable, it was an open range for cattle and sheep who grazed on the wild grasses of the Valley that grew green in spring and burned to tawny beige under the withering sun of summer.

In the Valley cotton production has been rationalized in a manner without precedent in the history of American agriculture. Americans had always insisted that, as part of their freedoms, they could do with their property as they pleased ('It's mine, ain't it?') subject only to the limitation that their actions did not injure neighbors. The Valley's cotton growers rejected this doctrine, and in 1925 at their behest, the California legislature passed the One Variety Cotton Act, making it unlawful to plant, harvest, or gin any strain of cotton except Acala. Thus the continued conformity of the dependable, high-yield strain is legally assured. Twenty-five years later (1949) nearly 10,000 cotton growers of the Valley switched as one man to a newly developed, improved strain known as Acala 4.42. Such a change-over has no parallel in the nation's farm annals.

The price of cotton is obviously important to the grower, but profit or loss is sharply affected by yield per acre. Here the San Joaquin Valley has gone ahead of other cotton-producing areas, with the exception of Arizona. If the other cotton states equaled the Valley's yield, the nation's cotton production would be doubled without the addition to cultivation of a single acre. Thus in 1952, the Valley's average yield of 632 pounds of lint cotton an acre was almost double the national average of 324 pounds.

Increased yields per acre generally reduce unit costs of output — including, of course, costs of cotton picking. When a Valley mechanical cotton picker harvested 200 acres a season, the cost of picking per bale was $24.50 if the yield was three-fourths of a bale to the acre. This cost dropped to $8.20 a bale when the yield was one and one-quarter bales to the acre, while a further increase in yield of one bale to the acre saved an additional $6.50 a bale for picking. These are some of the advantages of high productivity; advantages possessed to a higher degree by the Valley than any other cotton-growing area except Arizona.

California is perhaps the nation's most richly endowed state with its wide diversity of terrain, climate, and natural resources. It has a large and growing industry. The country's richest agricultural state, its range of production is without rival. In the decade 1940–50, swift-growing California became the union's most populous state, second only to New York. But in this roaring commonwealth farming is still the principal activity. Cotton occupies a predominant place, outranking in money value any other California farm product, and accounting for about one-sixth of the total value of its farm output.

A great change occurred in nearly every phase of our national life when men — including those in gold-rich California — made the eye-opening discovery that there is more gold above ground than under it. The San Joaquin Valley's inexhaustible gold mine is its climate. Hot and dry, it is ideal for cotton growing.

In the Southeast cotton planting may be retarded by wet fields that deny entrance to men and their machines. Sometimes, because of weather vagaries, the crop may have to be replanted at considerable expense. Or, as the crop grows, excessive rains may slow its progress, stimulate the growth of noxious plant life, and foster the multiplication of insect pests. Then, when the rains stop, the farmer is confronted with the expensive task of eliminating grass and insects. Or conversely, in the weather-capricious Southeast, rainfall during the growing season may be insufficient to produce a good crop.

Suppose that the Southeast farmer has had a good season and

at harvest time anticipates a large crop. Rainfall may keep his pickers out of the fields, and while he cusses, the rains damage his cotton and cause him terrible losses. In the Southeast, moreover, picked cotton must be protected from rains and heavy dews. It cannot be hauled to the gins in rainy weather unless secured under canvas covers because wet cotton cannot be ginned. Over most of the cotton belt, therefore, weather plays a vital but unpredictable role in the farmer's life.

In the San Joaquin Valley the situation is different. There, with rare exceptions, the cotton grower knows that day after day, from planting time to picking time, will come an unbroken succession of hot, dry, rainless days. He may, therefore, plan his daily operations almost as precisely as the assembly-line industrialist, free of the erratic curves of work and enforced idleness that often plague the Southeast farmer.

The Valley has other blessings. Over much of the cotton country the boll weevil has sometimes done great damage to cotton growers. Always a latent threat to the crop in the huge areas where it thrives, it multiplies to astronomical numbers in cool, rainy seasons. Then the farmer, at whatever expense, must destroy the boll weevil or be destroyed by it. But the hot, dry Valley climate offers this insect no haven and it is unknown in the area. Yet every earthly Eden, however outwardly fair, has its serpent, and the Valley is unwilling host to such destructive insects as cotton daubers, bean thrips, red spiders, and aphids.

The Valley's potentially fruitful soil had always been tempting but unproductive. There was insufficient rainfall in the area for growing field and orchard crops, and while it yearned for water as the hart panteth for the water brooks, its life languished and it was an empty, nearly sterile place. Irrigation has changed all that so radically that today the Valley's cotton grows under carefully controlled flows of water, and the local maxim is: 'There is no such thing as a cotton-crop failure provided the farmer and his pumps keep working.'

'Because of the high certainty of crop success,' *Fortune* reported in 1949, 'an amazingly liberal system of credit enables the grower to borrow in advance 100 per cent of his growing costs. He is part

of a self-financing industry. No bank, not even the aggressively enterprising Bank of America, can claim any laurels for the beneficial
terms he enjoys. Thanks to easy financing and high agricultural
prices, approximately 75 per cent of the state's cotton is grown by
landowners, and the remainder is farmed on a leased-land basis.
Sharecropping is unknown.'

The Valley has two kinds of irrigation because of its varying
water conditions. On its eastern side water is drawn from the San
Joaquin River and other streams flowing out of the Sierra Nevada
snowpack. Farmers buy water from water companies and irrigation
districts, or take it from shallow wells. The ready availability of
water makes capital outlay and operating costs relatively low. Thus
there are large numbers of small farms, usually operated by one
man and his family aided by one or two hired hands and seasonal
workers.

This area is perhaps the New Jerusalem of the small farmer. It
produces 90 per cent of the world's raisins, a huge supply of wine,
the nation's largest peach output, nuts, olives, and other specialty
crops including turkeys, dairy products, and alfalfa. Yet out of this
apparently inexhaustible cornucopia there pours an annual cotton
crop of approximately a million bales. It is the produce of 12,000
farmers.

The farmer of the east side of the Valley may own 20, 40, or 80
acres. But the combination of cheap water, fertile soil, generous
climate, and his skills enable him to gain more than a mere subsistence from his modest land holdings. He may attain an economic independence that is beyond the reach of men of similar
status in most of the other farming areas of the country.

Going from the east side of the Valley to the west side is almost
like going from one world to another. The west side is no domain
of the small proprietor. Its farms (ranches, in the California
idiom) vary from large holdings to those of majestic proportions.
Here, unlike the east side, the coastal ranges gather no water. It
may be had from other sources but only at a cost beyond the reach
of small farmers.

Cotton farmers of the Valley's west side go underground for
water. They sink wells of large capacity that employ high horse-

power turbine pumps to lift water from depths as great as 700 feet. The annual use approximates a million acre-feet of water. (An acre-foot is an acre covered with water to the depth of one foot.) Such operations may be undertaken only by men (or corporations) of means. The outlays are great. The cost of sinking and equipping a large, deep well, capable of lifting water 500 feet and irrigating one section of land (640 acres), may be as much as $70,000. Hence the cost of ten such wells for a 6,000-acre farm — and some of the west side farms are even larger — would be $700,000. And since still greater outlays are entailed for land and equipment, the capital requirements of a big west-side cotton farm approach those of a medium-sized industry.

Successful irrigating involves careful planning with respect to the topography of the land. Direct irrigation consumes enormous quantities of water and the Valley farmer must also count great losses of moisture caused by the area's hot, dry climate. For plant fruitfulness alone it takes, on the average, three and one-half acre-feet of water to bring an acre of cotton to maturity. Or, stated another way, a well flowing at a thousand gallons a minute can irrigate 150 acres of cotton during the growing season.

Yet even the high productivity of the Valley farmer might not enable him to earn a profit on his high capital investment if, like the Southeast farmer, his expensive equipment had to lie idle during much of the year. The Valley's climate rescues him, however, by permitting almost constant use of land and apparatus throughout the year. Hence, after gathering cotton, the farmer can cultivate acreages of melons, barley, and so forth. Spreading his capital costs over almost continuous production, his costly 'mules' do not eat their heads off during long periods of idleness in the barn, but more than pay for themselves by almost constant productivity.

The west side of the Valley is the promised land of the technician for it is further advanced in mechanization than any cotton-producing area of the country. In this treeless area, there are no cutover lands such as those of the Southeast where stumps must be grubbed out if machine operations are to be highly efficient. Huge, almost flat expanses of land lend themselves ideally to mechanization, and the large outlay for machines is spread over farms of great size. This mule-less area does not have the scattered barns and cabins of the Southeast farms, nor the languid airs characteristic of summer-drowsy, old-fashioned farming. This is engineers' country, a community of mechanics, technicians, and cost accountants among whom the rule of thumb has given way to the slide rule. Stakes are large. Permitted 'tolerances' are small.

On the Valley's great cotton farms are equipment depots containing tractors, mechanical pickers, assorted machines, supplies of parts, and oil tanks. There are repair shops which quickly return to the fields machines that may have broken down. Often there is a radio-telephone to enable the farm manager to communicate constantly with his far-flung subordinates. And there is frequently a hangar sheltering one or more airplanes that permit management to supervise wide areas and also get a bird's-eye view of growing crops.

These obviously are not the contented-proprietor-sitting-under-his-own-fig-tree farms of the Jeffersonian dream. They are, rather, farm-factories; rationalized expressions of large-scale agriculture. Such operations are plainly beyond the means of the small farmer. (Thus, for example, one cotton farm of 5,600 acres has invested $154,000 in 14 cotton pickers alone.) On the Valley's west side it is believed that to be successful the cotton farmer must cultivate at least 3,000 acres and employ four irrigation wells; wells that may cost in excess of $250,000. Many of the cotton farms exceed 3,000 acres; some contain more than 10,000 acres. These large-scale operations require not only great capital outlays but also managerial abilities of a high order.

But for all the brilliant technical achievements of the Valley's farmers, the life of the west side hangs upon an indispensable element over which they have little control and not too much knowledge: water. Men who irrigate an area almost the size of Rhode Island are worried. In June 1955, one of them told a *Wall Street Journal* reporter: 'The water table has been receding as much as 25 feet a year. Now it's getting near out of sight . . . I may be able to go on for five to 10 years like this. But some people . . . can't farm this year.'

Costs rise sharply as the water table falls. Old wells fail and newer, more expensive wells must be sunk. But sometimes a well fails and is too expensive to replace. Then nature reclaims her own and the land reverts to desert.

The reporter visited a 16,000-acre farm that grows cotton, barley, melons, and so forth. Here the assistant superintendent aired his worries in these words: 'Since we came out here in 1935, the water table has dropped about 250 feet. About a third of our ranch is in critical condition. On this part of the ranch it's taking 11 wells to do the work seven did in 1947.'

This being the case, the Valley's farmers are associating in grandiose schemes to assure themselves of an inexhaustible water supply. These include the Feather River project that would deliver huge quantities of water to the Valley. But since it would take 20 years to complete and innumerable legal-financial questions have to be solved before it can be started, the Valley must find more water relatively soon or suffer the unhappy consequences of moisture scarcity.

Whether or not California can produce cotton more efficiently, and therefore more cheaply, than the older cotton states is warmly debated by partisans of both sections. Time — and water — will resolve the issue. At present it is doing brilliantly. In 1953 the Valley's farmers grew 1,780,000 bales of the country's total production of 16,470,000 bales.

Nearly 150 years ago, Thomas Jefferson foresaw that the almost unknown regions beyond the Rockies would eventually become a transmountain empire. But it was beyond the surmise of anyone that the Far West, rivaling the Old South, was to become the site of a lesser cotton kingdom with flourishing provinces in California, Arizona, and New Mexico.

If California's development of cotton culture has been swift and successful, she has a not unworthy rival in the neighboring state of Arizona. Many of us regard this state in terms of metals — notably copper — cowboys, dude ranches, or sunny playgrounds. But the cotton trade, if not the public, recognizes Arizona as a new, important cotton area.

Arizona produces approximately 40 per cent of the nation's copper, and its annual value long had no rival in her economy. But in 1953 — only 36 years after her tiny 23,000-bale crop of 1917 — the million bales of cotton she produced approximately equaled the value of her copper production for that year. The phenomenal growth of her cotton culture parallels in many respects that of the San Joaquin Valley. She has the same hot, dry, cotton-ideal climate and also relies upon irrigation. She has brought cotton to a high place in her economy as the Valley has brought it to a high place in the California economy. And her farmers, like the Valley's farmers, are enterprising.

The only limiting factor to agricultural development in Arizona is water supply. The principal cotton areas of the state are irrigated by water pumped from ground-water storage. Yet — and this is a sobering reflection — it has long been realized that the annual rate of discharge from many of these reservoirs has been in excess of their rate of recharge.

Arizona's cotton growers have lowered production costs by spectacularly increasing average yields per acre. Double the national average, they excel those of the San Joaquin Valley. Increasing water costs because of higher pumping lifts have not discouraged continued expansion of irrigated acreage. But water scarcity has emphasized the importance of using water efficiently so that the largest acreages possible may be put into production.

We come now to the third province of the Western cotton kingdom — New Mexico. Like her sisters, she has a hot, dry climate, ideal for cotton culture, relies upon irrigation, and operates highly mechanized farms. Only yesterday — 1922 — the state produced an insignificant crop of 12,000 bales. But by 1953, the New Mexico output reached the respectable total of 310,000 bales.

If we compare the output of the new cotton kingdom in 1953 to the total production in that year, we shall see what extraordinary strides it has made in so short a time. The total United States cotton crop was 16,470,000 bales. Most of it came from states that had been producing cotton when the present Western cotton-producing states were almost empty parts of an almost unknown frontier region. But so swift has cotton culture developed in California, Arizona, and New Mexico that about one-fifth of the crop of 1953 came from their farms.

As cotton marched from the Southeast to the Southwest, it found an ideal home in Texas where the soil and climate are excellent for cotton. Rivers provided transportation before the railroads came. Local seaports gave farmers easy access to international trade. Texas had grown some cotton before the Civil War and after 1866, it received a great influx of cotton-wise men from the Old South. Ruined by the war or searching for better opportunities than were to be found at home, they flocked to Texas to do what they knew best: grow cotton. Here were millions of acres that could be had for low prices, the acres of a potential cotton empire whose development was to be on a herculean scale. For Texas has long produced approximately one-fourth of the nation's cotton.

Although Texas has long grown cotton, she is far from exhausting her cotton-growing potential. Recently an extraordinary expansion of cotton culture has occurred in the high plains. This area may be described as a tilted plain ranging in altitude from about 3,700 feet above sea level in the northwest to 2,500 feet in the southeast. The surface is almost flat except in the western and northwestern sections. The separation between the high plains cotton area and the rolling plains area immediately to the east is sharply defined by a steep escarpment several hundred feet high called the 'cap rock.' It protects the eastern boundary of the high plains cotton area from the destructive erosion that appears in many parts of the rolling plains.

In its virgin state, the area is treeless; a large proportion of the land is tillable, and it is easily put into cultivation. Plowing the native sod is often the only step necessary except on certain sandy-loam soils that require some grubbing to eliminate scattered growths of dwarf mesquite and catclaw. Most of the soils are fertile, and high crop yields accompany favorable growing conditions.

At the turn of the century this area was used almost exclusively for cattle grazing, and the first significant increase of the harvest crop came in the period 1909–19. But by 1929 crops were growing on slightly more than two million acres. The farmer was coming in with a rush and the rancher was going out. Now all or part of many cattle ranches, often comprising thousands of acres, have been subdivided into relatively small parcels for farming purposes. What caused the break-up of cattle ranches for crop production?

For one thing, it had early been demonstrated that, under farm conditions, cotton and grain sorghums could be grown successfully. It was further demonstrated that they possessed drought-resistant qualities which made them superior to other crops that could be grown in the area.

Associated with this was the westward movement of land-hungry settlers, and the building of transportation facilities. But here, as so often in men's affairs, change was enormously affected by war. The factor that caused the heaviest influx of settlers was the high price of cotton during the First World War and, in the early post-war period, high cotton prices and relatively low cattle prices. Then ranchers sold out to farmers and the nature of the area's economy rapidly changed. But its establishment as a cotton country and its continuing prosperity flow from the fact that its soil and climate are favorable to low-cost cotton production.

Before the high plains cotton area could become fruitful, it had to solve its water problem. Lack of moisture had long limited production. An annual average rainfall of less than 20 inches was bad enough, but, to make things worse, variations in its quantity and distribution from season to season caused extreme fluctuations of crop yields and farm incomes.

Consider, first, the variation in the amount of rainfall. Around Lubbock, commercial capital of a great cotton area, the average annual precipitation is little more than 18 inches. This is near the lower limit for successful dry-land farming. But the sparse rainfall is sharply varied. Thus, during ten years of the period 1932–51, it was less than 15 inches, and in 1941 it was 40 inches.

But, as farmers know, even abundant rainfall is not enough for crop abundance unless it is well distributed. Indeed the disadvantage of below-average rainfall may be partially offset by good distribution. This usually means sufficient moisture during May and June to get the crop up and well established. Conversely, benefits of normal or above-normal rainfall may be lost because of poor distribution.

Nor is this all. Much of the area's rainfall comes in the form of local showers, especially in summer. And the rains, despite the old saw, do not fall on the just and the unjust alike. Life-giving showers may fall on the lands of the wicked and pass by the acres of the best church member in the county. Indeed the difficulty is that the rains vary in timeliness from farm to farm. Farms in one part of a county frequently receive sufficient moisture, while others in the same county receive too little moisture.

The capriciousness of rainfall in the high plains is illustrated by Lubbock's experience in the period 1947-9. Some rain was reported during 326 days. But in 80 per cent of the cases it was not enough to 'settle the dust.' During the remaining 20 per cent of the period a quarter inch or more fell. Yet for only nine days was there more than an inch of rain. This is ineffective rainfall and the more so because moisture that falls in light showers is quickly lost through evaporation and contributes little to moisture supply.

These conditions resulted in wide variations in production and farm incomes. Farmers of the area therefore turned to irrigation on a wide scale. The movement was slow during the 25 years after drilling the first well in 1911. But with the coming of the Second World War, a pressing demand for cotton, high prices, and the removal of production controls, there was an extraordinary change. By 1940, 250,000 acres were irrigated. At the end of the war in 1945, there were 4,300 wells and 550,000 irrigated acres. Now the area has more than 25,000 wells that represent a capital expenditure of approximately $100 million. This huge outlay, however, is spread over an immense area. In the high plains more than three million acres are planted to cotton alone.

This marks a phenomenal expansion yet, given adequate water supplies, there is room for further expansion. In the plains area irrigation has been extended to approximately only 40 per cent of the total acreage. But the irrigated lands account for 75 per cent of its production. The remainder comes from dry-land farming.

Fortunately for plains farmers, wells come relatively cheap. By contrast with the outlay of $70,000 for a deep well on the west side of the San Joaquin Valley, the plains farmer may consider himself a bargain-counter customer as he pays $4,000 to $6,000 for a shallow well.

Because of this bargain-cheap water and its availability to many people, the plains area, like the east side of the San Joaquin Valley, is the home of the small farmer. Many holdings run from 160 to 330 acres, with an average of about 240 acres.

Americans long ago learned that some of their 'inexhaustible' resources are exhaustible. This may be true of the water supply of the high plains cotton area, and the United States Geological Survey and State Board of Engineers have been studying the question since 1936. The water engineers predict that 'The supply of water available for irrigation on the High Plains can in time be exhausted by continued heavy use. Also, owing to physical limitations of the wells or to changes in price-cost relationships, it may become unprofitable to operate many of the wells long before the supply is exhausted.'

Time alone will resolve the question. The while the area has had a fabulous cotton career. Only yesterday it was the home of the cowboy and cattle. Yet so swift has been its transition from ranching to farming that annually a white sea of cotton pours out of it. Within less than two decades high plains area farmers increased their output from small proportions to approximately 7 per cent of the total American cotton crop.

Let us now sum up what has been done by the newer provinces of the cotton kingdom — California, Arizona, New Mexico, and the high plains. In a sustained, dynamic burst of energy continuing over the past three decades, they have achieved a remarkable farming phenomenon by increasing their cotton production to the point where it constitutes about one-fourth of the national production. Its future obviously depends upon two unpredictable factors. The first is an adequate water supply. The second is an adequate market for cotton at profitable prices.

X

Front Street: Cotton Row

In 1881, COLONEL WILLIAM FALKNER, grandfather of William Faulkner, the Nobel Prize-winning novelist, wrote a novel entitled *The White Rose of Memphis*. Gallantry informing accuracy, the Colonel said, 'Cotton bales and pretty women seemed to be a spontaneous product in and about Memphis.' Some 75 years later, pretty women and cotton bales still seem to be a 'spontaneous product' in and about Memphis and — an improvement on the past — the pretty women are more in evidence than the bales of cotton.

Memphis was born of cotton and the westward expansion of the South. Before the War, the Mississippi River, the building of railroads in the early 'fifties, the construction of planked roads, and the central location of the town amid a huge cotton-growing area had made it the largest inland cotton market in the United States. Into it poured cotton from the Yazoo Delta of Mississippi, north Alabama, the fertile valleys of the White, the St. Francis, the lower Arkansas, and even the Red River in Louisiana. By 1857, so great was the traffic in cotton that Memphis had 26 buyers of cotton and 28 factors listed in the city directory. By 1860 it handled 400,000 bales of cotton, valued at $16 million in a single season.

Many of the leading citizens of Memphis grew rich as cotton

factors, cotton buyers, and cotton warehousemen. The city's wholesale and retail trade flourished on the patronage of consumers over a wide trade area who drew their livelihood from cotton. And dozens of cotton planters from nearby Arkansas, Mississippi, and Alabama made their homes in the city either because they wanted to escape the malaria of the lowlands where their plantations were located, or because their wives and daughters, feeling socially cramped in Marked Tree, Arkansas, or Nitta Yuma, Mississippi, dragged their menfolk to Memphis and a plusher social arena.

Memphis, now a great industrial city, remains the nation's largest inland cotton market, and cotton still grows up to its outskirts. It is no longer, however, omnipresent in the city's streets as it was in the days when mule-drawn wagons took thousands of bales to the steamboat wharves. One might be in the city for days without realizing that it is a premier cotton market. Trains and trucks now move cotton to and from warehouses located in out-of-the-way parts of the city. He, then, who would see the workings of the Memphis cotton market must go to a street near the main business thoroughfare called Front Street. The old-fashioned, mellow, becomingly dilapidated buildings of Cotton Row have the appearance of the structures of such a town as Cherbourg, France, seen from a steamer's deck. As Cherbourg looks out on the Atlantic, so Front Street, high on the bluffs of Memphis, looks down to the Mississippi River sweeping southward to the sea. Here are located cotton merchants who deal in the produce of millions of acres of land, and the fruits of the labors of hundreds of thousands of men. This is an inner sanctum of cotton's kingdom.

Front Street businessmen no longer exert the function through which so many of them grew rich when they were bankers and supply merchants to planters and often buyers and sellers of their debtors' cotton. Changing methods of cotton-financing and supplying have left them the sole occupation of buying and selling cotton. Their plainly furnished business places are occupied by rows of long tables covered with batts of cotton. These are samples, and this is the sales display of the firm, cottons of like kind being grouped together for the convenience of the buyer. And as tea firms have tasters who, at a sip from a cup, can determine the quality of tea and where it was grown, so cotton merchants employ the indispensable experts known as 'cotton classers.' As tea tasters earn their living by the sensitivity of their palates, these men earn their living by discriminating eyesight and the sensitivity of their fingers. There is a Front Street legend that Cain killed Abel because Abel classed Cain's cotton as low middling, when to Cain it was strict low middling.

Whatever the legend, buyers and sellers, before the establishment of standard grades by the federal government, vigorously argued about grades, and antebellum planters complained that British factors to whom they consigned cotton classed it unfairly. Yet cotton classing is not, and cannot be, an exact science. Before considering its complexities, let us answer the question: why is cotton classed?

There are many variations in the cottons grown on approximately a million and a half farms scattered over millions of acres with differing soil and climatic conditions. Each cotton-goods manufacturer, however, needs certain qualities in the cottons to be used for any particular product, and he wants them to be consistent from year to year, or even from decade to decade. He gives his specifications to cotton brokers who search for the kind of cotton desired by the manufacturer. Cotton classing, therefore, is a method of valuing raw cotton to make marketing and selection for manufacturing simpler and more accurate.

Sampling is the first step in classing. The jute covering of the bale is cut and samples are drawn from opposite sides to make certain that the bale contains the same type of cotton throughout. Each sample is a large handful, from 8 to 12 inches square, weighing 8 to 16 ounces.

Regulations of the United States Cotton Futures Act provide that classing shall be performed only when the samples are in 'proper condition.' This state is reached by leaving the samples exposed on a classing table so that they may loosen up and reach a moisture content in keeping with the balance of the classing room, for dry samples may absorb moisture and damp samples may give it off. Classing, moreover, is done under conditions of light most favorable for accuracy.

The term 'staple length' refers to the length of the fiber. Cotton of a given variety will produce fibers within a more or less definite length range. Since the length of fibers in a single bale may vary, the designated staple length is that which the classer considers predominant.

In spinning, one staple length cannot be substituted for another differing more than a small fraction of an inch without readjustment of the machinery. Difference in staple length also affects the strength of the yarn and the fineness to which it can be spun.

On the basis of staple length, cotton may be divided into five commonly used but unofficial groupings:

> *Very short cotton* (not over ¾ inch). This is mostly unspinnable and is used mainly in batting and wadding.
>
> *Short-staple cotton* ($^{13}\!/_{16}$ but less than $^{15}\!/_{16}$ inch). Readily spinnable, this cotton is used for many of the coarser and cheaper kinds of goods.
>
> *Medium-staple cotton* ($^{15}\!/_{16}$ but less than 1⅛ inches). The bulk of United States production is this kind of cotton. It is widely consumed domestically and great amounts are exported.
>
> *Ordinary long-staple cotton* (1⅛ to 1⅜ inches). The United States produces most of its own cotton requirements in this category but it occasionally imports small quantities.
>
> *Extra long-staple cotton* (1⅜ inches and longer). Domestic production of this type is relatively small and the United States gets much of its supply from Egypt.

In the United States, the last two groups are classified as long-staple cotton but they account for only about 3 per cent of our domestic crop. Medium-staple cotton ($^{15}\!/_{16}$ inches to $1^{13}\!/_{32}$ inches) outranks all others in American production, and accounts for 83 per cent of the total. Very short cotton ($^{29}\!/_{32}$ inches and lower) and short-staple cotton make up 14 per cent of the nation's output.

Grade and staple length usually determine the use of cotton and the competition of one variety with another, but character also affects the selection of cotton for a particular purpose. The term 'grade' here refers to color and brightness of cotton, the amount of foreign matter present in it, and ginning preparation. Standards for grading cotton have been established by the federal government, and they are invariably used in the trade and occasionally revised. For white cotton, the grades in the order of their highest value are Middling Fair, Strict Good Middling, Good Middling, Strict Middling, Middling, Strict Low Middling, Low Middling, Strict Good Ordinary, and Good Ordinary. The first two grades appear on the market in insignificant quantities, and the largest percentage of American cotton falls below the classification Good Middling.

The layman's eye may see all cotton as white, but the eye of the classer or the federal government does not. The Official Cotton Standards for Grades of American Upland Cotton comprise the following color classifications:

> *White cotton.* It usually has a creamy tint which, from a strict color definition, would class it as a very light yellow or cream. In the lower grades, white cotton includes enough dust and foreign matter to give it quite a gray color. The cotton itself may be a dull white, but should not be seriously discolored.
>
> *Spotted cotton* is that in which faulty color has developed from frost damage, boll-weevil damage, or in which some of the bolls have been colored brown by contact with wet bolls, leaves, or stems. This cotton mixed with white bolls will show brown spots in the white.
>
> *Tinged cotton,* damaged in somewhat the same manner as spotted cotton, is that in which the brown discoloration is more extensive than in the spotted samples.
>
> *Yellow stained cotton* is that in which the fibers are almost entirely discolored, giving the sample a slightly mottled tan color.
>
> *Gray cotton* is cotton that is discolored by exposure to rain or fog, followed by long periods of cloudy weather, producing a gray shade.

The term 'character' refers to the strength, body, maturity, uniformity, and smoothness of the fibers and to all other qualities not covered by staple strength or grading. There are no official standards for these qualities, but uniformity in all of them adds a high value to cotton, where lack of uniformity is a serious detriment.

As the determination of cotton color tests the classer's eyes, so the determination of the strength of cotton fibers, in connection with staple determination, tests his fingers. The classer takes a tuft of cotton drawn for staple determination, grasps both ends and breaks the fibers. Considerable experience is necessary to enable him to estimate even roughly the cotton's strength, and the final test is left, of course, to machines.

Since classers determine the approximate value of each bale of cotton and since it is ready for sale only after they have finished their task, the guild of classers, working with color-accurate eyes and sensitive fingers, is indispensable to the cotton trade.

Antebellum planters complained that buyers depressed the market by circulating false rumors or gathering information about the growing crop through private sources. Such procedures have, however, long been impossible both because of federal crop reporting and the rapidity of modern communications. Nor is this all. To aid in disseminating accurate information concerning cotton prices, the Department of Agriculture has designated Atlanta, Augusta, Charleston, Montgomery, New Orleans, Memphis, Little Rock, Dallas, Houston, Galveston, Lubbock, and Fresno as bonafide cotton 'spot' markets. A quotation committee in each city daily surveys the market and reports prices to Washington and to the other exchanges.

The term 'spot' cotton was first applied to cotton actually in a warehouse, at a port, or on the spot at any market. The term now applies to all bales actually bought and sold, as contrasted with 'futures' — the buying and selling of cotton for future delivery in some stated later month. Spot quotations come from the spot exchanges and mill centers and may differ according to locality. Spot prices are indications of what buyers will offer and what sellers will accept for cotton.

Spot cotton prices are published daily on the market pages of many newspapers, and in the cotton South a man may turn to the 'cotton page' even before looking at the headlines. Prices are stated in cents per pound to the nearest hundredth of a cent. Middling cotton with a staple of one inch is the base quality and prices for quality are measured from this base.

'Futures' bewilder because they seem to involve a fantasy more proper perhaps to Alice in Wonderland than to the businessman in his office. They permit one who has no cotton to sell it to another, or to buy cotton from one who has no cotton. Yet futures, for all their appearance of fantasy, are a rational part of the cotton industry, and futures exchanges operate in New York and New Orleans. These, like spot exchanges, are associations of buyers and sellers, formed to facilitate cotton trade. The members may buy or sell for themselves, or act as agents for their customers. Exchanges not only aid in the marketing of cotton by making price quotations available, but they act also as a barometer in reflecting prices for several months in the future, tending to stabilize and stimulate business.

Cotton futures exchanges are sometimes erroneously regarded as gambling rooms operating under a cloak of respectability, and they are, of course, used by the speculator. But they also perform the invaluable function of enabling users of raw cotton to protect themselves against future losses, a device without which mills and merchants would be subjected to inordinate risks and the market would approach a state of disorder.

In order to assure themselves of an adequate cotton supply, mills must contract for delivery months in advance. A futures contract is a legal agreement to deliver, on the part of the merchant, and to accept, by the spinner, cotton at any agreed price during a specified month. It thus guarantees both sale and delivery.

In contracting for future delivery, merchants and spinners 'hedge' to protect themselves against loss from price fluctuations. A bale of cotton may change considerably in value en route from the farm to the retail store. Each businessman who handles the bale expects to make his normal profit by providing a particular service — marketing, spinning, weaving, and so forth. But he seeks to avoid a loss — which could cancel his profit — caused by a drop in the price of cotton while the bale is in his hands. By hedging, he insures himself against a speculative loss.

The principle of hedging is to maintain an even or balanced position in the market at all times. This is done by selling for future delivery on the futures exchanges against unsold holdings and by buying for future delivery on the futures exchanges against forward sales.

When a merchant buys an actual or 'spot' bale of cotton, he hedges by selling a 'future' bale. When he sells a 'spot' bale, he hedges by buying a 'future' bale. Prices on both the spot and futures exchanges tend to move up or down together. Thus, what the merchant loses in one transaction is largely offset by a gain in the other.

This may be illustrated by an example. In November a merchant buys a bale of cotton — at a price per pound that makes the cost come to $200. At the same time he hedges by selling for $190 a 'future' bale for delivery the following July. The price of cotton falls. By March, when the merchant sells his bale to the mill, he finds it is worth only $180, or $20 less than he paid for it. But he can buy back a July futures bale for only $170, or $20 less than he paid for it. The $20 profit he makes in the futures market offsets the $20 loss he suffered in spot cotton.

Hedging is therefore a form of insurance which reduces the risks in the cotton business to a minimum. It shifts the risks to speculators who are the professional risk-bearers in cotton trading.

It is a common trick of demagogic politicians, when the prices of farm commodities sharply decline, to yell 'speculation!' Mr. Justice Holmes, however, said that speculation is 'the self-adjustment of society to the probable,' and added that 'its value is well known as a means of avoiding or mitigating catastrophes, equalizing prices and providing for periods of want.' The evil of speculation, he concluded, is that 'the success of the strong induces imitation by the weak, and that incompetent persons bring themselves to ruin by undertaking to speculate in their turn.'

Certainly — contrary to the politician's views about speculators — no one is big enough to set, even for a moment, the price of cotton. Cotton prices on the American exchanges are in a constant state of flux from minute to minute, from day to day, in accordance with supply and demand and the combined judgments of hundreds of thousands of men throughout the cotton world.

The merchant's job is to assemble many grades of cotton at the fall harvest to meet the particular requirements of textile mills during the year. His profit comes from performing this service for his customers. He hedges by selling future contracts as he buys raw cotton. Otherwise he would have to charge much more for his services to cover the risk involved in stocking a large supply of cotton and tying up a large amount of capital.

The mills also do much hedging. A mill with a large inventory of cloth may sell futures to protect itself against any drop in the price of raw cotton. As the cloth is sold, the mill buys futures. Another mill may make a sale of cloth for future delivery before it obtains the cotton required to fill the order. The mill can hedge the sale by buying futures so that if the cost of its cotton turns out to be higher than expected, a profit on the futures transaction can make up the difference.

A cotton farmer can also hedge. In the spring he may find the price of December futures attractive, and sell as many bales of them as he expects to grow. When he sells his cotton, he will buy back his December futures. Thus he protects himself against the risk of a sharp drop in cotton prices between planting time and harvesting time, but he also foregoes the possibility of gaining from an advance in prices.

In 1877, Lafcadio Hearn stayed for several days on Front Street 'in a great big dreary room of the great big dreary house. It overlooks the Mississippi.' Continuing, he wrote: 'I hear the puffing and the panting of the cotton boats and the deep call of the river traffic.' He boarded a steamboat and watched Negro roustabouts loading cotton, but the spectacle displeased him and he said:

'The sight, at first novel, became actually painful as the afternoon waned and the shadows of the steamboat chimneys lengthened on the levee. Cotton, cotton, cotton — thump, thump, thump — bump, bump, bump; until everything seemed a mass of bagging and iron bands, blotched with white, and one felt as if under the influence of a cotton nightmare. Just when the boat was leaving the levee, it suddenly occurred to me that the color of the face of the bluffs and the color of the new cotton bales piled along the slope were almost precisely the same; that the irregularly broken brownness of the bluffs themselves helped out the fancy that Memphis was actually built upon bales of cotton. Allegorically speaking, this is strictly true.'

Front Street, high on the bluffs above the Mississippi, still looks down upon the great river as it has for a century. The great cotton steamboats of another day are gone and with them has passed the gorgeous dynasty of the steamboat captains. Gone, too, are the once picturesque, flamboyant, free-spending, hell-raising cotton merchants who, in the Gilded Age, attempted to give gilt a new dimension as they dowered themselves with a touch of the baroque in their personal lives.

Their successors are quiet men, even men who are tamed. But in 1955 — as in 1855 — Memphis remains the center of a cotton empire, and annually hundreds of thousands of cotton bales pass across the black sample tables of Front Street.

There the visitor recalls Thackeray's apostrophe: 'Cotton Dealers, Brokers, Merchants, what's the word . . . ? They are tremendous men these cotton merchants.'

XI

Southward the Mills

Europeans, visiting early American cotton mills, could not believe their eyes. The high caliber of factory girls and their comfortable living conditions astonished them. To Anthony Trollope the mills of Lowell, Massachusetts, seemed 'the realization of a commercial utopia.' Workers were 'taken in, as it were, to a philanthropical manufacturing college, and then looked after . . . more as lads and girls at a great seminary than as hands by whose industry profit is to be made out of capital.'

Harriet Martineau wrote of the Waltham, Massachusetts, mills: 'The establishment is for the spinning and weaving of cotton . . . Five hundred persons were employed . . . The girls earn two and sometimes three dollars a week. The little children earn one dollar a week.'

The visitor was impressed by the housing of the workers: 'Most of the girls live in the houses provided by the corporation . . . When sisters come to the mill, it is a common practice for them to bring their mother to keep house for them and some of their companions, in a dwelling built by their own earnings. In this case, they save enough out of their board to clothe themselves and have two or three dollars a week to spare. Some have thus cleared off mortgages from their fathers' farms; others have educated the hope of the family at college; and many are rapidly accumulating an independence. I saw a whole street of houses built with the earnings of the girls . . .'

As for working time, 'The people work about 70 hours a week . . . All look like well-dressed young ladies. The health is good; or rather — is no worse than it is elsewhere.'

Early New England textile-mill owners concerned themselves with the private, religious, and cultural lives of their female workers. The Waltham Mills, for example, 'built the church on the green,' and established a lyceum 'which they have furnished with a good library and where they hear lectures every winter.' These philanthropies of the mills invariably were praised by lady writers and male politicians.

Mill owners carefully chaperoned women employees. They lived in boardinghouses under the watchful eyes of matrons. On the walls of their rooms hung pictures of 'inspirational' Biblical texts. Curfew came nightly at ten. Church attendance was obligatory. And although godly mill owners might have seemed to be doing all this to shelter 'pore lambs' against the winter winds of man's perfidy, the drab fact is that they did it for a sound business reason: to assure themselves of a supply of female workers by allaying the fears of rural parents that their daughters might suffer a fate worse than death at the hands of city slickers.

'By the erection of boarding houses,' writes Francis Hunt in *Lives of American Merchants*, 'under the control of the factory; putting at the head of them matrons of tried character, and allowing no boarders to be received except the female operatives of the mills; by all these precautions they gained the confidence of the rural population, who are no longer afraid to trust their daughters in a manufacturing town. A supply was thus obtained of respectable girls . . .'

Mill work, therefore, did not make a lady less a lady or mar her marriage chances. 'It was soon found,' says Hunt, 'that an apprenticeship in a factory . . . was no impediment to a reputable connection in marriage. And it soon came to be discovered that a few years in a mill was an honorable mode of securing a dower.'

It seemed indeed that a hard-working, chaste mill girl, who was saving her money, was a good catch for any young man with a head

on his shoulders, and a mill-town newspaper addressed itself to
local swains on this subject. 'Young farmers and mechanics, before
you go a-courting just sit down and cypher out the difference' between the usefully productive mill girls 'and the yarn of simpering
misses with novels in hand, loitering on the ottoman or gadding
in the streets for their weekly routine.'

The overwhelming majority of the mill workers in the early
period were girls and young women. In mill towns they found
companionship and comforts unknown in the austere households
from which most of them came; such comforts and even luxuries
as were depicted in a contemporary advertisement: 'BATH
HOUSE. Gentlemen wishing for warm baths can be accommodated
on Friday and Saturday each week. Price twelve and a half cents.
Ladies . . . can be accommodated on Wednesday of each week.
Lady in attendance . . .'

There were other luxuries. An ice-cream parlor offered 'a pleasant place to resort to on a hot day . . . to eat an Ice Cream.'
One's vanity could be pampered as a photographer, offering
'Daguerrotype miniatures,' set up shop. And something that must
have fascinated the girls was open to them — a 'shampoo parlor.'
The mills, severe though they were by modern standards, were
bringing some of the amenities of living to stern New England
towns and villages.

Twice annually the village of Biddeford, Maine, became festive
because of the Pepperell Mills. During six months of the year mill
work stopped at 7:00 or 7:30 p.m. During the other six months
work stopped at sunset. Two festivals marked the changeover. In
a day when candles and small lamps lit homes, the great whale-oil
lamps of the mills burned with such brilliance as to move local
poets to verse in praise of bright mill windows. On 20 September
as the mill's lamps were lit for fall and winter a 'Lighting-Up Ball'
was held, and parties were given in village homes. On 19 March
when the lamps were 'blown out' for the last time of the season,
they were festooned with flowers, and a 'Blowing-Out Ball' was
held.

It is therefore understandable that despite paternalism, long
working hours, poor working conditions, and wretched pay, women
flocked to the mills for town life may have seemed to offer appoint-

ments of fairy land to girls come from remote, bleak, often storm-bound, New England homes. The harsh side of the case is that wages, after deductions for board, were $2 a week. Girls worked in noisy, dusty, fire-dangerous buildings for 70 hours a week. The black list was used to weed out the disaffected, and mill owners combined to fix hours and wages.

But this petty despotism concealed by the silken glove of benevolence was to last only until the middle 1840s. By that time male operatives had succeeded the country-girl workers and the new despotism, not even attempting a façade of benevolence, was naked and harsh. The mill towns became full company towns. And, says Louis Hacker, 'Churches, newspapers, local politicians were owned by the industrialists; the terror of the black list meant starvation and not simple banishment to the country . . .'

In 1825 the Massachusetts legislature noted that children toiled in textile mills from 12 to 13 hours daily except Sunday. It came to the accurate conclusion that such hours 'left little opportunity for instruction.' There the matter ended. Only after a century of struggle did the good, kind American people make it legally impossible for good, kind employers to break the bodies and destroy the spirits of good, kind American children.

In 1846, Lowell cotton-mill workers toiled 13 hours a day in summer, and from daylight to dark in winter. During the period 1830–60, men workers earned about $5 a week and girls $2 to $3 a week. Southern wages were even lower.

Finally a spokesman for labor came to the fore — Seth Luther. A textile worker himself, he became a 'labor agitator' as secretary of the Boston General Trades' Convention. In 1832 in his *Address to the Working Men of New England,* he set out 'Conditions on which help is hired by the Coheco Manufacturing Company, Dover, New Hampshire.'

The employee agreed 'to work for such wages as the Company may see fit to pay, and BE SUBJECT TO THE FINES as well as entitled to premiums paid by the Company.' Two cents weekly was deducted from the worker's wages for the sick fund. If he left the company without giving two weeks' notice, he must forfeit two weeks' pay. But if the company discharged him, he must not expect final pay before two weeks had elapsed. And, finally, he agreed 'not to be engaged in any combination . . . whereby the work may be impeded.' If he did, he would forfeit wages due him.

Commenting on these terms, Luther made the argument that was later to be used by proslavery advocates in the South; namely, that Negro slavery in the cotton fields was little worse, if any, than working conditions in industrial New England. He said: 'We . . . know something about Southern slavery, having resided in slave country at various periods, and we know that children born in slavery do not work *one half* the hours, or perform *one quarter* of the labor, that white children do in cotton mills, in free New England . . . If the children in mills . . . are almost entirely deprived of education, will the gentlemen show us the great advantage *they* possess over *slave* children . . . ?'

Early in the nineteenth century, the United States imported, usually from Britain and France, large quantities of cotton textiles. In 1813 only one shop in Boston sold domestic cotton cloth, but this condition was soon changed. Britain continued to have a great cotton-textile market here, but no longer one of near monopoly.

Although the Revolution had stimulated American household manufacture of textiles, afterward British goods were again imported and domestic manufactures momentarily declined. Britain, moreover, forbade the export of textile machines with the hope of keeping the United States an agricultural economy. Yet the secrets of the industrial revolution could not be kept or the movement monopolized. Soon cotton-textile machines smuggled out of England, or made from drawings, began to appear in the United States.

Great change may go unnoticed when it is just beginning. Hence there was no stir in the young republic when, in 1790, there arrived in Pawtucket, Rhode Island, a young English cotton-mill mechanic named Samuel Slater. Financially backed by the merchants Almy and Brown, aided by a carpenter and a blacksmith, he reproduced from memory some of England's efficient machines. Then he began to run America's first cotton-textile mill.

Native factors accelerated American cotton-industry progress. The new republic had a Yankee Doodle pride. The Continental Congress had indeed considered (but rejected) a resolution to the effect that this was 'the greatest country in the world.' But native pride did not impede mechanical advance. Throughout the modern world workers have sometimes opposed the coming of machinery from fear that it might deprive them of jobs or cause lower wages. But American textile workers welcomed foreign-made machines, and labor-saving devices were generally approved because of the rapidly growing domestic market, the country's rising standard of living, and the mechanical aptitudes of native workers.

A great change in textile manufacturing followed the visit of Francis C. Lowell and Nathan Appleton to Edinburgh in 1811. These men were New England shipping magnates who had become interested in the textile industry. In Scotland they tried to buy something that was forbidden to be exported — a power loom. Disappointed but not deterred, the men came home and with difficulty constructed a power loom and other textile machines. Then in 1813, they formed the Boston Manufacturing Company with a paid-up capital of $100,000. It was the first American mill to perform all the operations necessary to convert raw cotton into finished cloth. Soon our first important industrial towns came into existence; towns such as Lowell, Massachusetts.

What were the sources of mill capital? When the first mills were founded there were few large fortunes in the country and little inherited wealth. By the 1850s there were reputedly 52 American millionaires, and John Jacob Astor — the richest man of his day — had left $20 million at his death in 1848. But even in 1860, a fortune of $500,000 was regarded as large and one of $100,000 as quite out of the ordinary.

Men who had worked hard and saved money were not inclined to risk it. They sought only conservative investments in local enterprises where they could watch them. Yet occasionally factory workers founded small cotton mills, sometimes in conjunction with farmers and neighbors who contributed sites and often worked in the mills.

The South was an agrarian economy whose funds were concentrated in lands and slaves. The North was mainly a mercantile economy concerned with trade and its financing. New York's wealthy men were not industrialists but rather merchants, bankers, and real-estate operators. The wealthy of Boston had somewhat wider interests that included shipping, banks, mortgage companies, and cotton mills. In the mercantile economy of the times, merchants were therefore an important source of capital for building New England's cotton mills. For some they were an investment. For others they were a source of supply for their mercantile establishments. Thus in 1808, John Waterman erected a cotton mill at Canton, Massachusetts, with capital provided by a merchant who agreed to take the output and pay a stipulated price for manufacturing. This is a practice that, with many variations, continues to this day, factories being financed by distributors who take the output.

War generally accelerates the industry of a belligerent and cotton-mill building was stimulated by the somewhat farcical conflict that we call the War of 1812. Little merchandise left the country, little came in, and New England's great ocean-carrying trade fell stagnant. As a result such prominent merchants as Almy and Brown, Lowell and Appleton intensified their textile operations, and after the war, when shipping remained in eclipse, shipowners and sea captains took to cotton manufacturing at Fall River and in Rhode Island. Before the first two decades of the nineteenth century had passed, the cotton-textile industry had made great progress. In 1816, when capital invested in manufacturing was estimated at $100 million, about $40 million of the total was invested in cotton-textile mills. They employed 100,000 workers and consumed 27 million pounds of cotton in a year.

Wherever there was water power, shrewd men founded cotton mills. It remained, however, for the ancient seaport of Salem, city of witches, the famous clipper ships, and the China trade, to depart radically from this pattern. Salem men organized the Naumkeag Steam Cotton Mills that began to operate in 1847. A new industrial era began as industrialists no longer had to depend upon turbulent rivers for power.

Up to this time American cotton mills had produced only rather coarse fabrics: drills, duck, plain cloth, sheeting — items called 'domestics.' Finer fabrics came from France and England. The initial American venture into this phase of manufacturing came from a strange quarter — the famous whaling town of New Bedford, Massachusetts.

During the first part of the nineteenth century her vessels were known in remote ports of the world as they chased the whale and returned with cargoes of oil and bone. But in 1847, the whaling industry still flourishing, New Bedford men organized the Wamsutta Mills to make fine shirtings, and after an investment of $167,000 the mills opened in 1849. Immediately successful, they had an ample supply of labor at hand. Ten thousand men were engaged in New Bedford's whaling industry and many of their women worked in the mills.

Yet, though they were successful, few other local capitalists sought to emulate them. Whaling was their first interest and it continued to engage their money and talent until the Civil War. Then adversity struck. Confederate privateers seized their ships. A series of disasters occurred in the Arctic Ocean. These misfortunes might have been overcome, but whaling was also faced with obsolescence. Gas and petroleum were coming in to take the place of whale oil for lubricants and lighting. There was left only the use of whale bone for the straitjacket corsets of the times that insured the desired wasp-waist effect of 'tightlacing.' But this could not support an industry, so thereafter until the end of the first decade of the twentieth century, New Bedford built cotton mills.

New England early gave evidence of her future position as center and dominant leader of the nation's cotton industry. The home of nearly all American-trained operatives, it attracted many British spinners who, seeking their fortune in America, brought with them their invaluable skills. Energetic, risk-taking capitalists of high managerial and organizational abilities imported the best available foreign machinery and foreign brains, including men who knew the complicated process of calico-printing that Sir Robert Peel had used for his successful ventures in Britain. (This process, transplanted here, initiated the vogue for the calico with 'the big flowers.') And not content to manufacture entirely at home, New Englanders carried the cotton industry into the upper Mohawk valley and the central lake region of New York.

Yet New England's cotton mills were hundreds of miles from the fields of cotton. How was it in the South with respect to the cotton-textile industry in the beginning?

In the antebellum South were the plantation system and the farm. Coastal Plain planters concerned themselves little with

household manufactures, which were left to farmers of the Piedmont and the Great Valley. It was a difference that marked the
areas of the subsequent agrarianism and industrialization of the
South.

Small farmers, who hired free labor, could not, or would not,
compete with slaves. But in the Piedmont men had a great
energy source in the region's water power and those of small
capital could employ water power and run cotton mills. Many
turned to this expedient. Before 1820, Southern cotton mills
had been little more than plantation spinning houses producing
coarse yarns for local household looms. But within 20 years the
scene changed. Water power and the development of transportation, opening up distant markets, sharply stimulated the
cotton-mill industry, whose growth was based on the conjunction
of cotton, the water wheel, and the steamboat.

The James, the Savannah, the Chattahoochee, and the Tennessee were the principal streams of the cotton states that afforded
both industrial power and transit to distant markets. Near the
head of navigation upon these rivers, at Richmond and Petersburg
in Virginia, Augusta and Columbus in Georgia, at Huntsville,
Florence, and mill villages near Montgomery in Alabama, arose
the first Southern factory centers to feed the larger commerce of
the country.

What was the source of capital for these mills? It did not
come from planters. Their funds were usually tied up in land
and slaves. It did not come from cotton factors who were unwilling to take the risks of the new enterprises. Capital came
from local businessmen, merchants anxious to increase payrolls,
bankers, lawyers, and physicians. It took the combined investment of seven men to furnish the $45,000 capital of the Vaucluse
Mills. This may seem quaint to us but it is a representative phase
of American risk-taking. In the first decade of the twentieth century an obscure mechanic named Henry Ford had the devil's own
time before he found a miscellany of men and women to sub-
scribe $28,000 for his automobile venture.

Southern cotton mills sold most of their products at home. The
North made better goods than the South and, despite transportation costs, sold them in the South at the same prices asked for

inferior Southern products. Southern merchants, therefore, went North to buy, not only because prices were lower but also because they did not like Southern-made goods. *De Bow's Review* querulously complained that 'almost every country merchant who visits Charleston has a through ticket to New York in his pocket.' But Southern merchants nonetheless continued to buy fine-grade cottons in the North and Southern mills continued to produce low-grade merchandise; coarse yarns, bagging, and the coarse fabric known as 'nigger cloth.'

Yet they prospered. Their wage scales were even lower than those of Northern mills. They paid children from 10 to 20 cents a day; women from 40 to 50 cents a day. At mid-nineteenth century (1849), the wages of the 94 men, women, and girls employed by the Vaucluse Mills averaged 38 cents a day.

But low wages were not anywhere regarded as scandalous. In 1869, a New York *Herald* reporter said of Georgia cotton mills: 'The operatives are . . . white people, chiefly boys and girls from twelve to twenty years of age. On an average they are better paid, and worked easier than is usually the case in the North. Country girls . . . soon become skillful operatives, and ere they have been in the mills a year are able to earn from four to six dollars a week.'

Some of these mills were owned by Northern men. Other Northerners who contemplated building Southern mills spoke of the 'ignorant, half-fed, ill-clothed Southern people' whose sufferings would be relieved only if benefactors erected cotton mills where they could work. But despite such cant, the wretched wages of mill workers may have seemed attractive to them at a time and in a place where poverty was so widespread that social distinction was conferred by ownership of a carpet, and a popular ditty ran:

> I had a girl in Baltimore,
> Brussels carpet on the floor,
> Horse cars running by the door,
> What could a fellow wish for more.

Modern Southern cotton manufacturing may be said to begin with the founding of the Graniteville (South Carolina) Mills by William Gregg in 1847. A self-made, successful merchant, born in Virginia, he was living in Charleston when he started this venture. His efforts to found a cotton mill, despite the hostility of Charleston planters, illuminate prewar attitudes of the agrarian South and the industrial North.

Gregg was plagued by the South Carolina planter aristocracy, or 'plantocracy,' as Miriam Beard calls it. In A *History of the Business Man* she observes: 'The American landed gentry were more intransigent than the European; like all things in the New World, "aristocracy" was also carried to extremes.' The most extreme of the extremists lived in the South. There 'With a hauteur greater than that of Louis Quatorze, the planters . . . repudiated trade without giving it at least a patient trial; they showed less comprehension of economic matters than . . . even the ancient Romans, whom they so often invoked.'

No agrarian society had ever been less self-sustaining than most of the cotton plantations, but few planters drew significant inferences from the fact, and 'would not recognize that the basis of their wealth was the Machine.' Their failure to do so led them to a catastrophic decision: 'They prepared to defy industry and business in the United States . . . a decisive leadership was assumed by Charleston . . . *the home of political figures who, it has been said, probably had, for good or evil, a larger influence on American history than any similar number of people in the country.*' (my italics)

Charleston was strongly influenced by its Huguenots. In their native France and Switzerland they had been able, sober business-men and bankers uncorroded by aristocratic pretensions. But, 'In this city merchants, turned "aristocrats," were out-Bourboning the Bourbons . . . Rich merchants strove to emulate the planters . . . and outvie them in imported displays of millinery and coaches; adopting the duelling and hunting codes of the surround-ing gentry, and buying plantations . . . Though few of them had noble ancestry, they all became . . . "French aristocrats," notorious for extreme hauteur . . . Thus the French *ancien régime*, destroyed at home, was revivified in the Machine Age in America, the home of survivals.'

Charleston had long prospered. In 1816 it ranked next to New York in the export trade. It had well-managed banks and a population second only to that of New Orleans, the South's most populous city. But its prosperity dwindled as South Carolina farmers exhausted the soil; exports declined, and population was lost to newer cotton-growing areas. Yet Charleston would not countenance the coming of industry and in an attempt to keep it away from its door, forbade the use of steam engines in the city. Whereupon an angry William Gregg sarcastically wrote: 'This power is withheld lest the smoke of an engine should disturb the delicate nerves of an agriculturist; or the noise of a mechanic's hammer should break in upon the slumber of a real-estate holder, or an importing merchant, while he is indulging in fanciful dreams of building on paper the Queen City of the South — the paragon of the ages.'

Gregg saw — as did other Southerners — that the South could not raise the living standard of thousands of its poorest people without some measure of industry. He therefore attempted to reduce Charleston prejudice against industry by writing pamphlets, making talks, and fighting in the state legislature. By way of indicating that cotton-mill industrialists were not, because they engaged in industry, blackguards, he told the press that Lowell mill owners lived in fine houses and wore white gloves. Massachusetts mills prospered, he said, because of their organization, skilled superintendence, and specialized production. Southern mills could also prosper because these elements were potentially available to them. His projected mills, he added, would not only pay investors well but would also provide jobs for hundreds of poor people.

Finally in 1847, aided by Charleston capitalists, Gregg built the Graniteville Mill. The largest in the South before the War, it had nearly 9,000 spindles and 300 looms which were driven by a 116-horsepower turbine engine. It produced mainly sheeting and coarse cloths.

Gregg's mill village was no montonous, bleak horror, but was composed of comfortable, attractive cottages scattered along woodsy roads, and there were flowers planted on the mill grounds. In the manner of his New England counterparts, Gregg erected a boardinghouse for single workers, a church, and an assembly hall. But no liquor could be sold in the village. He also built a free school and in effect compelled his employees to send their children to it because when, for no good reason, children did not come to classes, he made deductions from their parents' wages.

The Graniteville Mill, immediately successful, became a training school for future mill foremen and executives who, in time, took their knowledge to other Southern mills.

In 1860 New England dominated cotton textiles and Southern production was relatively insignificant. Thus Lowell alone had 100,000 more spindles than all those in the South.

During the 20 years preceding the War, the number of spindles had doubled, and the cotton-textile industry had grown twice as fast as the population. On the eve of the great conflict an old man might still remember when power spinning had been introduced to America 70 years before. In this short time cotton manufactures had come to excel all the nation's manufactures in terms of capital and labor employed and value of output. Great Britain's spindles still outnumbered America's six to one. But this country stood second to Britain in cotton manufacture and for 30 years had been her principal rival in foreign markets.

Cotton consumption had increased from five million pounds annually to 423 million pounds. Americans had constantly improved their mills, bettered their factory organization, and introduced new fabrics. But cotton-knitted goods were still imported, generally from Germany, and British and continental looms satisfied most of the domestic demand for light fabrics of ornamental weave and coloring. American mills contented themselves with producing durable, substantial fabrics.

Before considering the continuing advances of the cotton-textile industry, let us note how it was affected by inventions. It is indeed a distinguishing mark of the nineteenth century that it may be said to have invented the method of invention.

During the late eighteenth century and the first half of the nineteenth, new inventions and manufacturing methods enormously increased cloth production, especially through the use of multiple spindles and power looms driven both by steam and water. These inventions and methods sharply lowered prices and opened wider markets. The lace power loom came into being and the embroidery machine. Chlorine was used as a bleaching agent and the roller printing machine was perfected. Then calicoes became so cheap that everybody could afford them.

Men had known how to spin, weave, and dye cotton for 5,000 years. But within less than a century mechanics and inventors — usually of European origin — had wrought more changes in these arts than had been made in the preceding 50 centuries. So great was the production speed-up that in 1844 an English authority said that 30,000 workers using current English machines produced more yarn and cloth than 30 million workers could have produced in 1770. And since the effect of all this was to lower prices every man, so to speak, could afford a shirt.

In 1846, Elisha Howe, Jr., of Cambridge, Massachusetts, received a patent for his sewing machine. It increased the sewer's capacity from a few stitches a minute by hand needle to a few hundred a minute on the machine. Ladies so eagerly demanded the new machine that 15 years later 111,000 sewing machines were humming in 12 states.

Machine production had lowered the price of cloth. Now the home sewer (or hired dressmaker) could make clothes more speedily and economically than ever before. Eventually the electric sewing machine was to become the mechanical basis of America's gigantic ready-to-wear industry. There would remain millions of home sewers. But great numbers of women (to their delight) were freed from one of their ancient functions.

During the Civil War domestic cotton consumption declined by about 50 per cent, but most Northern textile mills operated during much of the period of conflict. They had bought heavily of the 1861 crop, not because they anticipated secession but because they expected an abnormally small crop in 1862. Immediately before the War, moreover, the South was shipping more and more of her cotton north via Ohio River ports, instead of Gulf ports, because of improved railroad transport. Cotton was now being compressed, and cars carried 30 bales as against 20 previously. When the War started, therefore, large quantities

were in transit to New England and many mills had stocks that
enabled them to operate for a long time.

By 1863 Northern mills were getting 3,500 bales of American
cotton weekly and 500 Indian; approximately one-fourth the
quantity required for full operation. Some cotton was re-imported
from England, cotton was captured and bought in the South, and
in the spring of 1863, 14,000 bales passed through Cairo, Illinois,
bound north.

The War gave the country a new industry. It had imported
most of its thread from England, but unfavorable exchange rates
caused Holt's thread to sell for four times its prewar price. So
Americans started to manufacture thread, cotton hosiery, and knit
goods — much of which had been imported.

The postwar North was richer and more powerful than the
section had ever been, and in 1867 *De Bow's Review*, quoting a
Southern observer, said that the North's war boom could be seen
in "new furnaces, mills, factories, tanneries; in the increase of
iron, coal, copper, lead and zinc; in new railroads and countless
oil wells; in the multiplication of machinery and the establishment
of new industries; in the vast number of new vessels on lakes,
rivers and canals; in the extraordinary increase of elegant and
costly buildings in country and town.'

During the War, Southern cotton mills produced largely 'war
goods.' The Graniteville Mill, for example, made army clothing,
tents, and sailcloth. In July 1861, the Governor of Alabama told
the Confederate Secretary of War: 'There are three factories
within 25 miles of this place [Montgomery] which can turn out
5,000 yards a day of tent cloth.'

The South had huge stocks of cotton, but few cotton mills.
At the beginning of the War thousands of volunteers were
provided with uniforms made by household looms and village
workshops of their districts. The Confederacy and its state governments commandeered cotton mills and provided funds for their
expansion, but so small were their facilities, and so deranged
were they by the conflict, that it is estimated the South spun only
200,000 bales of cotton annually during the War. Most of it went

into coarse yarns that were woven into sheetings, drills, and osnaburgs. But part of the yarns went to country people for weaving on household looms.

The end of the War found Southern mills lagging farther than ever behind the North. In 1868 Northern mills consumed about 825,000 bales of cotton and Southern mills 60,000. Massachusetts turned out one-third of the nation's cotton manufactures, followed by Rhode Island, New Hampshire, Pennsylvania, Connecticut, and Maine. New England accounted for three-fourths of the country's production of cotton goods.

After the War as production rose, prices fell. Brown sheetings, priced at 32 cents a yard in mid-1865, went for 18 cents in 1867, and denims dropped from 65 cents to 35 cents a yard. Workers' wages were also cut, but mills North and South paid dividends. Yet there were cross currents amid the winds of prosperity. Northern merchants bought heavily of cotton goods to replenish their war-depleted stocks. But the South, oddly, was not anxious to sell raw cotton. The people, distrustful of the federal government, shocked the cotton world by generally holding onto their cotton. Prices rose sharply in Liverpool and much cotton was drawn there. But soon the bottom fell out of the market, to the great detriment of cotton mills.

New England continued its textile progress. During the late 1860s mills were erected throughout the state of Maine, at Lewiston, Augusta, and Biddeford. Manufacturing prospered along the Merrimac River where French-Canadians usually supplanted native American workers. But as cotton spinning expanded in New England, it declined in the Central Atlantic and Western states and prophecies which had been heard before the War of great textile centers arising in the West were heard no longer.

In the South, the Graniteville Mill, which had emerged from the War in bad condition and heavily in debt, was refinanced by Northern capital, and another large mill was erected at Kalmia, South Carolina, by local and New York capital. Shortly after the War, at Columbus, Georgia, mills that had been burned during Wilson's Raid, were rebuilt. More and more Southern leaders moved toward manufacturing.

It was generally believed that the South would become an

important cotton-manufacturing region as Northern investors realized the advantages. There was an adequate labor supply, equable climate, abundant water power, fair transportation, and inexhaustible quantities of cotton. Railroad building, enabling Southern manufacturers to reach distant markets, went forward rapidly after the War. The prewar South had approximately 10,000 miles of railroads. By 1867, despite the ravages of war 17,000 miles of trackage were completed or under construction. Fast freight now reached New York from New Orleans in six days.

But in 1870 the North's spindles outnumbered the South's by almost thirty to one; this at a time when domestic demand for cotton had become such that mills were annually consuming nearly 900,000 bales of cotton.

Between 1873 and 1893 the industrial United States grew rapidly. 'In some respects,' notes Clark in *History of Manufacturers in the United States*, 'this was from an economic point of view the Golden Age of our history. Uncle Sam could still give every man a farm and the hardships of the frontier had largely disappeared. Taxes were low, federal finance was more concerned with surpluses than deficits, the public debt was rapidly reduced and the spiritual unity of the nation was being gradually restored after the violent severance of the Civil War . . . Consciousness of progress and an unclouded optimism as to the future were well-nigh universal . . .'

These decades also witnessed the severe panics of 1873 and 1893, and a surge toward industrialization in the South. It was a movement for building factories in general, and cotton mills in particular. The South had fewer cotton mills in 1870 than it had in 1860. But by 1880 it had as many mills as before and twice as many spindles.

The period 1880–1900 was perhaps the most extraordinary in the South's economic history. Men no longer regarded cotton culture as almost the sole source of wealth. And — just as important — they no longer regarded the planter's estate as the sole source of social distinction (gentleman). They now looked upon industry as a potentially great source of wealth, and the industrialist as not less touched with social distinction than the planter. These factors made it easier to raise money for industrial development and, as the fevers of Reconstruction abated and white supremacy was assured, men were less preoccupied with politics than they had been and felt that local investments were politically secure. Many of them indeed believed — so greatly had attitudes changed — that their losses on the battlefield might be recouped in the factory.

Southern leaders clearly understood that the North's industrial apparatus had virtually doomed to defeat the agricultural Confederacy, and even before the War ended some of them had hoped that Northern capital would afterward come South. They were men of the 'New South,' a term invented by General Adam Badeau, a Northerner living in South Carolina. So it was that immediately after the War they lifted their voices for Southern industrialism and in 1868, Francis W. Dawson, the able Charleston editor, said that the disasters of war 'have taught the Southern planter that he cannot live by cotton alone.' Industry was also needed to make a prosperous region.

The South could offer industry abundant brawn and natural resources of many kinds. But it lacked capital, and the longed-for Northern investment funds came South in large sums only to finance railroads.

After vainly waiting for 20 years, 'New South' leaders urged the region to act on its own behalf, the group including such men as Walter Hines Page, Daniel H. Tompkins, and Richard H. Edmonds of the *Manufacturers' Record*. They suggested a radical change of course. It was that the South should turn away from its former agrarianism and pursue industrial wealth.

Many Southerners have a low kindling point. Hence, fired by prospects of the industrial heaven they were about to enter, Charleston merchants — a city that not long before had banned steam engines within its limits — toasted their state: 'South Carolina — a new era of prosperity is about to dawn on her.' Moved by the same spirit, industrial exhibitions at Atlanta, Louisville, New Orleans, and Richmond, in the period 1881-8, were devoted to Southern industrialism, present and future. Whether because it was regarded as bad business or bad form, no one pointed out that the new 'prosperity' would be based on dirt-cheap labor.

Propagandists of the new order advertised the notoriously cheap labor and for once did not distinguish between whites and Negroes. The region possessed, they said, a 'large body of strong, hardy, active, docile and easily contented negro laborers,' who were content with their wages and had no disposition to strike. But the other blessedness in the land, the 'hardy native Anglo-Saxon stock' of the region, was not a whit behind Negroes in physical strength, docility, contentment with wages, and lack of disposition to strike. The *Manufacturers' Record,* moreover, assured prospective investors in the New South that 'long hours of labor and moderate wages will continue to be the rule for many years to come.'

A rapid growth of the Southern cotton-textile industry began and within 20 years (1880–1900) mills increased from 161 to 401, spindles increased eightfold, and workers sixfold. This accomplishment had no parallel in the annals of American industry. For it was neither an expression of ordered industrial capitalism nor the result of a boom. Its origins were of a kind unanticipated by Karl Marx or any orthodox economist. The strange mixture of practicality and evangelism that, in heroics, occasional hysterics, and pathos made industrial accomplishment seem a fevered folk movement, sprang from the hearts of men in whom the American Dream was dying. It was compounded of the concept of progress and the ideal of building an industrial society that would create jobs for poor people and yet retain the old rural-agrarian values of the Old South.

As the movement got under way, it 'acted upon the South of the time,' writes W. J. Cash in *The Mind of the South,* 'as the sermons of Peter the Hermit acted upon Europe in the eleventh century. It swept out of the minds of the men who conceived it, to become in the years between 1880 and 1900 the dream of virtually the whole Southern people — a crusade preached with burning zeal from platform and pulpit and editorial cell — a mighty folk movement which already by the turn of the century would have performed the astounding feat (in a land stripped of capital) of calling into existence more than four hundred cotton mills . . .'

In the presence of this religio-industrial program with its Tolstoyan overtones, cynics might have doubted those who said that they wanted to start cotton mills not to exploit the cheap labor and abundant cotton of the region, but primarily in order to find employment for the many poor. But 'At Salisbury, North Carolina,' writes Cash, 'one Mr. Pearson . . . declares that "the establishment of a cotton mill would be the most Christian act his hearers could perform" — and next evening the village's first mill is actually organized, with another minister at its head. At Clinton, South Carolina, very much the same thing happened under the leadership of a preacher named Jacobs.'

Community after community was fired by what may be called industrial revivalism. Everybody wanted to be a soldier for the Lord. Farmers who were too poor to buy even a single share of mill stock pooled their pennies and bought a share in common. Workers agreed to put aside 25 cents a week toward the new enterprise. Each community tried to outdo the other.

These were the impulses of men's hearts in that strange time when they were building not cathedrals, but cotton mills. It is hardly to be expected that men so animated should also have applied to their undertakings the care and caution of trained businessmen. Thus it came about that these builders of cotton mills blithely disregarded even the most rudimentary business principles. An aspiring hamlet, for example, would build a mill without regard to the advantages of the locality for textile manufacturing. The hamlet merely selected men who had its confidence — whether grocers, undertakers, or livery-stable keepers — and drafted their services without regard to competence. Many of the new mills, therefore, were headed by men trained in almost every field except that of textile manufacturing. Among them were doctors, lawyers, teachers, planters, even clergymen.

Such procedure is inexplicable unless it is remembered that men were not embarking on a business enterprise, but on a social enterprise. If the mill proprietors made a profit, that was incidental. The important factor was the salvation of the dying community and the rescue of the poor whites. 'The record of those days,' says Gerald W. Johnson, 'is filled with a moral fervor that is astounding. People were urged to take stock in the mills for the town's sake, for the poor people's sake, for God's sake . . . In this evangelistic spirit dozens of mills were built. They would, it was said, become the salvation of the necessitous masses of poor whites.'

These mills, not constructed with an eye to profits, nonetheless earned them and additional mills were financed and built. But soon came a change in the ownership and management of many of the mills. From the late 1880s onward, the 'hard, pushing, horse-trading type of man' began to take over. Thousands of jobs had indeed been found for poor people but as the 'new men' succeeded the old management, the poor remained poor and dragged out miserable lives.

Men and women flocked to the mills from their bleak farms. 'As late as 1907,' writes Woodward, 'a study revealed that 75.8 percent of the women and children in Southern cotton mills had spent their childhood on the farm . . .' The cotton-textile South of the period was repeating the experience of England under the industrial revolution when the rising textile mills recruited thousands of farm workers and brought them to the towns. So, too, the manner in which Southern operatives were housed is reminiscent of the horrors of the housing of first-generation English mill workers. Woodward, in *Origins of the New South*, sketches the scene: 'As pictured by an investigator in Georgia in 1890 "rows of loosely built, weather-stained frame houses, all of the same ugly pattern and buttressed by clumsy chimneys," line a dusty road. "No porch, no doorstep even, admits to these barrack-like quarters." Outside, in the bald, hard-packed earth, was planted, like some forlorn standard, the inevitable martin pole with its pendant gourds. Inside were heaped the miserable belongings that had furnished the cropper's cabin: "a shackling bed . . . a few defunct split-bottom chairs, a rickety table, and a jumble of battered crockery." In certain mill villages of Georgia in 1890 not a clock or a watch was to be found. "Life is regulated by the sun and factory bell" — just as it had once been by the sun and farm bell . . .'

What were the wages of workers who lived in this wasteland?

In the 1890s North Carolina adult males received 40 to 50 cents a day. Children competed with their parents in the mills and thereby reduced wages for both. Their pay varied considerably but some North Carolina mills paid 10 to 12 cents a day for child labor.

The profits and capital of many mills rose, but wages lagged. The hourly pay of adult male spinners in the South Atlantic states was about three cents in 1890. But despite the pitiful pay and horrendous conditions under which textile workers lived, mills easily filled their company houses. Strikes were rare. Few workers ever returned to the farm.

The twentieth century came and in ever optimistic America, men who believed in the perfectibility of human nature and the improvement of men's material condition looked forward to a new day of enlightenment, prosperity, and progress. But few rays of the rising sun of the twentieth century penetrated the darkness of the cotton mills. In 1904 Edgar Gardner Murphy, writing of Southern mill workers, said he knew mills in which 'for ten or twelve days at a time the factory hands — children and all — were called to work before sunrise, laboring from dark to dark. I have repeatedly seen them at labor twelve, thirteen and even fourteen hours a day . . . I have seen children eight and nine years of age leaving the factory as late as 9:30 at night, and finding their way . . . through the unlighted streets of the mill villages, to their squalid homes.'

These twentieth-century industrial scenes recall England's 'dark satanic mills' of the 1840s. The backbreaking toil, undernourishment, and wretched housing produced a kind of lower-depths human being. W. J. Cash describes him: 'By 1900 the cotton-mill worker was a pretty distinct physical type in the South; a type in some respects perhaps inferior even to that of the old poor white, which in general had been his to begin with. A dead-white skin, a sunken chest and stooping shoulders were the earmarks of the breed. Chinless faces, microcephalic foreheads, rabbit teeth, goggling-dead fish eyes, rickety limbs, and stunted bodies abounded . . . The women were . . . stringy-haired and limp of breast at twenty, and shrunken hags at thirty or forty. And the incidence of tuberculosis, of insanity and epilepsy, and above

all, of pellagra, the curious vitamin-deficiency disease which is
nearly peculiar to the South, was increasing.'

Men decayed but mills multiplied.

Cotton mills kept pace with advancing technology. They were
among the earliest large factories to employ electricity for driving
machinery, and in 1894 the Columbia Mills, at Columbia, South
Carolina, became the first large factory to depend entirely upon
electricity, the current being generated by the mill itself.

The use of electricity spread rapidly. The new power could be
economically delivered to any point, an asset that permitted mills
of a new design to be built. These were single-story factories of
large floor areas that did not need long lines of shafting. Mill
sites could now be selected with a view to cheap foundations
and convenient access to transportation and lighting, and the new
design minimized many of the risks of fire and accident that were
incurred in older establishments.

The rising Southern mills paralleled the rising alarm of Northern cotton manufacturers, more and more of whom predicted that
cotton manufacturing would soon be concentrated in the South.
Labor, fuel, water power were all cheaper than they were in New
England. Yet the South had no advantage in transportation
costs, and the New England mills were better organized and
benefited from marketing economies. Many businessmen concluded that neither section had a marked advantage over the
other. But the South could unquestionably produce coarse goods
more cheaply, while New England — especially the Fall River
district — could make fine goods at less cost than the South.
Southern competition affected the coarse-spinning area of New
England, and Merrimac Valley firms began to establish mills in
the South before the turn of the century.

In 1894 the Massachusetts Mills of Lowell organized a corporation with a capital of $600,000 to build a Southern mill. The
Dwight Manufacturing Company of Chicopee Falls appropriated
$500,000 to construct a mill in Alabama. In 1896 the American
Net and Twine Company of Canton, Massachusetts, built a plant
at Anniston, Alabama, and the Merrimac Company of Lowell
erected a large mill at Huntsville in the same state.

The South, weaving coarse fabrics, built a large export market in China and other parts of Asia. Then, to the distress of the North, it also turned to producing finer fabrics than it had ever made before. Before the turn of the century bleacheries and print works became common in the southern Appalachian textile districts.

When the First World War started in 1914, more than a century had passed since the opening of the first American cotton-textile mill. Britain still led the world in cotton manufacturing, with American spindles numbering about half of hers. She also dominated the export cotton-textile trade; a dominance based upon the inherited skills of her workers, abundant capital and low interest rates, worldwide banking relations, and a merchant marine that carried British goods everywhere. The United States in 1914 was second among cotton-manufacturing nations, but while Britain exported 75 per cent of her output, the United States exported only 5 per cent, and ranked fourth among cotton-goods exporters.

At home domestic producers of cotton goods fared well. Tariffs gave them virtually a monopoly of the home market since they averaged more than 40 per cent on most fabrics. The nation imported a few million dollars worth of cotton goods annually but excepted laces, embroideries, and similar specialties, it always exported more cotton goods than it imported.

The years between the two great wars of our time mark the shift of dominance in cotton-textile manufacturing from New England to the South. In the last year of the First World War New England's spindles exceeded those of the South by about four million. But at the beginning of the Second World War the South had 12 million more spindles than New England.

Today, 80 per cent of the nation's spindles, and 82 per cent of the looms, are in the South, and North Carolina is the heart of American cotton-textile industry. The nation's leader in terms of numbers of spindles in place, it is followed by South Carolina, Georgia, and Massachusetts.

Although Southern capitalists began to erect mills near the turn of the century, and are still building them, many New

England mills moved South and Northern capitalists built mills in the South to avail themselves of the region's manufacturing advantages. Chief among these were an abundance of electric power at low rates, low taxes, proximity to raw-cotton supplies, an equable year-round climate, tender treatment by local legislative bodies, and an abundance of labor at wages generally lower than those prevailing elsewhere. The assumption — real or fanciful — was that because living costs were lower in the South than in other sections of the country, Southern textile workers suffered no diminution of their real wage even if their money wage was less than that of their Northern counterparts.

A principal obstacle to the industrial South had been railroad freight-rate discrimination against it in favor of the East. In 1945 relief came. The Interstate Commerce Commission advanced 'class freight-rates' 10 per cent in the North and East, and reduced them 10 per cent in the South and West. This was highly beneficial to Southern cotton mills most of whose output went to other sections of the country or to seaports for export.

Some Southern states, such as Mississippi, had remained primarily agricultural for decade after decade. Even poorer than their sister states, they lagged far behind other sections of the Union. They suffered severe leakages of the heart as thousands of their young people left to find jobs elsewhere. But about 20 years ago they set out to lure industry by offering it compelling subsidies of many kinds. These included freedom from local taxes for a specified number of years, mill buildings erected by local capital and rented cheaply to enterprisers, and — above all — labor at wage scales lower than those of the North. The states which were offering this program attracted a large number of industrial plants, including cotton-textile mills and fabricators of cotton goods.

Perhaps the largest factor in the rise of the industrial South was its 'new men.' They began, as one observer noted, 'to substitute the research laboratory for the wailing wall.' The Old South might have regarded them as vulgar, brassy, pushing, and — not quite gentlemen. They did not hate Yankees but were eager to outwit them in business deals. They did not look backward to the War as the source of their troubles, but to the future as their hope. Able, energetic, aggressive, they built and maintained efficient cotton mills.

The South still had its magnolias. But by now they had become merely beautiful flowers indigenous to the region — no longer a symbol of its 'romance' or dreaminess.

The American textile industry, during most of its long life, has been a sorely troubled one, with a record for recurring deficits matched only by coal and wool. Operating in a country that usually moves frenziedly forward, it has been the melancholy distinction of the textile industry to go backward for years at a time. This was true of it during the period 1923–40. Its cumulative net income before taxes barely balanced its total losses and it sustained a net decline in assets upwards of $580 million. The last really profitable era in cotton textiles goes back to the early years of the century. 'Since then,' wrote *Fortune* in July 1947, 'only wars have bailed the industry out. This [cotton] is one of the world's great basic fibers, more versatile than any, which, in spite of backward development, cutthroat competition, and the inroads . . . of synthetic fabrics, still retains 70 percent of the total textile market in this country.'

During the First World War, the industry saw a 'wild expansion of capacity' that overhung it not for a year or two, but for the next two decades. It was also the victim of its method of manufacturing and selling. Mills produced mostly gray goods — the unbleached, uncolored, unfinished product of the looms. These were sold through Worth Street brokers, commission houses, and selling agents to converters, who determined the design, style, and color for the goods and sent them to finishers for bleaching, dyeing, or printing. Converters then sold the finished cloth as yard goods to wholesalers or as piece goods to garment makers.

What was the effect of this tangled pattern of manufacturing and marketing? *Fortune* tells us: 'The mills operated far from ultimate markets. Since they were as close-mouthed as they were closely held, and all stages of the industry were ruggedly independent, they operated largely blind. Inventories could start piling up on wholesalers, garment makers or converters, and before the intelligence crept back to millmen, gray goods . . . were coming out of their ears.'

During this period of cheap cotton and low wages when, says *Fortune*, 'mills generally held mill towns in vassalage,' many of them continued to produce, not in the hope of making a profit, but in the hope of covering overhead. The result was that 'Through most of the twenties and terrible thirties, with overproduction rolling up as rhythmically as tides of the sea and pounding gray-goods prices to pieces, the mills were at the mercy of . . . converters and big retail buying combines, which often dictate prices in a chronically distressed market.'

This condition led to a massacre of textile properties. In the period 1925–39, nearly one-third of the mills were closed out. So great was the distress that the abandoned spindleage equaled the total Japanese cotton-textile plant. Yet even after this gargantuan purge, idle capacity and overproduction plagued the cotton mills. The survivors were to be saved, not through their own skill or foresight, but through the circumstance of world tragedy — in the same manner that so many other men in so many other industries became rich.

A fantastic turnabout was in store for them. Business improved with the outbreak of the Second World War in 1939, becoming still better when the United States entered the war in 1941. It rose to frantic boom proportions as the war went on. Domestic consumption of cotton goods increased enormously. And mills turned out endless quantities of goods for the armed services. In the circumstances, yesterday's suicidal folly of the mills became today's saving wisdom. They cashed in handsomely on their vastly expanded capacity, and by 1942 hit an all-time high production record of 12 billion square yards of cloth.

A few years before mills had been sold on the auction block for what they would bring. Now their profits were enormous. They were so high that *The American Wool and Cotton Reporter*, a trade journal, applied to them the ugly term — 'unconscionable.' And profits continued to pile up for a while after the end of the war. For 1946 they were about 270 per cent above those of 1945. No other section of the manufacturing industry equaled this rise of earnings.

Converters, too, grew fat during the war. Their average profits jumped 950 per cent between 1939 and 1943. Noting these rich pickings, mills shouldered converters away from the trough and grabbed everything possible for themselves. They began converting their own gray goods and reduced supplies to converters. By the end of the war gray goods had almost disappeared from the open market, producing a frantic scramble to buy mills. Big converters bought to assure themselves of supplies of gray goods. Commission houses bought mills whose products they sold or entered into consolidations with them. Big mill groups purchased small mill groups. Between 1944 and 1946 there was a tremendous turnover of mill properties — 20 to 25 per cent of the total cotton-textile equipment of the country changing hands and over 290 recorded sales of cotton-mill companies. The traffic was mainly in old plants and equipment because new mills could not be built during the war and postwar costs made construction almost prohibitive. Under the pressure of heavy buying, prices shot skyward. In the depression of the 1930s, spindles had sold as low as $16. Now they brought from $60 to $125 a spindle, 20,000 spindles considered a fair-sized plant.

When this frenzied episode of the industry had been played out, many mills moved toward great and greater integration. They took over the converter's function, became their own sales agents, and often fabricated their own cloth into various forms of clothing and household articles. If a mill employs vertical integration, there can be a continuous follow-through from the cotton bale to the ultimate consumer, the mill manufacturing cloth, operating styling and merchandising divisions, and employing direct-to-the-consumer national advertising of its products. It may concentrate its efforts on a single product such as bedspreads, or may center its attention on a branded, nationally advertised line of bedsheets, towels, and similar items. The integrated organization may involve both cotton and synthetic fiber mills producing a wide range of merchandise for diverse customers.

There is no magic in integration. But integrated mills are more likely to be profitable than non-integrated mills.

The uses of technology were familiar to the great agrarian, Thomas Jefferson, but he believed that the coming of cities and factories to the nation would lead to its moral decay. On his farm, Jefferson sought a measure of self-sufficiency for his neighbors and himself by erecting a flour mill, a nail factory, and a small cotton mill that produced cloth for his slaves and homespun for sale to merchants.

The South's industrial revolution springs from technology, and as a measure of devotion to it the section has even permitted revered memorabilia of the Confederacy to be removed. In Richmond, Stonewall Jackson's stuffed horse, Old Sorrel, was taken out of the vacant Confederate Old Soldiers' Home that has become the new Virginia Institute for Scientific Research. In Camden, South Carolina, the twelve-foot, marble Confederate Monument was removed from the center of town and placed in a park to clear streets for the increased traffic from du Pont's huge orlon plant. Orlon competes with cotton grown by South Carolinians, but in its pursuit of the dollar the South no longer plays favorites.

We have repeatedly shown that the feudal prewar South did not encourage the growth of industrialism or the sciences. The postwar South was absorbed for many decades in the effort to make a bare living. Aspiring Southern-born scientists went North for training and usually found employment and spent their lives there. One result of this was that in the years preceding the Second World War the South held only 2 per cent of all United States patents, and employed about 2 per cent of all industrial research workers.

More gravely, the South lacked scientific schools; 20 years ago only six Southern institutions granted the doctor's degree in science, and few degrees were given. The region had long been aware of its need for educational facilities that would help to balance agricultural and industrial achievement. And even though agricultural experiment stations had been established at an earlier period, funds were pitifully small and as a result achievements were limited.

From a certain point of view, the South's economic collapse in the 1930s was fortunate because it set in motion a train of events that marked its industrial renaissance. This was the gift of the Roosevelt Administration and the New Deal. For, writes *Fortune*, 'Not until the New Deal's broad farm, crop, and land rehabilitation programs finally halted the long erosion of resources was the ground prepared for the seed's growth. And not to be forgotten is TVA, which, thrusting its mighty system of hydroelectric dams down the Tennessee Valley, initiating research in superphosphates, quick-freezing, farm mechanization, and regional land use, and attracting great industries to its side, probably did more than any other Agency to show the South its latent powers.'

The awakened South was stirred in 1940 by a speech entitled 'Scientific Research — The Hope of the South,' by Dr. George D. Palmer, retiring president of the Alabama Academy of Science and professor of chemistry at the University of Alabama. Five years later the Southern Research Institute was created. Now nearly 200 research organizations function in the South under the aegis of government, university, and private sponsorship.

In addition to private and university research in cotton and cotton textiles, a broad program is conducted by the United States Department of Agriculture Southern Regional Research Laboratory. Opened in New Orleans in 1941 to apply scientific research to specific Southern crops, nearly three-fourths of its work concerns cotton. Today's young Southerner who aspires to a career in textile manufacturing need not go North in search of an education. He may attend Southern textile schools that rank among the nation's best — including Clemson College, North Carolina State, the Georgia School of Technology, and Alabama Polytechnic. In terms of enrollment, Clemson is perhaps America's largest textile school. Hence the South is finally coming into step with the rest of the country in the all-important field of scientific research.

The South now leads the country in the production of cotton textiles and cotton manufactures of every kind, and the mark of its overwhelming leadership is that it processes approximately 90 per cent of all cotton consumed in the United States.

Wages of textile workers contribute importantly to the prosperity of many Southern states. In the two Carolinas, for example, about half of the workers (*nearly all of whom are women*) engaged in manufacturing are employees of textile plants. In terms of dollars, the textile payroll for a full year is approximately $1.5

billion in the four leading cotton-textile states of North Carolina, South Carolina, Georgia, and Alabama.

The great hegira of the cotton mills from New England to the South has brought the region an enormous industry, big pay-rolls, and, so to speak, an industrial-ideological split personality. A longtime producer of farm products such as cotton and tobacco that are mainly to be exported, the South had always been the proponent of low or liberal tariffs as opposed to high tariffs sought by the industrial North. Today, although the cotton farmer must still seek a large part of his market abroad, the region's cotton mills are vehemently seeking high tariffs to 'protect' their domestic sales. When the reciprocal trade program, backed by the Eisenhower Administration, was considered by Congress in 1955, it was strenuously opposed by the South's textile mills but it passed, by a narrow margin, over their shrill protests against the 'slave labor competition' of Japan and other countries. The facts of the case, however, were that:

> Most cotton cloth enjoys tariff protection only one-third below the high rates of 1930.
>
> In 1954, although the American textile industry held more than 99 per cent of the domestic market, it sold more than 6 per cent of its production abroad.
>
> In 1954 we exported eight times as much cotton cloth as we imported.
>
> Two hundred thousand of the more than one million textile workers, it is estimated, are involved to some extent in export trade.

The threat of Japanese 'slave labor' to the American cotton-goods industry was first seen in 1954 when the United States imported 17 million square yards of Japanese cotton cloth. This 'Japanese invasion' was announced in frightened tones in December 1954 by W. Ray Bell, president of the Association of Cotton Textile Merchants of New York. He said: 'The mounting inflow of goods . . . would indicate the long-dreaded Japanese invasion is on in earnest. It could well become an avalanche . . .'

Apparently it does not take much activity to make tariff

protectionists fear an invasion. *Japanese cotton-cloth imports for 1954 amounted to less than one-half a per cent of American production.*

It was also said by textile-industry lobbyists that the men's shirt industry was being destroyed by imports fabricated, of course, by 'foreign slave labor.' What was the truth? In 1954, the United States imported shirts valued at less than a million dollars ($915,836). But at the same time we exported more than six times this amount, nearly six million dollars worth ($5,881,300).

We have heretofore observed that even before the Civil War, when the South manufactured little of the cotton it grew, a politico-economic contradiction had arisen because of the conflicting interests of cotton manufacturers and cotton growers. The former sought protective tariffs to make secure their home markets. The latter sought liberal tariffs in order to foster export markets for their cotton. Thus, as we have seen, when in 1827 owners of a textile mill near Athens, Georgia, plumped for high tariffs on cotton goods, the local newspaper editor, painfully aware of the disagreement between manufacturer and grower, wrote: 'A sense of safety . . . combined with an expectation of profit have urged gentlemen to an undertaking with which their political convictions are at war . . .'

Nearly 150 years later the conflict of interest between the manufacturer and the grower was still raging and the former were able to persuade the legislatures of two Southern states to pass laws whose effect is to boycott Japanese textiles. In March 1956 South Carolina decreed that sellers of Japanese textiles, or garments made from them, must post a sign reading, 'Japanese textiles sold here.' The sign must be displayed 'in a conspicuous place upon the door' in letters 'not less than four inches high.' Alabama's legislature passed a similar bill in April 1956.

These statutes — as Tokyo has pointed out to our Department of State — violate our 1953 treaty of amity and commerce which accords to Japanese goods in the United States market treatment no less favorable than that received by exports from any other country. They, therefore, undermine the validity of the pledged word of the United States, formally given. So, too, they flout the basic tenet of United States postwar policy for the Far East: to help a friendly and politically reliable Japan to establish a sound economic system. And they obviously run counter to the interests of the American cotton farmer.

Japan is the largest single market for United States raw cotton. It is a doubly valuable market in that Japan is a large buyer of American cotton in a period of declining exports and rising surpluses. In 1955, the Japanese bought 647,000 bales, or 26 per cent of the total exported. It follows that if Japan's textile exports encounter discrimination in the United States she may reduce raw cotton imports in retaliation.

All this is of considerable importance for the future economic and political policies, not only of the South but also of the nation. As Southern mills grow in power and influence, it may be expected that they will exert their power more and more to push high tariff legislation through Congress in collaboration with Northern protectionists. If they succeed, the effects will be multifarious throughout a free world that is so dependent upon us for trade, and they may also be lethal to the hard-pressed American cotton farmer. He is looking for markets wherever he can find them, including the great markets of the world beyond our shores.

If today's Southern cotton-textile mills bear little resemblance to those of the past physically or organizationally, neither are pay scales and working conditions like the dark days when cotton-mill workers endured in the wretchedness we have hitherto observed. Child labor — once the horror and shame of the nation — disappeared long ago from the scene. The Federal Wage-Hour Law fixes a minimum hourly wage rate for workers whose products move in interstate commerce. A growing enlightenment among employers, a rising social conscience in the nation, a limited unionization of mills plus the threat of larger unionization — all these have brought about relatively high wage rates for cotton-textile workers. They are not among the country's best paid workers for the textile industry has never been a high wage-paying industry. But it has markedly improved and in the period 1939–53, cotton-mill wages rose from an approximate average of 39 cents an hour to $1.30 an hour.

The Southern textile industry is unionized to the extent of only about 10 per cent. How far unionization may ultimately extend in the Southern mills, no one knows. But a visitor would no longer see either the poverty-corroded textile workers of a former day or the hovels in which they once dragged out painful lives. Many of the textile companies support communities of workers who own their houses or rent them at reasonable rates from the companies. These houses are usually well built, trim, surrounded by flowers, trees, and vegetable gardens. Their tenants have access to schools, churches, and civic activities of a superior quality. Many of the firms maintain health, vacation, and insurance plans and paid holidays. They run cafeterias at cost, conduct athletic contests, and encourage activities beneficial to children. But many companies have divested themselves of all activities that might come under the heading of 'paternalism.'

The capital of cotton-textile America is Charlotte, North Carolina. More than 250 cotton mills function within a hundred-mile radius of the city. A decade before the Civil War, Southern leaders, as we have seen, hoped to hasten the day of more factories in their region. They especially wanted mills to weave and spin the cotton of its fields. This hope was not realized in their time. But a century later, as the visitor to Charlotte may see, it has been realized far beyond their modest expectations.

XII

The Great Turning Point

AMERICAN COTTON CULTURE has been marked by several great phases. From its eighteenth-century beginnings until 1866, cotton was produced by both slave and free labor. After 1866, slavery vanished and sharecropping flourished. But it was disappearing, too, giving way to wage systems and mechanization of farms. Always 'restless,' cotton culture spread widely in the Southeast and Southwest during the nineteenth century. In the twentieth century it progressed beyond the Rockies to the shores of the Pacific where it has become an important economic factor.

Throughout the nineteenth century, American cotton dominated world markets. But today it is confronted with the increasingly severe competition of more than 50 countries which also grow the staple. Some have produced it for centuries, others began only yesterday.

Men were growing cotton when Ecclesiastes wrote, 'There is nothing new under the sun.' The fiber was regarded for centuries as not only indispensable but also irreplaceable. Now, however, cotton growers are faced with the massive, unrelenting, ingenious competition of something new under the sun: man-made fibers. And to these have been added another serious rival in the form of paper products.

Cotton culture has not been exempt from the staggering changes of our age. Technologically, recent decades have brought marked improvement in the qualities of cotton fiber, yields per acre, and mechanization of production.

Ideologically, cotton culture has moved out of its ancient state of *laissez faire* into the novel one of state subsidy and state regulation. The grower in return for such benefits as price support (various percentages of 'parity') limits his acreage. This condition, except for a period during the Second World War when production was untrammeled, has prevailed for nearly 25 years.

Sociologically, the history of cotton production has differed from that of such crops as wheat and corn-hogs. In antebellum days these were generally produced by free white labor, but cotton culture was dominated by Negro slavery. In postbellum days, wheat and corn-hogs, primarily Middle Western products, were 'white men's crops.' Prominent among their producers were men of Teutonic and Scandinavian heritage. But the whites who produced cotton in the antebellum and postbellum South were overwhelmingly English, Irish, and Scottish in origin.

The antebellum South maintained that Negro slavery was essential to cotton culture because white men could not endure the Southern sun. Indeed it was so hot that in some parts of the cotton country — as the Mississippi Delta — it was the custom, when the day was at its hottest, to stop work for a while, not for the comfort of the Negro plowman, but to 'shade the mule.' Yet eventually whites exceeded Negroes in the cotton fields.

Cotton is unique among our field crops in that it produces both fiber and food. It is historically linked — as no other segment of our agriculture or industry — with some of our characteristic institutions. These include the plantation system and the rise and fall of slavery. And cotton culture was, of course, vitally involved with the vast tragedy of the Civil War. Cotton growing, moreover, as no other form of our agriculture or industry, affected — may even have shaped — the culture of a great region. Thus the well-known Southern romanticism was one of the psychological results of slavery and the plantation system, and slavery was conducive to the development of a patriarchal, aristocratic organization of society, excessively individualistic and passionately fond of rhetoric.

W. J. Cash remarks that in the South rhetoric became 'not only a passion' but a 'primary standard of judgment,' the '*sine qua non* of leadership,' and love of oratory was associated with 'love of politics.'

From colonial days until 1920, ours was a rural-agricultural society. The United States political system was originally created by and for an agricultural democracy, but with passing time it has been adapted to the needs of an urban-industrial society. In 1920, for the first time in the history of the nation, more people were living in towns and cities than on farms.

The South remained more agricultural than any other great region of the country, but it also began to change, and the more it became industrialized, the more its cities grew. From 1930 to 1950 Southern population in cities of 50,000 or more increased at three times the rate for the nation as a whole. Southern farm population in the single decade 1940–50 declined by more than one-fourth. Decade after decade the condition (generally ailing) of agriculture has been discussed and debated by farmers, the press, state legislatures, and Congress. The United States has never been as rich and populous as it is today. But the 'farm problem' remains perhaps the nation's greatest, most stubborn domestic question.

There are now approximately six times more people in cities and towns than on farms. Industry and finance dominate the nation's affairs. Annually, fewer farmers produce a larger fraction of the country's agricultural output. In 1930, 25 per cent of the American people lived on farms. In 1955 — 25 years later — only 13.5 per cent of the people lived on farms. And these had grown so much larger and more productive that in 1950 approximately 40 per cent of all farms accounted for 90 per cent of all farm sales. At the same time, however, farm output is becoming more and more a relatively small item in the vast American economy. It now accounts for only 4 per cent of the total national product.

In spite of this situation, both great political parties continue to woo the 'farm vote' with bridegroom fervor, and many who seek it are persuasively eloquent. Yet the antebellum plantation system produced the most articulate, as well as the most passionate, defenders of the agrarian way of life the country has ever known.

Let us now turn to some of the things that have been occurring in American cotton culture since the turn of the century.

In Enterprise, Alabama, stands a monument of a rare kind — a monument to an insect; one, moreover, that is an enemy to man. The insect so memorialized is the boll weevil. Grateful men raised the monument on the theory that the weevil, by reducing the cotton crop, raised the price of the fiber and kept many farmers from going broke.

We have noted some of the obstacles that confronted cotton farmers, but perhaps nothing has caused greater losses or compelled a more constant, costly effort than the boll weevil. Shortly after the turn of the century it dealt the cotton South a catastrophic blow. On its long march from Mexico, beginning in 1892, it settled in Southern cotton fields — 'just lookin' for a home' — in the words of the song made famous by Carl Sandburg. Less lyrically, the Department of Agriculture writes: 'The cotton plant is unusually attractive to insects and probably no other cultivated crop has as large a list of insect enemies. Among these are some of the most destructive pests in agriculture.'

When the boll weevil struck, federal entomologists went into the field. But, writes Harris Dickson in *The Story of King Cotton*, 'Some planters got mad and said, "I don't believe in spectacled professors galavanting around the country preaching calamity and scaring our Negroes. T'aint the weevil but this infernal agitation that's ruining us."

' "Huh!" Negroes commented . . . "It's jest a trick o' dese white folks to keep from givin' us niggers any grub." '

The boll weevil was no trick. In 1904, it cost Texas cotton growers $50 million and the Texas legislature offered a reward of $50,000 for a remedy that would dispose of it. Half a century later no one had claimed the reward.

The insect effected the gravest destruction, and although statistics prove it, they cannot illuminate the human misery implicit in them. In Louisiana, for example, five years after the boll weevil appeared there, the cotton crop was reduced by three-fourths. Mississippi had an average crop of approximately 1.5 million bales for the period 1904–8. But after the boll weevil struck, seven of the next ten crops were below a million bales and one was only 604,000 bales.

Georgia suffered severely. Within ten years after its appearance the boll weevil reduced the cotton crop by two-thirds. The 1930 Census reported a ten-year decline of 250,000 in Negro farm population, and a lesser decline for whites. 'The whole economy of the State,' writes H. P. Todd, 'built largely on cotton production, suffered disruption and destruction: wholesale and retail trade, gins, compresses, oil mills, banks and transportation. Doctors and lawyers lost their accounts. There were tens of thousands of foreclosures; the very basis of credit was undermined. There were bank failures and bankruptcies . . .'

In the unending struggle against this pest, the federal government, state governments, agricultural colleges, chemical companies, and plant breeders have aided the farmer to make a profitable cotton crop despite its presence. Yet it remains a latent threat to most of the cotton South. It still causes direct losses of millions of dollars annually, and the costs of fighting it run into more millions — the damage and costs rising or falling as climatic conditions, favorable or unfavorable to the boll weevil, vary from year to year.

Since American cotton was grown more for export than for domestic consumption, it was inevitably affected by foreign affairs. But on 28 June 1914, when a man few farmers had ever heard of — Archduke Ferdinand, heir to the Habsburg throne — was shot by a Serb nationalist, the incident did not evoke even a ripple of talk in the South's country stores. A month later, however, there was some talk when Austria-Hungary declared war on Serbia. Two days later there was still more talk as Russia mobilized its military forces. Men said: 'Looks like it's gonna be trouble over yonder.'

The next day — 31 July 1914 — there was trouble over here; unanticipated, unprecedented trouble. The cotton exchanges closed. The United States economy was confronted with an unforeseen war on a world scale. Frightened investors dumped stocks, bonds, and commodities. Thousands of bales of cotton that had been sold to central Europe and Russia could not be shipped and contracts were canceled. It was bad enough to be unable to sell cotton, but it was worse perhaps to be unable to ascertain what it was 'worth.' There were no official market quotations and there were to be none for four months until, on 16 November 1914, the exchanges reopened.

The 1914 crop was the largest ever harvested up to that time — approximately 16 million bales. But the cotton trade was demoralized by the sudden, severe shock to its export business. When the New York Cotton Exchange again opened its doors in mid-November, it opened them on disaster. Cotton was selling at 5.5 cents a pound. Cotton exports in the autumn of 1914 fell to less than one-fourth of those of the same season of 1913. In the presence of a sledgehammer blow to its economy, the cotton South improvised many relief plans. Perhaps the most spectacularly futile of them was the Buy-A-Bale movement. In hundreds of towns and cities cotton bales were displayed in hotel lobbies and public places bearing placards reading:

BUY-A-BALE
of
COTTON
at five cents a pound
AND
HELP THE FARMER

So tiny a remedy for so great a problem availed nothing. The important German market remained cut-off by the Allied blockade, but in 1915 the overseas cotton market saw some improvement. Yet the 1914–18 war reduced world consumption of American cotton an average of 12 per cent below consumption in the three years preceding the conflict even though there was an increase in domestic use of the fiber.

At no other time during the war did cotton acreage match the 36 million acres of 1914. In the five years preceding the war, American cotton exports averaged approximately 8.5 million bales but exports during the conflict averaged approximately six million bales, or less than three-fourths as much.

The price of cotton, however, slowly rose. Business in the United States had been poor in 1913, but as the war progressed, we sold huge quantities of materials to the Allies and began to supply their former export markets. Direct trade with Germany soon ceased because of the Allied naval blockade; however, if goods that we sold to neutrals found their way into Germany, it was not our concern. We sold to all who could pay.

When we entered the war in 1917, our already roaring business received a gigantic impetus. 'War babies' on the New York Stock Exchange rose to dizzy heights and the general boom, the rise in commodity prices, and inflation boosted cotton prices. For three years the average price was about 25 cents a pound. In 1919 it was 35 cents a pound and some especially fine growths brought more. That was the year of the South's memorable, and unprecedented, two-billion-dollar crop.

War is for many of us a moral holiday. And in the frenetic boom, millions of people went on a protracted spending spree whose emblem was the $15 silk shirt. Southerners were no exception to the general rule. But the days of easy-come-easy-go were ending. Evil times soon confronted a large part of the population, including cotton growers. For an understanding of the period, a brief glimpse at some aspects of its fiscal history may be helpful.

Some of us believe that the United States — the world's richest nation — has immemorially been a giver or a lender to others but never a debtor to foreigners. The truth is quite the opposite. Always potentially rich beyond calculation, nonetheless, as Arthur Bryant tells us in *The Age of Elegance*, 'in July, 1813, the United States, then at war with Britain, was unable to borrow as much money as more than one English nobleman could raise on his private credit.'

In 1914, a century later, Americans owed $3.4 billion more to foreigners than foreigners owed to us. We had borrowed large sums abroad to use in building this country. Foreigners were, for example, heavy investors in our railroads. In 1914, Britain was the world's leading international banker, ocean carrier, and insurer. The Dutch, too, were eminent in international banking — London and Amsterdam being the world's principal money markets. The French were, per capita, perhaps the world's wealthiest people.

This was soon to change. During the First World War the fortunes of the United States underwent an unparalleled transformation. The once debtor country emerged a net creditor with foreign states owing her government and nationals about $14 billion. At first foreigners paid for American goods with their reserves of gold and dollars and sales of their investments in American companies. When these assets were exhausted, we lent them money. In the period 1914–19 our excess of exports over imports reached the colossal sum of $15 billion.

As a debtor nation we had exported more than we imported. Chief among these exports was raw cotton. The social-economic logic of the postwar situation demanded that we should import more than we exported. Instead we embarked upon nationalism. 'BUY AMERICAN!' became the cry of most industries and newspapers. Then we raised tariffs against hardpressed foreigners who desperately needed American goods that they could get only by selling us their goods and services. Our actions flouted the basis of international trade by which men have lived since the Phoenicians traded to Cornwall for tin — namely that trade is bilateral or multilateral, and that he who would sell must buy. Ignoring this, we raised our tariffs from 1921 until in 1930 they reached their peak in the highest tariff law the country had ever enacted — the Hawley-Smoot Act. It became law just about a century after South Carolina — a prime cotton-growing state — had threatened to secede from the Union because of the 'Tariff of Abominations.'

High-tariff proponents did not worry about the huge sector of our agriculture that was bound up with foreign trade. In 1929 approximately 59 per cent of America's total crop acreage was planted to wheat, cotton, and corn; crops that were in large part meant for export. This was notably true of cotton. Before the First World War we usually exported approximately 66 per cent of our cotton crop. In the period 1926–30 we exported 59 per cent of it. At the same time most of our great farm and orchard crops were deeply involved in foreign trade which took, for example, 50 per cent of our prunes, 34 per cent of our tobacco, 54 per cent of our raisins, and 18 per cent of our wheat.

In the fall of 1932, when farmers were struggling against wholesale evictions from their lands, President Hoover spoke to them at Des Moines. He told them that the way to save American agriculture was to raise farm tariffs. 'Ninety percent of your market,' he said, 'is at home and I propose to reserve this market to the American farmer.'

This must have been news to cotton farmers. At no time had 90 per cent of their market been at home. Historically cotton had always been primarily an export crop. But even if 90 per cent of a crop is consumed domestically and the remaining 10 per cent designed for export cannot be exported, the 10 per cent may make the difference between profit and loss on the whole crop.

When Mr. Hoover spoke, wheat sold for 35 cents a bushel at Chicago and 20 cents on the farm. Suppose that some mad foreigner had then wanted to ship us wheat. Because our wheat duty was 42 cents a bushel, he would have had to give us the wheat, pay carrying charges, and add 7 cents a bushel because the wheat tariff alone was 7 cents more than its Chicago price. Yet the country was told that higher tariffs were the farmer's salvation! As for alleged menace of foreigners to our farms, in 1932 (the year of Mr. Hoover's address) we imported only 241,000 bushels of wheat and 233,000 barrels of wheat flour. At the same time we produced 24 million barrels of flour.

Consider corn. The 25 cents a bushel duty on it then equaled, or exceeded, its farm price. In 1932 we grew 2.5 billion bushels of corn; 70 per cent of the world supply. We imported 185,000 bushels; special types of flint corn for feeding poultry. If the troubled farmers who heard Mr. Hoover talking nonsense had been subscribers to the Cartesian doctrine that 'It is immoral to believe in the truth of a proposition which cannot be demonstrated,' they might have indicted him for gross immorality. He certainly could not demonstrate that the farmer was being destroyed by foreigners.

Cotton was in a bad plight. It was losing, or was in danger of losing, much of its export market. At home an ineffective buying power deprived it of an active market capable of consuming cotton that once went abroad. Everywhere in the country farm surpluses went up and prices went down. Farmers are perhaps the most stable group in American society. But nearly the whole farming community became desperate. There were strikes, mob formations, violence. Men stopped mortgage sales with shotguns. They threatened the lives of sheriffs and judges.

Farm prices of *export* crops dropped more than the prices of crops on a domestic basis, and the gulf widened between prices farmers received for their produce and prices of things they bought.

One did not need statistics for proof: the visible sufferings of people in the cotton country showed it.

Farmers needed markets. But they got — tariffs. The absurdity of this was noted by the cotton grower and cotton economist, Oscar Johnston, of Scott, Mississippi. When he was chief of the Federal Cotton Pool and Assistant Secretary of the Treasury, he said in the *Cotton Trade Journal* (International Edition, 1935): 'The major cause of the shrinkage (in cotton exports) is due to the inability of foreign consumers to obtain American exchange.'

Cotton importers tried either to buy from those who would take their goods in exchange or to find cotton substitutes. Raw cotton was Italy's principal import until after the passage of the Hawley-Smoot tariff when her imports of American cotton dropped by 51 per cent. The problem of exporting American cotton hinged upon its price relative to foreign growths, and the ability of foreigners to lay their hands on dollars. High tariffs would not help here. Nor would it avail anything to restrict cotton production. Twenty years ago Oscar Johnston wrote: 'Production control . . . cannot alone accomplish anything approaching a permanent improvement of the position of the cotton planter.'

This concept has been proved accurate by the experience of the 20 years since it was stated. So, too, wars — aside from the calamities they bring to mankind — create abnormal cotton demands which cannot permanently improve the position of producers.

When the Second World War began, a large cotton surplus lay in government warehouses. This proved to be a blessing for out of our surplus we supplied the cotton needs of ourselves and our allies, and it melted under war demands. Not only was it liquidated at a profit, but all restrictions on producing cotton were removed when we entered the war. By the mid-1950s, however, cotton production was again being severely restricted by Washington.

Let us now continue to trace the course of events that preceded the breakdown of American agriculture, its turning away from *laissez faire* to state intervention, state subsidy, and state control of the nation's great crops, including cotton.

Nationalism in one place tends to breed nationalism elsewhere, especially if one of its most ardent practitioners is the world's richest nation; the greatest producer of factory and farm products; the earth's richest, most compact market. In order to understand the resentment which the Hawley-Smoot tariff aroused overseas, and its inevitable effects on the American cotton economy, it is necessary to glance briefly at the post-World War I situation into which it was hurled.

There were many new and struggling states: Poland, Finland, Czechoslovakia, Yugoslavia, Estonia, Lithuania, Latvia. Alsace-Lorraine had been detached from Germany and handed back (or over) to France. The Saar rested in a League of Nations limbo. The Polish Corridor was something new in diplomatic arrangements of territory. New seaports, such as Gdynia, arose, and old seaports, such as Hamburg, declined. Germany suffered successive revolutions. The Austro-Hungarian empire had been dismembered. Titanic forces of unknown direction were at work throughout the vast regions of the former Russian empire. Turkey had fought a new war with Greece and become strong again. Greece dethroned its king and became a republic. Medieval Spain, affected by modern ideas and intolerable losses of men and money in futile Moroccan campaigns, exiled King Alfonso and elected a republican president. In Italy, the House of Savoy lay in the shadow of Mussolini's jutting jaw. England seized Germany's former colonies in Africa and the South Seas. She extended her sway over much of the Middle East. Syria became a French dependency. Japan emerged from the war richer and stronger than before and thirsting for more spoils of victory. China's millions were ravaged from within and without. A dictator seized Persia's throne. The Emir of Afghanistan was exiled. India seethed with revolt. Governments tumbled in Latin America.

In this postwar world there were tremendous changes of governments, shiftings of peoples and boundaries, and alterations in trade channels. There were new commercial rivalries, new technologies, and new owners of raw materials. There were huge debts, repudiations of debts, loans, abandonment of the gold standard, depreciated currencies, barter agreements, and various schemes designed to keep stumbling nations erect. Basically, however, their economic recovery depended on a revitalized export trade, and if that were strangled by tariffs, they would sink deeper into poverty and discontent.

The United States had emerged from the war unscathed and

wealthy. The world's richest, most compact market, it was also the source of materials that others desperately needed, including cotton. These materials, in the absence of gifts or loans, could be had only if the United States took foreign goods and services in payment. But when high tariffs made this impossible, foreigners had to struggle for trade in contracted markets. They felt, therefore, that the United States was wronging them by her essential withdrawal from international business at a desperate moment in their lives.

In protest they moved to bar American goods from their markets, and in England, Sir Arthur Salter said: 'The ratification of that tariff [Hawley-Smoot] was a turning point in world history.' Canada moved so effectually to exclude American goods that within ten months after the enactment of our new duties, 74 American companies were forced to open Canadian branches in order to maintain their business.

France acted in a similar manner. Our exports to her soon fell to half their former value; imports to one-fourth. Italy raised rates on American cars, the duty on a Ford, for example, rising from $350 to $815. By November 1930, all Italian agencies selling American cars had been liquidated, and Ford closed its assembly plant at Trieste. Switzerland, deeply disturbed by our new high watch duties, established a virtual boycott on American goods. Thus she increased duties on American typewriters by 400 per cent.

The United Kingdom had been our largest customer and the principal buyer of American cotton. Now she not only erected a tariff system, but also sought Commonwealth preference in trade through the Ottawa Agreements of 1932. Empire purchases were diverted from the American to the British market. In all, 61 countries, 18 of which were British dominions or possessions, either raised their duties on American goods or established some more stringent form of import restriction.

Slightly more than a century, we repeat, had passed between the 'Tariff of Abominations' and the Hawley-Smoot tariff. To the extent that foreigners now bought foreign cotton, the American cotton grower lost his export market. To the extent the tariff hurt domestic business in general, he found a smaller demand for cotton goods. And even if he still was able to export cotton through the device of loans to foreigners (or give-away programs), he could not rationally count on it as a permanent condition for prosperity. Meanwhile he could stare at a bleak fact of life. In 1870 foreigners produced 37 per cent of the world's cotton supply. By 1934 they were producing 57 per cent of the total.

As the country emerged from the First World War into peace, cotton experienced a dizzy fluctuation of price. In 1919 the return was $60 an acre, and throughout the years 1915–19, the average annual return per acre had been nearly $50. But by 1920–27, this return had fallen by almost half — to $29 an acre.

These receipts are fiscally better than the $21 average return in the eight year period preceding the First World War. But the appearance of improvement is somewhat illusory. The real income of farmers was reduced by inflation, as well as the high costs of lands that many had bought in the boom years. The cotton kingdom had expanded to majestic proportions. In the 1930s its domain embraced 40 billion acres plus millions more that were planted in crops to feed work stock. So, too, cotton had leaped the Rockies and taken ultimate roots on the shores of the Pacific.

The cotton South has annually added a huge increment to the nation's wealth. Yet as the nation moved toward the great depression of the 1930s, the South — certainly relative to other sections — seems to have been in a long continued state of depression.

The collapse of cotton prices in the 1930s was bound to bring great suffering to the cotton region because the majority of its people were attached to the land. The following figures (round numbers) indicate the percentages of its rural population in 1930:

Mississippi	83%
Arkansas	80%
South Carolina	79%
North Carolina	75%
Alabama	72%
Georgia	70%
Tennessee	66%
Oklahoma	66%
Louisiana	60%
Texas	59%

As the table shows, the rural population of the cotton states ranged between 59 and 83 per cent. But that of the Northeastern industrial and the Middle Western industrial-agricultural states ranged from 8 to 33 per cent. The differences in occupations among these areas often led to diverse and even conflicting economic interests. At the same time the South had undergone little urbanization. The Census of 1930 showed no Southern city with a population of as much as 500,000. Mississippi, a state of approximately two million residents, had no city of as many as 50,000. North Carolina, with more than three million people, had as its largest city Charlotte, with a population of 82,000.

The livelihood of most of the South's people, therefore, was bound up with agriculture, and agriculture that produced not only for the home market but also for world markets. The urban-industrial population, on the other hand, was dependent on the fortunes of the industrial market. Let us see now the position of cotton in the Southern economy in 1929, just before the nation plunged into the depression of the 1930s.

> Cotton was the principal crop on 62 per cent of the farms.
>
> Cotton was planted to 44 per cent of the available crop lands in the cotton states.
>
> Cotton and cottonseed produced 56 per cent of the total income received by farmers in the cotton states.
>
> Cotton was the most important cash crop in all of the important cotton-growing states except North Carolina and Tennessee. Even in these states it was second in value.

If cotton income is compared with the income of American farmers from all crops, the tremendous importance of cotton in the United States economy becomes strikingly apparent. In the predepression years 1924–8, the gross income for all field and orchard crops was approximately $6 billion annually. During the same period the annual value of cotton and cottonseed was more than $1.5 billion. This was one-fourth of the total value of all United States crops.

Looked at in another way, we see that in 1930 there were

6,330,000 American farms. And two million of the farms — approximately one-third of the total — grew cotton, which was the principal crop of 1.6 million farms. Considered in relation to the 360 million acres of crop lands, about one-ninth was planted to cotton. Adding the acreage devoted to work stock fodder, cotton culture involved about one-fifth of the nation's crop lands.

The cotton industry together with the rest of the country moved toward the great depression. It occupied the predominant place in Southern economy and a high place on the national level. But the South was especially tried by the depression. Its reserves were slender; its people were America's poorest. We shall now consider a few relevant statistics.

In 1922 the ten great cotton states had 22 per cent of the nation's population, 24 per cent of its land area, but only 12½ per cent of the total wealth. Their per capita wealth was $1,635. Poorest of the 48 states was Mississippi with $1,216. But the per capita wealth of the 38 states outside the cotton area was $3,313, or more than double that of the cotton states.

Ten years passed and 1932 came. How did the cotton states fare then with respect to wealth? If we note the federal income taxes paid, we shall have the answer.

North Carolina	$4,018,000
South Carolina	313,000
Georgia	1,692,000
Tennessee	1,699,000
Alabama	770,000
Mississippi	134,000
Arkansas	216,000
Louisiana	1,424,000
Oklahoma	1,204,000
Texas	5,743,000

The total is slightly over $17 million. But a large part of the payments of Louisiana, Oklahoma, and Texas derived from petroleum profits, and those of North Carolina from tobacco manufacture.

What was the condition elsewhere? The New England states alone during 1932 paid federal individual income taxes of more than $30 million, or nearly twice as much as those paid by the cotton states.

At about this time, Mr. Alfred Sloan, president of General Motors, voluntarily reduced his salary from $500,000 a year to $340,000. His cut of $160,000 was more than the federal individual taxes then paid by two million Mississippians. Their direct contribution to the Treasury was about 6 cents each!

During this period the average farmer's cash income in cotton-growing Mississippi was about $200 a year or less than 50 cents a day, and the average monthly outlay for clothing per family was $1.75. (It is generally believed that it would be difficult to clothe a family of jaybirds on this sum throughout the year, including the cold months.) In the golden days of 1929, the per capita amount spent on retail sales in the cotton states was $245. In the other states it was nearly double, or $444.

If we enter the schoolrooms of the nation, we find that in 1930 the national average wealth per school child was $10,200. In the Southern states the median was $4,900, or less than half the national average.

The cotton states were long on children and short on money for their education. Expenditures per white school child ranged from a high of $47.64 in Texas to a low of $20.83 in Arkansas. Elsewhere expenditures per school child ranged from $125.43 in California to $64.65 in New Hampshire.

In the circumstances, it was the melancholy distinction of the people of the cotton states to lead the nation in illiteracy. The rate ranged from 14.9 per cent in South Carolina to 6.8 per cent in Texas — this in contrast with the national rate of 4.3 per cent.

We have seen that the cotton grower tended to restrict himself to that one crop and to buy what he might have grown. The Federal Bureau of Economics recommended that 83 per cent of an adequate farm diet should be home grown. But poorer cotton farmers bought as much as 58 per cent of what they ate. Thousands of them existed on a diet of the infamous three Ms: meat, meal, and molasses. This condemned them to early death or misery from such diet-deficiency diseases as pellagra, rickets, and anemia. The death rate among Southern whites from malaria, typhoid, and childbirth was much higher than it was among Northerners. For Negroes it was appallingly higher. Hence the average Southerner was younger than other Americans, and South Carolina startlingly illustrated the fact. In 1930 it was the only state in the Union with half of its population under 20 years of age.

This is not to say that the South, including its cotton areas, had not progressed since the Civil War. When Olmsted made his famous antebellum journey through the South, he complained of the lack of comforts he found and the mean way in which thousands of people lived. But what if he had returned to the back country in 1930?

'Had he come again then,' writes Howard W. Odum in *An American Epoch*, 'he would have passed thousands of home and suburban places surpassing all that he had seen in the ante-bellum country . . . he would have found comfort and surcease . . . He would have found Southern wealth and resources beyond the limit of any ante-bellum dream.'

There had been marked progress in the South since 1865. But it was still corroded by a poverty more widespread than in any other section of the nation. Some understanding of this requires the repetition of an awesome fact of cotton culture. The compelling reason that had kept the South a one-crop economy was that cotton was the easiest of all commodities to turn into money. This led to the neglect of other products for home use. Thus the South of 1930, writes Odum, had 'the lowest ratio of income from livestock production, the lowest per-capita purebred livestock, the lowest production of milk and dairy products, a low ratio of pasture land, a low carrying capacity for pasture lands.' It was almost as though time had stood still since the 1870s. Poorly fed men suffered disease and fell prey to physical and mental lassitude. The soil was neglected. *In 1930 nearly half of the nation's eroded lands were in the South.* 'In many of its areas,' writes Odum, 'vast gullies and gulches, wagon wide and tree deep, spotty hillsides and great stretches of fields marred like some battlefield — each year destroyed more and more, each decade added ugliness and havoc to the landscape.'

Eroding men living on eroded lands did little to stop the soil damage. Yet they had to eat and they got something out of the

soil through extensive — and expensive — use of commercial fertilizers. The Southeast's fertilizer bills were twice those of the rest
of agricultural America.

Along with all this was a long-continued leakage from the heart
of the section. The 'seed bed of the nation,' the South often overproduced cotton and constantly overproduced children, bringing
them to life in areas that offered few opportunities for material
advancement. In 1920 the average number of children under five
years of age per thousand white mothers in the 11 former Confederate states east of the Mississippi was 724. The comparable figure
for the nation was 538.

We are accustomed to reading of the tremendous emigrations of
Europeans to this country, for example, the Irish. We are less
given to contemplating the huge Southern emigration that arose
primarily because great numbers of young Southerners could not
earn a living where they were born. Millions of 'surplus' children
left the South when grown. In the period 1900–1930 the surplus
of emigrants over immigrants was nearly 3.5 million. This was a
grave loss to the section. The South's emigrants — like emigrants
generally — tended to come from the more imaginative and bolder
part of the population. It had cost the region about $2,000 to nur-
ture each of them to maturity, and their departure represented
a money loss of billions. But the indirect loss of nearly 3.5 million
vigorous persons cannot be calculated.

Still the South's population grew because of its high white birth
rate and its even higher Negro birth rate. The surplus population
attracted industry to the South and also created the low wages
that kept much of the population from sharing in the nation's
general prosperity.

The population pressed upon the land. In the first decade of the
twentieth century there was an increase of nearly 350,000 farms
containing less than 100 acres. By 1930 almost 80 per cent of
Southern farms contained less than 100 acres. This seemed to indicate that the section was moving into an era of the widest owner-
operator relationship to the soil. What was the situation?

From 1900–1930 land prices rose. It might be accounted for in
part by population pressure, men's desire to satisfy their land hunger, the continuing existence of the notion that land possession is

synonymous with gentility, or the persistence of the belief that
next year would bring a big crop that would sell at a high price.

The period of the First World War made the dream appear to
have come true. Cotton rose in price and few men are more addicted to the illusion that 'the only way is up' than are cotton
growers. During the boom, farmers and townsmen borrowed what
they could and mortgaged what they had to buy land that they
would sell tomorrow to another borrower and mortgagor. By 1930
half the land in some of the cotton counties was mortgaged. Cotton prices had long since slumped from their war levels, but the
notion persisted that war prices were 'normal' prices and the market would return to them. Now the sons of small farmers whose
patrimony was too small for them 'owned' land. (The narcosis of
possession, through mortgages, creates the illusion of ownership.)
Yet the average value of Southern farms was less than half that of
Middle Western farms. Thousands of those which still counted
on paper as farms, moreover, were of little value because they had
been either taken over by the boll weevil or had been affected by
erosion. In 1930 there were 150 million acres of eroded lands in
the United States and at least 75 million of these were in the
South. This would partially account for the fact that the pressure
for relatively fertile lands drove their price up from $50 to $200 an
acre.

Could men meet their mortgages on land bought at such figures?
Even if we assume a relatively high price for cotton, against this
were the high costs of an inflationary period, high credit charges,
and large bills for commercial fertilizers. Thousands of farms
failed. Many former owners became sharecroppers and the figures
tell the story.

In 1880, 36.2 per cent of Southern farms were run by tenants.
In 1920, the figure was 49.6 per cent. By 1930, it was 55.5 per cent.
More than half of *all* Southern farms were in tenancy; but on cot-
ton farms the percentage was still greater — 60 per cent.

By 1930, cotton culture, usually associated in the public mind
with the Negro, was becoming more and more a white man's occupation. Rupert B. Vance estimates that in the 1930s about 5.5
million whites and slightly more than three million Negroes constituted the cotton-tenant group. White tenantry increased as

Negroes moved North or left the fields to work in Southern industry. The rural South was becoming a white man's problem, and by 1940 two-thirds of all Southern tenants were white.

As for Negro land ownership in the South, Rupert B. Vance, in *All These People*, writes: 'Whatever assistance Negroes encountered in a cotton system heavily weighted against peasant proprietorship, it seems safe to assume that economic factors offered barriers to an unpropertied group as great as those offered by racial barriers. The rise of Negro peasantry out of slavery to the ownership of 173,000 farms in the census South valued at 250 million dollars in 1940 remains . . . an outstanding fact in the history of race relations.'

Sixty-five years after Appomattox, and 125 years after the beginning of cotton culture in this country, the cotton South was an area of low incomes, low per capita wealth, low farm values, low educational attainments, and a low standard of living. Soon the weakened people of the cotton fields were to face the chilling winds of economic depression that blew over the whole country.

For a decade after the First World War we made private and governmental loans to foreigners until the situation became so grotesque that we were lending our debtors money to pay interest on loans we had made them. The while our trade policies made it difficult, if not impossible, for debtors to repay us. But our 'prosperity' continued. From 1922 until 1932 American tourists annually spent more than $500 million abroad. Our immigrant citizens sent $300 million a year to the old folks at home. These sums, plus our loans, enabled foreigners to buy American products, including cotton. In 1928 we abruptly stopped these loans. The shadows of depression, beginning in Austria, lengthened across Europe and traveled around the world. The catastrophic depression of our age had begun.

Let us pause and review the fabulous change of America's international debt situation. In 1914, Americans owed $3.4 billion more to foreigners than foreigners owed to them. But in 1930, foreigners owed Americans (and their government) $8.8 billion more than the foreign debts of Americans.

If we turn back to the cotton fields, we see that for some time after the First World War cotton production could not be significantly increased because of boll weevil ravages. In 1929, they were estimated to have reduced the crop by 30 per cent. But while many Old South areas lost acreages there were large additional plantings in Oklahoma and Texas and cotton culture was extended to semi-arid, boll weevil-free Western sections. In the period 1921–6 Texas brought 7 million additional cotton acres into cultivation and the nation's total cotton acreage increased from 30 million to 46 million.

Foreigners, too, were growing more cotton in the Orient and South America. American cotton farmers watched the rise of new cotton regions and increased production in the older regions. They also watched the rise of an even more potent rival as rayon production increased from 33 million pounds in 1920 to 458 million pounds in 1930.

Before dealing with changing attitudes on the part of federal government and farmers that led to the abandonment of *laissez faire* by growers of the nation's great crops in return for something approaching 'security,' it is necessary to show the times in perspective.

Perhaps the greatest of the economic maladjustments of the 1920s was the unstable nature of international economics. They especially affected cotton because of its importance as an export crop. American loans tided western Europe over a number of post-war years, and her recovery in the period 1925–30 was a large element in American prosperity. Yet Europe's financial dependence upon the United States remained. Hence when we stopped our loans, her new-found prosperity collapsed.

American farmers had not shared in the general postwar prosperity. On the contrary, the long agricultural depression that began in 1920 had impoverished some of them and compelled others to operate unprofitably for a decade. As farm incomes and farm values fell, great groups of people could buy little and a bad situation was made worse by the widespread failure of country banks. Even conservative Republican leaders were alarmed by agriculture's plight, the more so as Middle Western farm states carried their battle into the 1928 Republican National Convention and threatened rebellion against the domination of the party by 'industry and finance.' They were not successful. But Herbert Hoover entered the White House committed to 'do something' about the farm problem.

The Hoover Administration, before the depression of the 1930s affected everyone, realized that agriculture had long been in a depression of its own, and in April 1929, Congress approved one of its great farm relief measures — the Agricultural Marketing Act. This created the Federal Farm Board with a revolving fund of $500 million to be lent to farm-marketing co-operatives and builders of warehouses. The money was also to be used to hold farm products off the market in the event of price decline, for the Board was empowered to *establish corporations to stabilize farm prices through direct market intervention.*

This marked a sharp break with the past. The farmer had been the very symbol of American individualism, the independent-as-a-hog-on-ice-American. He had lived by the great pioneer doctrine of 'Hoe your own row.' Certainly he would not have been beholden to anybody, including the 'guvment.' So, too, men had felt it was somehow wicked to raise prices by controlling production because that interfered with 'God's law of supply and demand.' The farmer had believed in the Lord and in himself and this had been the nation's faith. Once, when Congress appropriated $10,000 for the relief of Western farmers whose crops had been destroyed by storms, President Grover Cleveland, a Democrat, vetoed it. He told Congress it was the duty of farmers to support the government, not the duty of the government to support farmers. The veto stuck.

The Hoover Administration embarked upon an unprecedented program to stabilize farm prices and support the farmer. From 1929 to 1931 the Farm Board organized producers of the great crops — including cotton — into national co-operatives and established corporations to stabilize farm prices through large-scale market operations. By lending to co-operatives and buying great quantities of cotton and wheat, the Board held domestic prices slightly above the world price level until the summer of 1931. But as Europe's purchases of American farm products dried up, prices fell heavily. In 1932 cotton sold for about one-third of its 1929 price.

The Farm Board got down on its bureaucratic knees and begged farmers to reduce their output: 'Grow less, get more.' This availed nothing. Since the Board did not have the power to compel or the eloquence to persuade, output increased and prices continued to fall. In 1929 the United States had produced 15 million bales of cotton which, added to 11 million foreign-grown bales, depressed further an already depressed market. But the worst was yet to come. Hellbent to grow cotton, farmers ignored the Farm Board's warnings. In 1931 they planted cotton to the ditchbanks. Their misdirected energy brought a dubious blessing in the form of more than 17 million bales of cotton. Now there was an awesome glut of cotton in the world: 39 million bales. But annual world consumption was only 23 million bales.

The sequel to the farmers' bullheadedness, indiscipline, or passion for fruition — call it what you will — was written in the impassive numerals of cotton-exchange tickers. Cotton stood at five cents a pound, or the price of a bottle of Coca-Cola.

The cotton economy was particularly vulnerable to the price collapse, not only because it had long been on 'short rations,' but also for a reason stated by *The Report of the President's Committee on Farm Tenancy* (1937): 'Highly commercialized types of farming . . . depend for their very existence on a balanced and stabilized set of price relationships. When prices drop while operating costs remain constant, or decline very little, the consequences are dwindling savings, declining equities and finally foreclosure sales.' This echoed the ancient pleas of Southern leaders who vainly urged diversification on cotton growers; the economic virtues of 'living at home.' Much of the sense of the *Report* was put more trenchantly and picturesquely by a rural Negro preacher. He told his congregation of field hands, 'If you don't git out in the blackberry bushes and scratch yo' foots and put up some preserves, you ain't gwine have much t'eat this winter.'

Desperate conditions demand desperate remedies. In 1931 the Cotton Corporation proposed a radical medicine for the ills of overproduction, a remedy unprecedented in the history of American agriculture. *Every third row of growing cotton should be 'plowed under.'* This nostrum of the Hoover Administration was rejected. But later, as we shall see, it was adopted by the Roosevelt Administration.

In 1932 the Farm Board, despairing of helping the farmer by getting the farmer to help himself through voluntarily reducing his output, urged Congress to establish a system for regulating acreage and production, the alternative being continued agricultural bankruptcy. Again the Board was rebuffed. But Congress — departing from the past — indulged in some patchwork relief. It released 85 million bushels of wheat to feed the unemployed, and 500,000 bales of cotton to be made into clothing for the unemployed.

By the summer of 1932, however, the Farm Board had lost $354 million, mostly in wheat and cotton, and admitted that it could not do much about the farm problem. Its policy had been to buy surpluses of 'overproduced' crops in order to sustain prices until things should again be 'normal.' But what if conditions were such that American agriculture was not to become 'normal' during the foreseeable future? A number of factors made a quick return to normality unlikely.

Agriculture ever since the First World War had produced far more than could be sold profitably at home and abroad. The reason for this was clear. New agricultural areas were being opened up in various parts of the world. The transition of the United States from a debtor to a creditor country made it difficult for foreigners to buy here; a difficulty increased by our high tariffs. Changing consumer habits were also affecting many segments of our agriculture. The result was that the government piled up mountains of wheat and cotton and prices continued to drop. The Hawley-Smoot tariff, which Richard Hofstadter calls 'a virtual declaration of war on the rest of the world,' was Hoover's attempt to help the farmer, but it proved futile. Industrial lobbies saw to it that while the Act provided about 75 increases for farm products, it contained 925 increases for manufactures.

Then came the crash. National income fell from $81 billion in 1929 to $41 billion in 1932. Five thousand banks closed. Nine million savings accounts were wiped out. The condition of the country — potentially rich beyond calculation — illuminated Carlyle's phrase, 'poverty in the midst of plenty.' As for farmers, 1932 was probably the darkest year in their history. The cotton South faced definitive disaster as many banks closed and mortgages in great numbers were foreclosed. Some farmers abandoned their lands, or left them to be tilled by tenants. Others flocked to towns searching for jobs that did not exist. Thousands of tenants and sharecroppers wandered aimless and directionless on the cold crust of a cold earth. The planted cotton acreage declined by 11 million acres from the 1929 plantings.

In January 1932, Congress set up the Reconstruction Finance Corporation to lend $2 billion to banks, insurance companies, railroads, agricultural credit organizations, and other enterprises. By July 1932, President Hoover accepted a relief bill of $2,122,000,000 of which $1.8 billion could be lent to states and municipalities for relief and public works, with the remainder earmarked for federal construction.

Mr. Hoover had a somewhat peculiar attitude about relief. After the 1930 drought he approved a Congressional appropriation of $45 million to save the livestock of Arkansas farmers. But he opposed an appropriation of $25 million to feed the farmers, insisting that the Red Cross feed them. But when Congress appropriated $20 million for this purpose, it sought to satisfy the President's scruples by stipulating that the money should go as a loan rather than a gift. The President said that for the government to *give* money for relief 'would have injured the spiritual responses of the American people . . . We are dealing with the intangibles of life and ideals.' Then he went on to say, 'A voluntary deed is infinitely more precious to our national ideals and spirit than a thousandfold poured from the Treasury.'

Commenting upon this, Richard Hofstadter in *The American Political Tradition,* says: 'Even for a people brought up in the same folklore, it was becoming hard to understand the Hoover *mystique.* Hoover had never been so solicitous about the "spiritual responses" of the businessmen who had been beneficiaries of federal subsidies or of Secretary Mellon's handsome tax refunds. And the idea that money given by the federal government would demoralize reliefers, while money given by their neighbors or the Red Cross or local governments would not, seemed too fanciful to command respect . . .'

On 4 March 1933 began the New Deal and the age of Franklin D. Roosevelt. As the new President was being inaugurated, the nation lay prostrate in a state of economic collapse, benumbed with somber forebodings of the morrow. The country's economic system could not function with the banks of 47 states either closed or doing business under severe restrictions.

'So desperate was the crisis on March 4, 1933,' writes Arthur S. Link in *American Epoch*, 'and so frightened were congressmen and the people that Roosevelt possessed a power unprecedented in American peacetime history. Had he harbored imperial ambitions, he probably could have obtained dictatorial powers from Congress . . .'

Men of all classes, feeling their old world crash about them, knew that change — even sweeping change — had to come. They welcomed and gave themselves to it and thanked God and Franklin D. Roosevelt. Such was the spirit of the times.

During the Presidential campaign of 1932, Roosevelt said to Edward O'Neal, president of the American Farm Bureau Federation: 'One of the first things I am going to do is take steps to restore farm prices. I am going to call farmers' leaders together, lock them in a room, and tell them not to come out until they have agreed on a plan.' Immediately after his inauguration Roosevelt called the promised meeting of farmers' organizations, against a background of past, present, and promised future violence. By the spring of 1933 most American farmers were despairing or rebellious, and nowhere was agrarian discontent as dangerous as in the Middle West. There the Farm Holiday Association had been organized to persuade farmers to keep their products off the market until prices equaled cost of production. In 1932 mobs of farmers tried to prevent food from entering Sioux City and Des Moines. In March 1933, representatives from most of the Middle Western and Plains states met in a national convention of the Farm Holiday Association in Des Moines. They threatened to call a nationwide strike if the Roosevelt Administration did not meet its demands by 3 May 1933.

Meanwhile, farmers by direct action, or through state legislatures, sought to keep from losing their lands at forced sales. The Minnesota and North Dakota legislatures forbade forced sales of farm properties. Vigilantes threatened to shoot bank or insurance agents. They went in groups to foreclosure sales and bought back properties for nominal sums. The most violent outbreak oc-

curred at Le Mars, Iowa, on 27 April 1933. Some 600 enraged farmers dragged a foreclosing judge from his bench and beat him into
insensibility.

In this crisis involving what is usually the most stable element
of our community, the Roosevelt Administration moved quickly
in 1933 to save the farmers and remove the danger of violent rebellion. Cotton farmers were, of course, beneficiaries of the program.
Eventually it included measures for credit and debt adjustment,
crop control, soil conservation, parity payments, rehabilitation of
farm families through loans and education, encouragement of subsistence farming, aid to farm co-operatives, group medical care,
and aid for tenants who were buying homes. Experience proved
these measures to be of varying utility.

On 6 March 1933, the new Secretary of Agriculture, Henry A.
Wallace, began a series of conferences with farm leaders that resulted in the Agricultural Adjustment Act passed on 10 May 1933.
Known as the 'Triple A,' it was the most far-reaching agricultural
legislation in the history of the country. Its objective was clearly
announced in the language of the Act: to establish and maintain
such a balance between the production and consumption of agricultural commodities that farm income would have the same relative purchasing power that it had enjoyed during the period 1909–
14. In order to achieve so-called 'parity' prices, the act provided
for the 'adjusted reduction' of several crops, including cotton. The
farmer who made an agreement with the government to reduce
cotton surpluses, thereby boosting cotton's price, was to get 'benefit payments' on his restricted allotment. He would, that is, be
paid for *not* growing cotton. Large growers signed first; then smaller
farmers joined the fold. But there were many nonconformists and
many who held back because they were illiterate. Federal agents
were sent out to convert them to the true faith.

The Administration had hardly set back and caught its breath
when it received bad news. Cotton farmers were on another production spree. In the summer of 1933 they expected to gather 16
million bales from their planting of 40 million acres. In despera-
tion the Roosevelt Administration proceeded to do what the
Hoover Administration had not been permitted to do: plow under
much of the 'excess' acreage.

Hastily, 22,000 agents of the Department of Agriculture, mostly voluntary missionaries preaching the strange gospel of scarcity as the road to economic salvation, took to the field. Farmers agreed to plow up about one-fourth of their growing cotton crop in return for payment to them by the government of $6 to $20 an acre. And approximately 10 million acres were plowed under.

Many pious people interpreted the act of destroying cotton as being 'agin God.' In some places mules balked when, contrary to the teachings of a lifetime, they were compelled to destroy cotton instead of cultivating it. At least one man killed himself because of the plow-up decree. A *New York Times* report from Greenville, South Carolina, said: 'Rather than plow up three acres of cotton he had cultivated, R. B. Medlock, tenant farmer . . . shot and killed himself today . . . He had complained bitterly for several days over the plow-up order . . . Another tenant will plow up the cotton.'

Farmers plowed up the crop with one hand, and built up the remainder with the other. They fertilized the crop so heavily that 13,047,000 bales were produced in 1933 compared to 13,002,000 bales in 1932.

Farmers, however, complained that the Triple A did not sufficiently meet their needs and in the autumn of 1933 the Administration announced that it would grant loans to cotton growers. Loans of approximately 10 cents a pound on warehoused 1933 cotton were offered, and about $120 million was lent on 2.3 million bales. These advances were made only on condition that borrowers promised to sign Triple A production-control contracts in 1934 and 1935. Under this plan the farmer could not lose anything and might gain much. If the price of his pledged cotton fell below the loan rate, he could let the government take the cotton for the loan. But if the price rose above the loan level, he could pay his loan, retrieve his cotton, and sell it in a favorable market. The effect of this was that Washington *guaranteed* farmers higher prices for cotton than could be obtained in ordinary markets, and exacted of them one safeguard by which it could control production to some extent.

Acreage reduction did not inevitably mean a corresponding crop reduction. Critics argued that farmers would increase production by intensively cultivating acreages left to them, putting their best lands into cotton and extensively using fertilizers, and 'non-co-operators' would expand their cotton acreages. Production esti-mates might be upset by favorable weather during the crop season. So the government moved toward coercion under the Bankhead Cotton Control Act. Effective during 1934–5, it permitted the Triple A to assign marketing quotas to cotton growers, and heavy penalties were levied on cotton ginned in excess of each farm's quota.

The Triple A and Bankhead Act sharply reduced cotton produc-tion. In the period 1933–5, it is estimated that the crop was smaller by 10 to 13 million bales than it would have been without controls. Even though cotton acreage was cut by one-third, had not controls and price supports been in effect the price of cotton would not have risen much above the depression level.

In 1936 the Supreme Court 'outlawed' the Triple A. Federal payments to farmers for reducing acreage were barred. The govern-ment now sought to compensate them by other means, notably through payments for soil conservation and 'parity' — the ratio be-tween the purchasing power of the net income of farm persons and that of the net income of non-farm persons that prevailed more than two decades before: August 1909 – July 1914.

'Parity income' became the goal of the government's farm policy nearly 20 years ago and continuing through the Roosevelt and Truman Administrations it remains, with some changes, a policy of the Eisenhower Administration. Under parity, Washington could make cash payments to farmers who shifted acreage from soil-depleting crops — among them, cotton — to soil-building crops, chiefly legumes and pasture, and who would practice other soil conservation measures. The aim was to lower production of the principal crops — including cotton — to raise farm income, and to conserve the soil. But Washington's farm planners were soon to be confounded by events.

In 1937, farmers, stimulated by relatively good cotton prices, increased plantings. They used more efficient machinery, better insect control methods, and better seed than ever before. The re-sult was an explosion of cotton: 19 million bales. It was the largest crop in the nation's history.

Cotton was giving Washington more trouble than any other

of the country's great crops. By 1938 the American carry-over had reached the tremendous total of 14 million bales. A loan of 8.3 cents a pound on 1938 cotton brought about 4.5 million bales — more than one-third of the relatively short crop of that year — into government storage. Loans had helped farmers. But what was their long-run effect?

In 1938 the United States no longer dominated the world cotton trade. Foreigners were growing more and more cotton. They bought our best farm machinery. They hired our cotton experts. Americans — including Anderson, Clayton Company, the world's greatest cotton firm — acquired large stakes in foreign cotton production. Our loan policy stimulated foreign cotton growers to greater efforts because it notified them that they might take much of the market by selling cotton slightly under our loan rate. The gold price of cotton on world markets fell to record lows, but American cottons were offered at higher prices than foreign cottons. In 1938–9 only 3.4 million bales were exported from the United States; the smallest movement of American cotton in 60 years.

Apropos of our loan policy, Mr. Henry Wallace, Secretary of Agriculture, said: 'It held the price of American cotton above its normal relation to the price of foreign growths, and thereby gave foreign growths a price advantage.' Or, as cotton men said, 'It held an umbrella over foreign producers.'

But if there had been no loan policy cotton prices might have been depressed to the levels of 1931 and 1932 with immense distress to farmers, widespread dispossessions, disaster to the Southern economy, and a great disturbance to the national economy.

In June 1939, the government held 11 million bales of cotton. Anxious to reduce this colossal supply, it announced a bounty of $7.50 a bale on new crop exports. But the way of planners is often hard. Just when they had their program ready, it collided with another plan: Hitler marched into Poland and the Second World War began.

Cotton boomed. The war was, we said, no business of ours. Yet it was good for business. It gave a tremendous impetus to cotton exports, and in 1939–40 we exported over six million bales, or almost double the exports of the preceding year. By trading 600,-

ooo bales of government-owned cotton for 85,000 tons of British-owned rubber, Washington reduced its holdings as of 1 June 1939 by about 6 per cent, and further reductions were made as domestic business conditions improved and more cotton was consumed.

Soon the country was to be faced with the problem of not how to dispose of surplus cotton, but of how to produce enough cotton to satisfy insatiable wartime demands.

When the United States entered the Second World War, controls went out of the window. It was patriotic to grow as much cotton as possible, and farmers did so within the limitations imposed by shortages of manpower and machines. Production for the years 1942–4 was between 11 million and 12 million bales. But for the years 1945–6 the crop fell to approximately 8.5 million to nine million bales. An immense pent-up demand for cotton goods readily consumed these postwar crops.

The production potential of American cotton farms is high. After the Second World War men and machines were available to farmers and they were subject to no controls. Cotton production forged ahead. By 1953 the crop was nearly 16.5 million bales, there was a carry-over of 5.5 million bales, and the cotton economy was rapidly reverting to its chronic condition of burdensome surpluses. And since 'all that changes is the same,' controls came back. Crops produced since 1954 have been grown on government-restricted acreages.

The acreage had been dropping since 1955, but in 1955 it just about equaled the acreage of 1909. And too 1955 was a fabulous boom year for the American economy. A huge and growing population bought more goods than any group of people had ever bought within a comparable period. In the midst of the boom, however, the cotton economy was producing, not for the United States of 1955, but for the United States of nearly 50 years ago. Yet even so, its future was dark.

Federal controllers slashed back the cotton acreage from a 1951 high of 28 million acres to 17 million acres in 1955. But the 1955 crop of approximately 12.5 million bales was only barely below the 12.9 million average for the 1944–53 decade that piled up the government's big surplus. Even as the government cut back the acres, better farming stepped up the yield per acre. The average yield in prewar 1935-9 was only 224 pounds an acre. In 1944-53 the average moved up to 279 pounds. In 1955 it was indicated at a never-before-attained 367 pounds.

Surplus cotton from past crops totaled 11.1 million bales in July 1955 — the greatest pile in ten years — and it is likely that the 1955 crop will add several hundred thousand bales to this white mountain.

In 1955, therefore, men still debated the values of nostrums to solve the cotton problem, but they agreed upon only one thing: cotton was a problem. More than 150 years had passed since the invention of the cotton gin. Cotton had been a 'problem' to those concerned with it during most of those years. Yet this is not because the art of cotton agriculture has failed to progress.

Today's cotton growers are generally more skillful than their predecessors. Many are college-trained. All are beneficiaries of modern technology. Thus, for one thing, today's cotton is superior to the cotton of even a decade ago in fiber length and fiber strength.

Twenty-five years ago men planted more than 500 varieties of cotton. Now ten varieties account for 89 per cent of the crop with three-fourths of it planted to four of these ten. This is no botanical whim on the farmer's part. Crop uniformity is profitable. It enables spinners to buy large quantities of even-running qualities of fiber. While improving the quality of cotton, farmers have so greatly increased the yield per acre that it is now almost double that of the long period 1870-1930.

Today's farmer no longer has to sell his cotton for what it may bring, in order to pay his debts. He may put it into a government loan and retrieve or abandon it as conditions dictate, certain that although he may gain by the loan, he cannot lose by it.

Every day the number of potential cotton consumers in the United States and the world increases as populations grow. In 1955 there were more than twice as many Americans as there were in 1900. And they could buy, within reason, almost anything they wanted, for the national income in 1955 was nearly five times greater than it had been in 1929. Nor is this all. Cotton remains the most extraordinary of fibers in versatility, durability, washability, cheapness, and so forth.

It would seem, then, that American cotton farmers ought to be among the most contented of men — efficient, productive, their financing costs reasonably low, the government loan at their disposal, supported by parity, and with an ever increasing group of potential consumers to buy, in myriad forms, the extraordinary fiber they grow. Yet though living in a fabulously expanding national economy, they are operating in a constantly shrinking cotton economy. In the summer of 1955, Mr. Lamar Fleming, Jr., chairman of Anderson, Clayton Company, told *The Wall Street Journal*: 'We are in a very bad fix, and we have to find a way out that will really get us out.'

Let us examine some of the factors that caused the farmer's 'very bad fix.'

Technology made the cotton grower more productive than he had ever been. But it also brought him the remorseless competition of synthetic fibers, a colossal industry that for the most part came into being only yesterday. During the First World War when the United States could not get German supplies, American manufacturers began large-scale production of organic chemicals, dyestuffs, and so forth. The industry, starred by such world famous names as du Pont, grew at dizzy speed. By 1950 it had accomplished the tremendous feat of displacing automotive manufacture as the country's premier industry. Then it went on to become a 'great, yeasty force at the center of the economy,' accounting for approximately one-fifth of the total national product.

In December 1939, the du Pont Company proclaimed the coming of a new chemical age in the name of nylon, a synthetic yarn derived from coal, air, and water. 'The real importance of nylon,' said *Rayon and Synthetic Textiles*, 'is that for the first time man had gone back to the elements and created a molecule that was meant to be a fiber. For the first time man had quit trying to imitate a worm, a plant or a tree and had struck out

. . . to create a fiber that was meant to be a stocking instead of a cocoon. For the first time man was free from the capriciousness of animal and vegetable materials for his textiles.'

The creation of synthetic fibers seems accompanied by the wizard's touch since some of them are partially drawn literally 'from the air.' Yet this is workaday magic having to do with man's increasing ability to convert the resources of nature to his own uses and thereby make his living more comfortable. For thousands of years man had relied upon animal or vegetable raw materials for fibers from which to fashion clothing: skins, wool, linen, silk, mohair, cotton, the coconut. But ever since he has used chemistry he has dreamed of creating clothing fibers from the basic elements. A few strangely wonderful things did emerge from these dreams — medieval armor, cloth of silver, cloth of gold, and Cinderella's slipper — but their rarity and intricacy of fashioning kept them severely limited.

It was not until the year 1884 that chemists began to realize their dream. A French scientist, Count Hilaire de Chardonnet, invented rayon. Some 25 years passed before commercial production of rayon began in the United States. Once begun, however, rayon consumption increased substantially year by year. The while there also came about the invention and production of many other synthetic fibers such as Nylon, Orlon, Dynel, Vicara, Acrilan, and so forth. So far as cotton farmers are concerned, the effect of all this may be expressed in these terms: the total United States synthetic fiber production in 1955 amounted to the output of about 5.5 million acres of cotton, when the synthetic poundage is translated into terms of cotton bales.

The largest single victory of synthetic fibers has been in the huge, ever-expanding field of automobile tires. Once tire 'cords' were made exclusively of cotton yarns. Now they are made almost exclusively of rayon and nylon yarns. This means an annual loss to farmers of a market of more than a million bales of cotton, or about $150 million. Tire makers changed to synthetic fibers because they were either better suited or cheaper than cotton, or a combination of these factors. It follows, therefore, that cotton might recapture the lost tire market if it were made superior or priced lower than synthetics — or both.

To accomplish this cotton must overcome two obstacles, neither of which is any larger than Texas. If cotton is to be made superior to synthetics, cotton growers must have at their disposal a research apparatus superior to that of the giant chemical companies. This is unlikely to occur for the cotton industry cannot command the huge sums that are at the disposal of the chemical industry; a group whose massed billions make the sums available to the cotton industry seem only nickels and dimes.

As for cotton competing in price with synthetics, cotton's price could be sharply lowered only if farmers were content to produce cotton in unlimited quantities and, abandoning government price props, let it seek its own price level in the market. Such a procedure might bankrupt thousands of farmers, and it is unlikely that cotton growers will adopt it during the foreseeable future.

In consumer's markets, textile makers say that 80 per cent of rayon sales flow from rayon's lower-than-cotton prices. This point of view finds partial confirmation in a statement by T. V. Houser, chairman of Sears, Roebuck and Company, the world's largest merchandising company. In April 1955, he told the annual meeting of the American Cotton Manufacturers Institute that the relatively high price of cotton kept cotton goods from selling in greater volume. If cotton were reduced, he said, by 10 cents a pound, typical cotton garments for men and women would be reduced at retail by 5 to 10 per cent, and articles such as sheets and towels would be 15 per cent lower.

American cotton, as we have repeatedly noted, is both a domestic and export commodity. Let us consider the Food and Agriculture Organization of the United Nations for a world view. In 1955, FAO reported that although the consumption of apparel fibers doubled between 1900 and 1948, the greatest increase was in the consumption of man-made fibers. FAO also makes a number of broad observations about synthetic fibers:

> There is a fairly consistent tendency for them to assume greater importance in industry and to invade an increasing number of markets.
>
> Newer types of synthetics are still gaining ground over natural fibers.

Competition between synthetic and natural fibers will become greater as time passes.

In 1955, the United States Department of Agriculture dipped into its ocean of statistics and brought up the following conclusions:

> As usual during wartime, cotton consumption increased sharply during the Second World War over the 1935-9 (prewar) period.
>
> In the postwar period cotton consumption has declined rather steadily, and consumption of synthetics has tended to increase. The result was unhappy. In 1954 cotton consumption was down to its 1935-9 level, and below the postwar level of 1949.
>
> Synthetics had only 10 per cent of the market in 1939.
>
> But in 1954 they accounted for 25 per cent of United States fiber consumption.

Longer term trends favor continuing increase of synthetic fibers consumption. Over the years, annual consumption of textile fibers has grown at the rate of about one-half pound per capita. But the bulk of the growth in the past quarter century has been in the man-made fibers. Compared with the late 1920s average annual consumption of cotton in the last three years has stood virtually unchanged at 23 pounds per capita. But consumption of synthetic fibers has increased from one pound per capita 25 years ago to more than eight pounds today.

Let us consider, in this context of growth, the spectacularly successful synthetic fiber called rayon staple. It is successful because its applications appear to be endless. Woven alone or in combination with other fibers, it is used in such items as men's work clothes, sport shirts, summer suits and slacks, women's skirts and blouses, children's wear, blankets and sheets, curtains and draperies. Blended with thermoplastic fibers, it is heated and melted into hundreds of non-woven fabrics including diapers, handkerchiefs, napkins, towels, vacuum cleaner bags, casket linings, filters, grain and fertilizer bags.

Cheaper than wool, more luxurious and durable than cotton, rayon staple is making great progress in the large rug market. In 1953, carpet makers used three times as much cotton as rayon staple. But in 1954, cotton's share of the rug market dropped to half that of rayon staple.

It has been called the most gregarious of all textile fibers. Strong and resilient, it is capable of accepting and retaining the widest variety of finishes, and it also takes dyes in colors ranging from pastels to the deepest, richest shades of the spectrum, and it blends easily with other fibers, natural or synthetic. For these reasons United States production of rayon staple hit a record 312 million pounds in 1954. This was an increase of 24 per cent over the 1953 figure.

Since American cotton is heavily dependent for its prosperity upon exports, any competition with it that restricts exports affects the farmer. But here again, cotton encounters the competition of synthetic fibers abroad. A few statistics illuminate the situation. In 1949, foreign production of synthetic fibers reached the equivalent of 4 million bales of cotton, this within three years of the ending of the Second World War when many foreign producers had not yet hit a steady production stride. But in 1954 — just five years later — the production had doubled, reaching the equivalent of 8 million bales of cotton.

What does this mean in terms of cotton acreage? It means that an additional 23 million acres of cotton planted outside the United States would have been required to produce the equivalent of the 1954 foreign output of rayon, cotton's most direct competitor among synthetic fibers.

All this relates to the past. What of the future? Let us turn to the authoritative publication of the Twentieth Century Fund, *America's Needs and Resources, a New Survey*, by Frederick Dewhurst and Associates, published in 1955. Here we are told: 'What the future will bring is anybody's guess, but it seems certain that the use of the newer synthetics in fabrics of all kinds will expand greatly. The President's Materials Policy Commission, reporting in June 1952, predicted a 1950–60 production growth for:

Nylon   from 100 million pounds to 300 million
Orlon   "   6.5   "   "   " 125   "
Dynel   "   5   "   "   " 100   "
Acrilan   " none   " 100   "
Dacron negligible amounts   " 150   "

If these estimates should prove accurate, 1960 will see the consumption of 825 million pounds of 'miracle fibers' alone, and although all of them are not directly competitive with cotton in actual and potential uses, there is little doubt that they adversely affect cotton consumption. Cotton still accounts for nearly three-fourths of all domestic fiber consumption, yet it must run hard just to remain in the same place.

'It is true,' Senator James Eastland of Mississippi, a large-scale cotton farmer, said in 1955, 'that domestic consumption of raw cotton has not declined appreciably, but that is only part of the story. Cotton has not held onto its share of the increase in total fiber consumption. It has lost some very important markets to synthetics and others to paper, jute and plastics . . .'

Then he spelled this out: 'Per capita consumption of all fibers,' he said, 'increased about 10 pounds from the average of the five pre-war years to the past four years. Cotton got less than one-third of the increase . . . *The per capita consumption of cotton went up about one-eighth while rayon and acetate consumption was more than two times greater.* If the rate of rayon increase could have been held to just one-half of what it actually was, domestic cotton consumption would be a million bales greater today.'

The cotton-growing Senator concluded sadly: '*In 1954,*' he said, '*per capita consumption of cotton in the United States declined nine percent. It is the smallest per capita consumption since 1938 . . . But last year's (1954) production of rayon staple fiber, priced 5 to 8 cents a pound less than cotton on the basis of useable fiber, increased more than 20 percent over the previous year.*' (my italics)

It is therefore obvious that if per capita cotton consumption had kept pace with the expanding domestic population alone, large additional plantings of cotton would have been needed to supply the demand.

What of future domestic consumption of cotton?

Projections made by *America's Needs and Resources* indicate little future change in the domestic demand for cotton. Compared with a consumption per capita of 30 pounds in 1948, a projection of cotton consumption to 1960 — more than a decade later — would show only a moderate increase to 32 pounds. But the same authority estimates that the consumption of synthetic fibers might increase to 14 pounds per capita by 1960, compared with 9.7 pounds in 1950.

Cotton suffers from the sharp competition of paper as well as synthetic fibers, but before discussing that phase, let us add a note about technology. Technology is obviously the nation's primary resource, for potential resources such as coal, oil, iron, and timber become actual only when technology converts them to the uses of men.

Technology consists of accumulated knowledge, techniques, and skills and their applications that create useful goods and services. Its efficiency may be judged by the living standard achieved and, since the United States has the world's highest living standard, we clearly have a skillful technology.

The paper industry is one of the principal beneficiaries of technology, using it lavishly. First, giants of the industry, such as International Paper Company, annually spend millions for research. Second, more than a hundred companies support the Institute of Paper Chemistry, and because of research new paper products are constantly coming on the market. The over-all result has been spectacular: per capita paper consumption, increasing at a greater rate than the population, jumped from 228 pounds in 1929 to 338 pounds in 1954.

Technology produced the paper towel, doilie, napkin, table-cloth — all of which compete with cotton. It also produced the multi-wall paper bag. The cotton bag consumed more cotton than any other product until this form of the paper bag provided an efficient container for sugar, flour, cement, and so forth, at a price nearly 60 per cent lower than cotton, an almost insuperable disadvantage for cotton to overcome.

Cotton is failing by ever-widening margins to meet the competition of synthetic fibers and paper. With a regularity sickening to the cotton grower and painful to the federal government that buys 'loan' cotton, cotton continues to fall behind in the struggle with its massive competitors.

'King Cotton,' reports The Wall Street Journal, 'loses further ground as newer synthetics capture the public's fancy.

'The once-proud monarch settled for two-thirds of the U.S. fibre market last year [1955]. That's the slimmest slice ever, just a sliver compared with the 90% chunk cotton had in 1913.'

The year 1955 was a black one for American cotton. The nation's rise in population and living standards increased its consumption of everything 27 per cent. But cotton consumption increased only 2 per cent. Nor is this all. In 1955, while consumption of other fibers rose an average of 22 per cent, cotton use went up by only 7 per cent.

All this is part of the relentless competition between materials such as steel and aluminum, coal and oil. No quarter is asked or given in this struggle. But a large part of the price of survival lies in unremittingly aggressive industrial-chemical research, and the spending of great sums for this purpose.

While cotton is fighting a losing battle for a diminishing share of the home market, it is fighting a spectacularly losing battle in the export market.

In 1912, forty-four years ago, the United States exported approximately 11 million bales, or more than five times the exports of 1956, and in 1955 the world took 3,445,000 bales. But now the export of American cotton is just about what it was more than a century ago. Yet even these sharply reduced exports are not entirely 'legitimate.' They rely heavily upon foreign aid programs, and 30 to 40 per cent of American cotton exports are financed through some form of government aid.

The effect of this, among other things, is to create curious behavior patterns among cotton farmers and the communities dependent upon cotton for their prosperity. The government subsidizes the cotton farmer. Then it subsidizes his exports. Large numbers of farmers and their fellows are alleged devotees of states rights, and vocally fierce enemies of what they call 'socialism in Washington.' Yet they are willing to accept government handouts — if only these are not called handouts. They are prepared to accept, or even to embrace, the status quo. But they seem unable to bring themselves to recognize it.

In this context, it is interesting to consider some remarks of the Memphis *Commercial Appeal,* published in a city that is the nation's largest inland cotton market. Determined to call a subsidy a subsidy, this newspaper says: 'THE UNITED STATES HAS COTTON EXPORT SUBSIDY DISGUISED AS SALES FOR FOREIGN CURRENCY UNDER PUBLIC LAW 480.' Then it observes: 'The United States is subsidizing the exportation of cotton . . . Public Law 480 and its acceptance of foreign currencies for cotton is an export subsidy . . . It is a limited subsidy . . . but it is a subsidy.'

The rich, powerful United States is selling cotton abroad, says the *Commercial Appeal,* through the same device used by one of its competitors: 'It is, in effect, the same device that has been used by Brazil to export its cotton.'

Yet should export sales of cotton be greatly increased through subsidies, it does not follow that what is good for the cotton farmer is good for all Americans, including cotton farmers. Indeed the State Department opposes subsidies to increase cotton exports because this might seriously harm friendly cotton-exporting nations such as Mexico and Egypt.

Artificially high prices for American cotton have enabled Mexico to become a relatively important cotton producer during recent years, and her 1955 crop was approximately two million bales, of which she will use only 350,000 bales at home. Cotton exports have become highly important to Mexico, constituting no less than 30 per cent of her total export trade. And since the price level of United States cotton is high, Mexican cotton sells abroad for 2 to 3 cents less a pound than is asked for comparable United States grades.

Hence when Congress discusses the possibility of directly subsidizing exports of United States cotton, Mexico and other friendly cotton-exporting countries become gravely alarmed. The State Department becomes deeply concerned lest a shock to the economies of friendly countries make them hostile toward us. Besides, asks the State Department, why build up the economies of friendly countries through various kinds of aid and then, when they are on their feet, wreck them through the use of subsidies to cotton farmers?

The dilemma of the cotton farmer stems not only from the difficulties that we have already surveyed, but also from a central fact of life. It is that whenever subsistence farming gives way to commercial farming, the farmer's status changes. As he devotes himself exclusively to producing crops to be sold in the market, he becomes subject to all the storms of the domestic system and, if he grows cotton, he becomes subject also to the storms of the international system.

'Indeed,' says V. O. Key, Jr., in *Politics, Parties, and Pressure Groups,* 'the key to the understanding of farm politics in the United States in the first half of the twentieth century lies in the practical unavailability to farmers of the weapons of economic defense used by industrial and financial interests. When over-production and lower prices threaten, business groups may with some success act together to curtail production and safeguard themselves against the economic storm without the interposition of government. Millions of independent agricultural producers find concerted action impossible; hence they enter politics to seek through government a way to collective action by which they can be assured of their "fair" share of the national income.'

The cotton farmer (along with other producers of staple crops) is in politics up to his neck as he tries to get his 'fair share' of the national income. From a short-term point of view, he has perhaps achieved this aim. But from a long-term point of view, he has compounded his difficulties. Unless the cotton farmer is to become a ward of government, the cotton producer must meet the price and quality competition of his rivals among makers of synthetic fibers and paper products and foreign growers of cotton. Yet, as is clear, he is moving farther away from his goal.

He receives artificially high prices for his cotton. This increases his vulnerability to the price competition of synthetic fibers, paper, and foreign cotton growers — all of which undersell him. Nor is this all. His high prices 'hold an umbrella' over foreign cotton growers who increase their output on the premise that they can easily find markets by underselling American cotton in foreign markets. Then the already subsidized farmer asks Congress to subsidize him again by dumping cotton abroad at a price lower than our domestic price. This alarms domestic textile manufacturers who are fearful that foreign competitiors may buy American cotton for less than they can and then undersell them in textile markets. Such suggestions also, as we have seen, alarm the State Department which believes that they are counter to the national interest. There the matter hangs, and the cotton economy hangs with it.

It is a risky, delicately sensitive economy. John Chamberlain describes it: 'The cotton trade is chancy in the extreme because it is interfered with by governments, subject to the vicissitudes of weather on five continents, and affected by changes in fashion in everything from women's gloves to the dungarees worn by U.S. college co-eds as well as by dock wallopers in Antwerp . . . It is also complicated for a very simple reason — just as "steel is not steel," so cotton, coming as it does in some 1,500 grades and types that are of shifting use in thousands of products, "is not cotton." A change in the taste for padded jackets in Asia could alter the market for short staple in the twinkling of an eye, and a sudden spurt in foam rubber could wipe out the profit in cotton linters — a fuzzy by-product of cotton seed used for upholstery — in a month.'

It is footling to attempt to predict the future of American cotton. Much will depend upon whether there is war or peace in the world, the price of American cotton relative to foreign growths, the ability of foreigners to get dollars with which to buy it, and the liberalizing, or further stiffening, of our trade policies.

Much will also depend upon the ability of cotton to meet the technological and price competition of synthetic fibers and paper products. Where the competition is strictly upon the basis of price and utility, it seems unlikely that cotton will recapture the ground it has lost to these competitors. It will indeed have difficulty standing its ground against them. But where the competition is in terms of such intangibles as taste and fashion — dominant factors of the important women's apparel field — the cotton industry is already successfully meeting its competition and may score vital victories over synthetic fibers.

As for price, cotton could certainly recapture some part of the great markets it has lost to paper products and synthetics, if it became less expensive. Sometimes the reduction would have to be extremely sharp; by as much as 60 per cent to compete with paper bags. But since farm costs are high in general, particularly high for the tens of thousands of small farmers, it is not possible to reduce substantially cotton prices except perhaps by bankrupting great numbers of farmers.

Meanwhile, smaller growers are especially hard hit as their acreage allotments shrink to tiny dimensions, and a desperate game is played between federal controllers and the mass of farmers. Controllers dictate the acreage limits beyond which the farmer may not go without incurring penalties. Then the farmer, determined to 'beat' the acreage allotment, uses only his best land for cotton, cultivates it intensively, fertilizes it heavily, and grows almost as much cotton on seven acres as he did on ten acres. The result is (as in 1955) that he excels himself in productivity per acre, and this can only lead — in the absence of a widening cotton demand — to more severe allotments and greater efforts on the farmer's part to 'beat' them, until the point of diminishing returns is reached.

There is no easy answer to the cotton problem. There may be, in fact, no answer to it at all. It is one of the oddities of our national life that, although as individuals we do not believe we can solve all our problems in relation to God, parents, wives, children, and country, we manage to lead relatively happy, useful lives. But as a nation we are somehow committed to the naïve concept that we can solve difficult international, social, or economic problems by finding a sovereign remedy that will dispose of the problem for all time. It does not matter that this is quite impossible as proved by the lessons of history and personal experience. Profoundly difficult problems may perhaps be ameliorated. They cannot be solved in the patent medicine sense.

It is obvious that cotton is no longer indispensable for many uses. It is reasonable to conclude that technology will find more and more substitutes for cotton as time passes. It is also reasonable to assume that foreigners will grow more and more cotton in the future, especially if artificially high prices are maintained on American cotton. Hence American cotton may be limited in the near future to the minimum needed for domestic and export consumption.

But the country may, for whatever reasons, decide to keep in being a greater-than-needed cotton culture by subsidizing it. So, retrospectively, 50 years ago the country might have decided to keep in business livery-stable people and buggy-whip people and growers of mules and horses and harnessmakers and mule-shoers and sparrows that lived on the mules' droppings — else they would surely be put out of business by the rise of the horseless carriage.

Yet, in so far as the future of cotton is concerned, there is a saving grace in such speculation. It is irrational to conclude that simply because men may arrive at rational conclusions, they will necessarily act upon them.

Index

Note: q. indicates a quoted source.